Catastrophe Disentanglement

Catastrophe Disentanglement
Getting Software Projects Back on Track

E. M. Bennatan

✦✦Addison-Wesley

Upper Saddle River, NJ • Boston • Indianapolis • San Francisco
New York • Toronto • Montreal • London • Munich • Paris • Madrid
Cape Town • Sydney • Tokyo • Singapore • Mexico City

Many of the designations used by manufacturers and sellers to distinguish their products are claimed as trademarks. Where those designations appear in this book, and the publisher was aware of a trademark claim, the designations have been printed with initial capital letters or in all capitals.

The book includes several references to software development survey data and analyses produced at the Cutter Consortium, Cambridge, Massachusetts. This material is copyright © by the Cutter Consortium (2000–2005), and is reproduced here with the Consortium's permission.

The author and publisher have taken care in the preparation of this book, but make no expressed or implied warranty of any kind and assume no responsibility for errors or omissions. No liability is assumed for incidental or consequential damages in connection with or arising out of the use of the information or programs contained herein.

The publisher offers excellent discounts on this book when ordered in quantity for bulk purchases or special sales, which may include electronic versions and/or custom covers and content particular to your business, training goals, marketing focus, and branding interests. For more information, please contact:

U.S. Corporate and Government Sales
(800) 382-3419
corpsales@pearsontechgroup.com

For sales outside the United States please contact:

International Sales
international@pearsoned.com

Visit us on the Web: www.awprofessional.com

Library of Congress Cataloging-in-Publication Data

Bennatan, E. M.
  Catastrophe disentanglement : getting software projects back on track / E. M. Bennatan.
      p. cm.
  ISBN 0-321-33662-3 (pbk. : alk. paper) 1. Software engineering. I. Title.

  QA76.758.B463 2006
  005.1—dc22

                                  2006000158

Pearson Education, Inc.
Rights and Contracts Department
75 Arlington Street, Suite 300
Boston, MA 02116
Fax: (617) 848-7047

ISBN 0-321-33662-3
Text printed in the United States on recycled paper at R. R. Donnelley in Crawfordsville, Indiana.
First printing, April 2006

CONTENTS

PREFACE

A story that I first heard several years ago tells of a Russian, a Frenchman, a Japanese man, and an American who were captured by cannibals. Before they were thrown into a pot of boiling water, the chief told his captives that he would grant them each one last request.

The Russian asked for one last glass of vodka. The Frenchman asked for one last kiss from a young native girl. The Japanese man said that he would like to give his talk about quality one last time. The American then requested: "Please boil me first, so I don't have to listen to another talk about quality!"

There is a time and a place for everything, and when a software project is in serious trouble, the last thing the development organization wants to hear is how they *should* have run the project. But when a software project is in serious trouble, there is no PMI, IEEE, SEI, or ISO rescue process to follow because these organizations offer preventive, rather than corrective, solutions. And as the project gets closer to being thrown into the pot of boiling water, its last request is "save me" and not "show me how not to get into trouble again."

This is the "save me" book. It deals with rescuing failing software projects and getting them back on track; though, admittedly, it does stray into preventive territory occasionally. The book describes ten steps to rescue (or disentangle) a failing software project (or catastrophe). It is intended for a broad audience, including software developers, project managers, members of senior management, and software project stakeholders (anyone with a significant interest in a software project).

The book is also intended as courseware, and each chapter includes a chapter summary and a list of review exercises.

While the book does occasionally expect some knowledge of software engineering, this is not a primary requirement for using the book. Thus, the book is as useful for software engineers who have limited knowledge about management as it is for managers who have limited knowledge about software development.

The book is divided into 13 chapters:

Chapter 1 contains an introduction to the concept of catastrophe disentanglement. It discusses when a project needs the intervention of a rescue process, and it explains several of the basic terms used in the book.

Chapter 2 describes the method for determining when a project is a catastrophe. For a troubled project, this is the chapter that determines whether the remaining chapters are required.

Chapters 3 through 12 describe the ten steps of the catastrophe disentanglement process (each chapter describes one step).

Chapter 13 is an epilogue called "Putting the Final Pieces in Place." This is where some of the worst straying into preventive territory occurs. It also provides a bird's eye view of the ten steps and shows how to fit the overall disentanglement process into a fixed schedule of two weeks.

This is not a read-as-you-go book. Many of the steps overlap, and each step is dependent on the steps that preceded it. It is also easier to understand each step if the reader has an overall grasp of the whole disentanglement process. Therefore, it is strongly recommended that you review all chapters before implementing the process. However, before becoming discouraged by the previous sentence, recall that each chapter concludes with a summary. You can get by with just the summaries as long as the chapter related to the disentanglement step that is being implemented is read in detail.

As this is a practical text (and not a theoretical one), many methods and techniques are described without their theoretical basis. Extensive references are provided throughout the book, however, for those interested in the theoretical background. A comprehensive list of references appears at the end of the book.

Before this book went to print, there was some discussion about whether a project can rightly be called a catastrophe when, in reality, we expect to rescue it (that is, is the state of being a catastrophe reversible?). The answer is evident to anyone who has worked at a large technology company and has heard a frustrated senior manager say: "This project is a catastrophe!" If the state could not be reversed, the project would be cancelled there and then. But what usually follows is, "We need to get it back on track immediately!" Well, that is exactly what this book is about.

The disentanglement concept is the product of many years of hands-on software project management at Motorola and at other technology companies, and the collection and analysis of software project development data from hundreds of development organizations. The book was preceded by a pilot paper with the same name, published in the U.S. Department of Defense Journal of Defense Software Engineering, *CrossTalk*.

I would like to acknowledge the tremendous assistance from Amir in producing this book. His contributions and reviews were invaluable.

E. M. Bennatan
January 2006

1

An Introduction to Catastrophe Disentanglement

Step 10 Early Warning System

Step 9 Revise the Plan

Step 8 Risk Analysis

Step 7 Rebuild the Team

Step 6 Can Minimum Goals Be Achieved?

Step 5 Define Minimum Goals

Step 4 Evaluate the Team

Step 3 Evaluate Project Status

Step 2 Assign an Evaluator

Step 1 Stop

In Spencer Johnson's *Who Moved My Cheese* [9], the little people keep coming back to where the cheese used to be even though it's not there anymore. It's a natural tendency to continue doing what we did before even when, to an outside observer, it no longer makes sense. This behavior is quite common when software projects get into trouble. We keep plodding away at the project hoping that the problems will go away and the "cheese" will miraculously reappear. In all too many cases, it doesn't.

Just as the smart thing to do when a ball of twine seems hopelessly entangled is to stop whatever we are doing with it (otherwise, the tangle gets worse), so it is with a disastrous project; the longer we keep at it, the worse it gets. At some point, we need to halt all activity and reassess what we are doing.

Disastrous software projects, or *catastrophes*, are projects that are completely out of control in one or more of the following aspects: schedule, budget, or quality. They are by no means rare; 44% of surveyed development organizations report that they have had software projects cancelled or abandoned due to significant overruns, and 15% say that it has happened to more than 10% of their projects (see Figure 1.1).

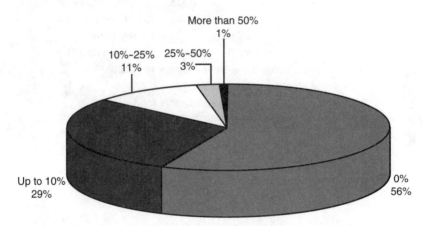

Figure 1.1 Percentage of surveyed organizations' software projects that have been abandoned or cancelled due to significant cost or time overruns in the past three years (source [12])

But obviously, not every overrun or quality problem means a project is out of control, so at what point should we define a software project as a catastrophe? What are the criteria for taking the drastic step of halting all activities, and how do we go about reassessing the project? Most importantly, how do we go about getting the project moving again? The answers to these questions are the essence of the concept of *catastrophe disentanglement*.

One of the best-known attempts to disentangle a multi-hundred-million-dollar catastrophe ended recently, more than a decade after it began. In August

2005, the plug was finally pulled on the infamous Denver airport baggage handling system, in a scene reminiscent of Hal's demise in the memorable Kubrick space odyssey movie.[1] This was a project that had gained notoriety for costing one million dollars a day for being late. One of the interesting questions about the Denver project is why didn't the repeated efforts to save it succeed?

Of all the problems that plagued the project (see [3], [4]), probably the most formidable was the project's unachievable goals. It is unlikely that anyone associated with the project could have brought about a significant change to the goals because the project's extravagant functionality had, in fact, become part of its main attraction. But the ability to define achievable goals is a cornerstone of any catastrophe disentanglement process, without which the process cannot succeed, and that is one of the main reasons the Denver system could not be disentangled.

As indicated by the above survey data, cases like the Denver project are not rare (although few are as extreme). Most development organizations know this even without seeing the survey data. This frustrating reality was expressed in a famous quote from Martin Cobb of the Canadian Treasury Board: "We know why projects fail, we know how to prevent their failure—so why do they still fail?" [10].

Cobb's quote highlights the conventional approach of software engineering. The objective of existing software engineering practices is to *prevent* the occurrence of software catastrophes—that is, to prevent the project from spiraling out of control. As such, the practices have an important role to play in software development. However, more than five decades of experience show that despite these methods, software catastrophes will continue to be around for a while.

When a software project is out of control, there is no PMI, IEEE, SEI, or ISO rescue process to follow because these organizations offer preventive, rather than corrective, solutions. But is such a project necessarily doomed? Will it inevitably collapse in failure? The following chapters will show that this is far from inevitable.

This book fills the void for corrective solutions in software engineering. It deals with projects that are already in serious trouble. In fact, this book is less concerned with how we got into trouble; it is more concerned with how we get out.

1.1   Overview of the Catastrophe Disentanglement Process

Before the first step in disentangling a project can be taken, we must first establish that the whole process is necessary. This means deciding that the project, as it is currently proceeding, has little chance of success without taking drastic measures.

---

[1]   Hal was the wayward computer in Stanley Kubrick's movie *2001: A Space Odyssey*.

Many software organizations have difficulty making this decision, and some avoid it entirely. In fact, there is a general tendency to let troubled projects carry on way too long before appropriate action is taken [6]. Keil [7] uses the term "runaways" to describe software projects that continue to absorb valuable resources without ever reaching their objective. Keil's runaways are, in effect, undiagnosed catastrophes that went on unchecked for much too long. Indeed, the ability to save a project is usually dependent on how early in the schedule a catastrophe is diagnosed. Furthermore, organizations that permit a runaway project to continue are wasting valuable resources. This reality is well demonstrated in the following case.

1.1.1   A Case Study

The FINALIST case, described next, demonstrates how difficult it is to acknowledge that a project is in serious trouble, even when the problem is obvious to almost anyone looking in from the outside. It is an interesting case because it is by no means unique; it demonstrates just how easy it is to become committed to a failing path.

> After the year 2000 passed, and the software prophets of doom faded away, a Canadian software company found itself with almost no customers for one of its small business units. The unit's main expertise was in supporting Cobol programs (where many of the bug-2000 problems were expected to be), and suddenly there wasn't enough Cobol work to support it.

> So the company decided to rewrite one of its core products, FINALIST, a large financial analysis system, but it chose to write it again in Cobol in order to retain the company's unique expertise for solving bug-2000 problems (which it still thought would materialize). The new project, appropriately named FINALIST2, was given a 30-month schedule and a team of 14 developers, eight of whom were veteran Cobol programmers.

> At the beginning of the second year of the project, two Cobol programmers retired and, soon after, three more moved to another company. With only three veteran Cobol programmers left, the FINALIST2 project began to experience serious problems and schedule delays. The company's management repeatedly resisted calls to reevaluate the project and attempted to get it back on track by conducting frequent reviews, adding more people to the team, providing incentives, and eventually, by extending the schedule.

> Finally, 28 months into the project, a consultant was brought in, and his first recommendation was to halt the project immediately. This drastic advice was based on the conclusion that little or no meaningful progress was being made and the project, as it was defined, would probably never be completed. There were not enough experienced Cobol programmers around to do the work, and it was unlikely that new ones would be hired.

Furthermore, it was unlikely that the new recruits would become sufficiently proficient in Cobol within any reasonable time frame.

The final recommendation was to either restart the project in a modern programming language or to cancel it entirely.

One of the key points in this case is that management failed to notice that what
was once a strength (Cobol) had ceased to be one—a classic example of "who
moved my cheese." This failure was clearly fostered by a strong desire to preserve
Cobol expertise within the company, but it was also the result of a natural reluctance to acknowledge a mistake (resistance to reevaluate the project). These two
factors obscured the solution. And so management attempted to fix almost everything (process, team, schedule) except the problem itself.

   This case illustrates the difficulties decision makers have in accepting the
need for drastic measures and is reminiscent of a gambler who cannot get up and
walk away. First, there is the natural tendency to put off making the difficult decision in hope that conventional methods will eventually get the project back on
track. A second difficulty involves over-commitment to previous decisions,
prompting the investment of more resources to avoid admitting mistakes (this is
known as *escalation* [6]).

   But troubled projects are never a surprise, and even those most committed to
a failing path know that something is severely wrong. But how severe is "severely wrong"? How can we know that it is time for drastic measures? Ideally, there
would be a decision algorithm (a kind of software breathalyzer) to which managers could subject their projects, and which would make the decision for them.

1.1.2   Deciding to Rescue a Project

There is no perfect breathalyzer for catastrophes. However, although it is difficult
to make a completely objective decision about a project, there are methods that
remove much of the subjectivity from the decision. These methods involve an in-
depth evaluation of the project and require significant effort. Unlike status reports
or regular progress reviews, they are not designed to be applied at regular inter-
vals throughout the development cycle. The process prescribed by these methods
is to be applied only when we suspect that a project may be in serious trouble, but
we are unsure whether it requires life-saving surgery.

   The procedure is based on the evaluation of three basic project areas:

- Schedule
- Budget
- Quality

The procedure examines whether serious problems have existed for quite a while
in any of these project areas and whether the situation is getting worse, not better.
Any one of these areas can trigger a catastrophe decision, but when this happens,

it is not unusual for serious problems to exist in all three. Chapter 2, "When Is a Project a Catastrophe?," covers this subject in detail and also discusses the tricky question of what quality is (the definition will be based on the level of product defects and the degree to which customers or users are satisfied with the product).

Once the decision has been made that a project is indeed a catastrophe, the options become more clear: save it or lose it. This is the time for the ten-step disentanglement process.

1.1.3 The Disentanglement Process

The disentanglement process is designed to rescue a seriously troubled project, provided it can establish business or strategic justification for doing so. The process is built around two main figures: the *initiating manager* (who initiates the process and oversees its implementation) and the *project evaluator* (who leads and implements the disentanglement process). The initiating manager is an insider, a senior manager in the organization that owns the project. The project evaluator is an outsider, a seasoned professional, reliable, and impartial.

The catastrophe disentanglement process consists of the following ten steps:

1. **Stop:** Halt all project development activities and assign the team to support the disentanglement effort.

2. **Assign an evaluator:** Recruit an external professional to lead the disentanglement process.

3. **Evaluate project status:** Establish the true status of the project.

4. **Evaluate the team:** Identify team problems that may have contributed to the project's failure.

5. **Define minimum goals:** Reduce the project to the smallest size that achieves only the most essential goals.

6. **Determine whether minimum goals can be achieved:** Analyze the feasibility of the minimum goals and determine whether they can reasonably be expected to be achieved.

7. **Rebuild the team:** Based on the new project goals, rebuild a competent project team in preparation for re-starting the project.

8. **Perform risk analysis:** Consider the new goals and the rebuilt team, identify risks in the project, and prepare contingency plans to deal with them.

9. **Revise the plan:** Produce a new high-level project plan that includes a reasonable schedule based on professionally prepared estimates.

10. **Install an early warning system:** Put a system in place that will ensure that the project does not slip back into catastrophe mode.

There are three main reports generated by the project evaluator during the disentanglement process:

1. **Step 4: The team overview document**

   The document contains a summary of the project team evaluation. It is used as input to step 7 ("rebuild the team"). The overview includes the main sources of information, the list of interviews, the reasoning that led to any significant findings, and any problems or incompatibles that arose during the evaluation.

2. **Step 6: The midway report**

   The document is generated midway through the disentanglement process after establishing the feasibility of the minimized goals. This provides senior management and other key stakeholders with a formal update on the progress of the disentanglement process. The report documents all major decisions, evaluations, and conclusions that produced the new reduced-scope project. It also includes summaries of the discussion that led to agreement among the key stakeholders.

3. **At the end of the disentanglement process: The final report**

   Producing this report is the project evaluator's last task. The report summarizes all information collected and generated, all decisions made, all major project documents produced, and lists all problems that were resolved or left unresolved. This report is produced even if the disentanglement process does not succeed or if the project is cancelled.

The sequence of the disentanglement steps is organized according to the logical flow described in Table 1.1. It is important to complete the steps in this sequence (though parts of the steps may overlap). The following points demonstrate why the sequence is important:

- There will not be enough information to propose new goals until the project has been evaluated (this includes both the project status and the team).
- There will not be enough information to rebuild the team until the new project goals have been established.
- There will not be enough information for a new plan (schedule and estimates) until the new project goals have been established, the team has been rebuilt, and the risks have been identified.

Table 1.1 Logical Flow of the Ten Disentanglement Steps

Phase	Steps
Launch the process	1, 2
Evaluate the status	3, 4
Introduce changes	5, 6, 7
Prepare to resume	8, 9, 10

Each one of these steps is described in detail in the following chapters. Their success is strongly dependent on the cooperation of all involved parties and the active involvement of the project team. But the main precondition for success is the support of the organization's senior management. As we shall see in the following chapters, without effective management support, the process will fail at almost every step.

The entire process should take no more than two weeks to complete (see the disentanglement timeline in Figure 13.1 of Chapter 13, "Epilogue: Putting the Final Pieces in Place"). This also represents the maximum amount of time that the project will remain halted.[2]

1.2   A Closer Look at the Data

We have seen in Figure 1.1 that software catastrophes are not rare, but the data in Figure 1.1 does not tell the whole story. Could these projects have been saved if a formal disentanglement process (like the one we described earlier) had been used in time? An indication can be found by looking at additional data related to the schedule, budget, and quality of the projects (these are the factors that would have triggered the process).

The data in Table 1.2 is based on a broad software development survey [8] that defined a schedule overrun of more than 50% as severe, a budget overrun of more than 50% as severe, and the quality problems of a product with critical post-release defects as being severe. These projects are considered failures even though they were permitted to run their course to completion (and many would submit that they should not have been permitted to do so).[3]

- **Schedule:** The data clearly shows that severe schedule overruns are far from rare. In a quarter of the surveyed software organizations, more than 10% of the projects had severe schedule overruns. In 13% of these organizations, the situation was much worse: more than a quarter of their projects had severe schedule overruns.

- **Budgets:** The data for software project budgets is just a shade better. In just less than a quarter of software organizations, more than 10% of the projects were severely over budget. In 8% of these organizations, more than a quarter of the projects were severely over budget.

---

[2] Unless, of course, the project cannot be saved and gets cancelled.

[3] The most common argument is that organizations that permit overruns of more than 50%, or the release of products with severe quality problems, have little chance of survival.

- **Quality:** The data for quality does not tell a good story. More than a third of software organizations (35%) had severe quality problems in more than 10% of their products after their release. Of these, 15% reported severe quality problems in more than a quarter of their products after their release.

Table 1.2 The Proportion in Software Development Organizations of Software Projects with Severe Problems (Source: The Cutter Consortium, 2005)

Severe Schedule Problems		Severe Budget Problems		Severe Quality Problems	
More than 10% of projects were very late	25%	More than 10% of projects were greatly over-budget	24%	More than 10% of projects had critical quality problems	35%
More than 25% of projects were very late	13%	More than 25% of projects were greatly over-budget	8%	More than 25% of projects had critical quality problems	15%

After a severely troubled project is completed or cancelled, there is, of course, no way of telling whether the outcome could have been different. However, we speculate that many of these severely troubled projects could have been rescued. At the very least, such projects would have greatly benefited from an early warning system. The survey findings are from projects that were more than 50% over-schedule or over budget or had critically severe quality problems. The warning system, which is further discussed in Chapter 12, "Step 10—Create an Early Warning System," is designed to trigger an alarm whenever such conditions begin to develop.

Interestingly, the survey found that 50% of software development organizations do implement some type of project rescue process. These companies reported that they handle early indications of project failure by initiating a formal project reevaluation process resulting in possible changes to goals, plans, and the development team. These are precisely the elements of the catastrophe disentanglement process presented in this book. Furthermore, according to another survey finding shown in Figure 1.2, 45% of organizations almost always succeed in getting troubled projects back on track. We can speculate that they overlap the 50% that conduct rescue processes.[4] These, then, are organizations that have independently developed catastrophe disentanglement processes, and have apparently applied them to great effect.

---

[4] Without the need to speculate further, we can state that the 45% is a low figure; there are certainly more successful project rescues within the 30% who responded that "some are saved and some are not." So the overlap may look even better.

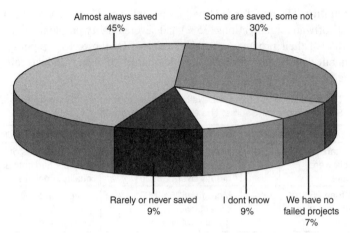

Figure 1.2 How frequently are troubled projects saved?

The survey also looked at the cost of catastrophes. When asked to assess the impact of software project failures on their organization, the most common response lamented the waste of funds, time, and other resources. Others reported a decline in the organization's motivation and prestige and the loss of customers and business opportunities. Clearly, the high cost of project catastrophes goes way beyond the cost of the failed project itself. With an effective disentanglement process, it is practically certain that much of these costs could have been avoided.

1.3 Tips Before You Proceed

There is no magic or mystery in the ten steps of the catastrophe disentanglement process. They are all familiar steps that many software developers will have used at various times in their careers. The strength of the process is in combining the steps together, implementing them as a single aggregate with each step building on the previous ones, and doing so within a short, fixed schedule.

Before proceeding with the implementation of the process, here is a summary of several of the tips that are provided throughout the discussion of the ten disentanglement steps. These tips and others are elaborated at length in the upcoming chapters.

1. **Work in parallel.**

   Though the ten steps of the process need to be completed in sequence, they do not need to start in sequence. In fact, parts of some of the steps can be implemented in parallel to others (this can save time). For example, step 8 (risk analysis) can begin as soon as step 3 (evaluate project status) is complete, and much of steps 5 and 6 (define and evaluate the feasibility of minimum goals) can be implemented in parallel.

2. **Expect resistance**.

   Expect resistance to change; it is natural. The best way to deal with resistance is by enlisting the support of allies from among the project stakeholders and the project team. In cases where resistance is particularly high, enlist the support of senior management.

3. **Be sensitive to the team and to the stakeholders.**

   Be sensitive to the emotional concerns of the project team and stakeholders. Team members will have legitimate job security and career concerns. Some of the stakeholders will have personal interests in the project that will not necessarily be financial or business related. Before proceeding, become familiar with the key stakeholders and team members.

4. **Keep within the schedule.**

   The process can easily slip well beyond the allocated two weeks; this will happen one day at a time, and at some point the delay is no longer manageable. Treat any delay (even of a half day) as a problem that needs to be immediately corrected.

   Overcome delays by working whenever possible at a high level (leaving details to be filled in by the team after the project resumes), by using a project evaluation *team,* and implementing the disentanglement steps in parallel. If delays are caused by a lack of cooperation, enlist the immediate help of the organization's senior management.

5. **Do not proceed without senior management support.**

   The disentanglement process cannot succeed without firm visible support from senior management. The process requires significant cooperation from all involved parties, and this will not be assured without such senior management support.

   The process also involves activities that will generate resistance from the project stakeholders and the development team. In some cases, it will be difficult or even impossible to overcome the resistance without the support of senior management.

6. **Encourage all involved parties to review the disentanglement process.**

   The disentanglement process is more likely to succeed if all involved parties understand how it works and why each step is being implemented. Thus, while the description in the following chapters is directed toward the project evaluator and the initiating manager, all parties involved in the effort to rescue the project will benefit by understanding the process.

7. **Document decisions and findings.**

   All key decisions and all major findings should be documented. This will save time, should the decisions need to be reevaluated or explained. The decisions and findings document should be maintained by the project evaluator and submitted to the initiating manager at the end of the process.

8. Be open and accessible.

Many of the concerns and much of the reluctance to cooperate can be overcome by conducting the disentanglement in an open and candid manner. This means no clandestine decisions and no behind-closed-doors meetings except in rare occasions when topics of a purely personal nature are discussed (they should be kept to a minimum).

9. Listen to arguments.

Be prepared to listen to arguments before decisions are finalized, provided they are of a professional nature (exclude political and personal interest viewpoints). After decisions have been made, be prepared to re-open them only if significant new information becomes available that was not previously considered. Be resolute about preventing undue delays in finalizing discussions and decisions.

10. Not all problems discussed will occur.

The following chapters provide guidelines for resolving many problems that may arise during the disentanglement process. This can be alarming. Remember, not all problems will actually occur—in fact, most will not. The guidelines are like a first aid kit; just because you carry anti-venom serum doesn't mean that you will be bitten by a snake.

11. The key to success is a good evaluator.

Of all the factors that affect the disentanglement process, the two that most contribute to its success are senior management support (discussed earlier) and a good project evaluator. Start the search for evaluator candidates even before a final decision has been made to proceed with the disentanglement process.

12. Read through the entire process.

Read through the entire process before proceeding. Many of the steps are inter-dependent. You can better implement each step if you understand the steps that follow.

One final point: There are no shortcuts. The disentanglement process is designed to be implemented in its entirety. Each step relates to the evaluation or resolution of a problem that, if left unsolved, is likely to disrupt the entire disentanglement process. Furthermore, several of the steps are inter-dependent. In fact, the final step (install an early warning system), which ensures that the project does not slip back into catastrophe mode, is dependent on the preceding nine steps.

1.4 Summary

Disastrous software projects, or *catastrophes*, are projects that are completely out of control in one or more of the following aspects: schedule, budget, or quality. But obviously, not every overrun or quality problem means a project is out of control, so at what point should we define a software project as a catastrophe? What are the criteria for taking the drastic step of halting all activities, and how do we go about reassessing the project? And, most importantly, how do we go about getting the project moving again? The answers to these questions are the essence of the concept of *catastrophe disentanglement*.

Before the first step in the disentanglement process can be taken, we must first establish that the whole process is, indeed, necessary. This means deciding that the project, as it is currently proceeding, has little chance of success without taking drastic measures.

There are methods that can help remove much of the subjectivity from this decision. The idea is not to define an algorithm and subject projects to it every week, but rather to provide a procedure to be applied only when we suspect that a project may be in serious trouble and we are unsure if it requires drastic life-saving surgery.

The procedure is based on the evaluation of three basic project areas: schedule, budget, and quality. The procedure examines whether serious problems have existed for quite a while in any of these project areas and whether the situation is getting worse, not better.

The disentanglement process is built around two main figures: the *initiating manager*, who initiates the process and overseas it as it is being implemented, and the *project evaluator*, who leads and implements the disentanglement process.

The ten steps of the catastrophe disentanglement process are

1. Stop.
2. Assign an evaluator.
3. Evaluate project status.
4. Evaluate the team.
5. Define minimum goals.
6. Determine whether minimum goals can be achieved.
7. Rebuild the team.
8. Perform risk analysis.
9. Revise the plan.
10. Install an early warning system.

The ten steps should be completed in sequence, and the entire process should take no more than two weeks to complete.

The following list summarizes several tips for the successful implementation of the disentanglement process:

1. Work on the steps in parallel.

2. Expect resistance from stakeholders and project team members.

3. Be sensitive to the team and to the stakeholders. Before proceeding, become familiar with the key stakeholders and team members.

4. Keep within the two-week disentanglement process schedule.

5. Do not proceed without senior management support. The process cannot succeed without it.

6. Encourage all involved parties to review the disentanglement process. The process is more likely to succeed if all involved parties understand how it works.

7. All key decisions and all major findings should be documented.

8. Be open and accessible. This will reduce concerns and any reluctance to cooperate.

9. Be prepared to listen to arguments before decisions are finalized.

10. Remember that not all problems discussed here will actually occur—in fact, most will not.

11. The key to success is a good evaluator. Start the search early.

12. Read through the entire process before proceeding. Many of the steps are inter-dependent.

There are no shortcuts in the disentanglement process. The process is designed to be implemented in its entirety. Each step relates to the evaluation or resolution of a problem that, if left unsolved, is likely to disrupt the entire disentanglement process.

2

When Is a Project a Catastrophe?

Step 10   Early Warning System

Step 9   Revise the Plan

Step 8   Risk Analysis

Step 7   Rebuild the Team

Step 6   Can Minimum Goals Be Achieved?

Step 5   Define Minimum Goals

Step 4   Evaluate the Team

Step 3   Evaluate Project Status

Step 2   Assign an Evaluator

Step 1   Stop

?

A software project catastrophe is like a train coming at you; if you look, you can see it coming. In fact, with the right tools, you can see it coming from quite a distance. The problem is that when software projects are in deep trouble, we often choose not to see the approaching train, and even when we do, we tend to hope that it will go away if we ignore it. Indeed, in many cases, we find it difficult to admit that we have been hit.

This chapter describes a process for determining if a software project is in the danger zone (in railway terms, either the train is bearing down on us or we are already under the wheels). Knowing that we are in danger is a prerequisite for any survival procedure, and according to traditional wisdom, is half of the solution. This is as true for disastrous software projects as it is for trains.

In Chapter 1, "An Introduction to Catastrophe Disentanglement," a disastrous project, or *catastrophe*, was described as a project that is completely out of control in one or more of the following areas: schedule, budget, or quality. We also conceded that not every overrun or quality problem means that a project is out of control (unfortunately, overruns are quite common, as shown in Figure 2.1).[1] So at which point should we define a software project as a catastrophe? What are the criteria for taking such drastic measures as halting all development activities?

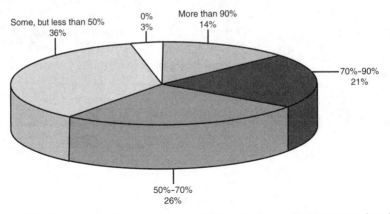

Figure 2.1 Percentage of surveyed organizations' software projects completed within 10% of the original estimated time (source [1])

There are methods for establishing thresholds (or alarm triggers) beyond which project schedule and budget overruns are considered severe and the project is regarded as a catastrophe. But establishing quality thresholds is often more difficult because some aspects of quality, such as customer satisfaction, are thought to be less tangible. This can sometimes lead to customer satisfaction being overlooked as a measure of quality, as in the following case:

---

[1] To be statistically accurate, the results may have also included some projects that were finished early, but we risked the speculation that such cases (if any) would only represent a small fraction of the results.

A Chicago software consumer products company was struggling recently with increasing customer complaints. This was at a time when the demand for software consumer products had begun to soar and customer expectations were changing, driven not just by a growing software market, but even more so by increasing competition. Consequently, many consumer software companies were becoming more sensitive to customer complaints, and some of those that were not (and one such was the Chicago company) were witnessing a sharp drop in business.

As is often the case when a company is not sure why things are not going well, they brought in an external consultant.

But the software development manager was uncertain why his boss had brought in the consultant and why his development process was being reviewed. "We do a fairly good job," he told the consultant, "and most of our software projects are successful." He continued rather proudly: "Our projects rarely overrun their budget or schedule, and we always follow our requirements faithfully."

When asked why then he thought the company felt the need to bring in a consultant, the manager added almost as an afterthought: "We do seem to get many complaints from our customers, but that has nothing to do with my department."

This limited definition of project success—on time, within budget, and according to requirements—has been widely used since the early days of software development. But, in reality, this is not enough; a project cannot be considered successful if its quality is poor and its customers are dissatisfied.

Even if they appear intangible, customer satisfaction and other aspects of quality *are* measurable, and we shall see that thresholds can be established for all three factors: schedule, budget, and quality. The main problem, though, is deciding when to trigger an alarm (that is, where to set the threshold) because the level of tolerance for overruns is highly dependent on the characteristics of the development organization and the nature of the project. The expectations from mission critical, life support, or banking software are significantly different from most consumer- or Internet-based software applications.

So can we determine that a software project is headed for failure (that is, it has become a catastrophe)? It would certainly be great if we could run the project through a set of evaluation criteria that could warn us if the project was going to fail. But while there are no such universal criteria, experience shows that in virtually all cases, projects are in deep trouble if serious problems have existed for quite a while and the situation is getting worse, not better. The remainder of this chapter shows how this is reflected in terms of schedule, budget, and quality.

> **Advisory:** The process of determining whether a project is a catastrophe is a precursor to the disentanglement process (if the project is a catastrophe, disentanglement follows). It is not intended to be a periodic or regular process and should be initiated only when there is strong suspicion that a project may be in serious trouble.
>
> More general project status reviews are an important management tool and *should* be conducted regularly (this is discussed in Chapter 12, "Step 10—Create an Early Warning System").

2.1 Schedule

Unfortunately, there is no shortage of software schedule catastrophe examples. In most cases, severe schedule problems also led to budget and quality catastrophes, though it was not always clear where the problems really started. Here is one such case:

> In 1994, the Canadian Government awarded a large Income Security Program Redesign (ISPR) software project to EDS, Canada, for the design, development, supply, integration, test, delivery, and installation of the ISPR's Client Service Delivery Network. The development schedule was 35 months, though since its inception, the project experienced several problems related to scope and design changes, which created the potential for rework.
>
> In 1995, the Canadian Auditor General's office reported that the project was being plagued by multiple problems and was constantly in need of corrective action to manage various project risks. This led to a revision of the schedule, the budget, and the contracted deliverables.
>
> By month 15 of the 35-month schedule, the project had used up the entire contingency for schedule slippage and the schedule was again extended. Reports blamed poor management controls as well as completion and cost targets that were too easily moved.

The following year's report indicated that things were getting worse; it said: "Risks remain very high that further changes in schedule, cost, or requirements will be necessary to complete the project."

In 1997, after concluding that they could no longer determine when the project would be completed, the Canadian Government contracted an external company (Alltel) to independently assess the ISPR project. Alltel's report concluded that the ISPR project was in serious trouble and that the overall risk was indeed high. The report went on to evaluate several options, including termination of the contract.

In March 1998, long after the original end-date of the ISPR project, and with the completion date and cost still unknown, the Canadian Government decided that they would no longer risk additional delays and cost overruns. The ISPR project was cancelled.

The ISPR project is a classic example of an unfolding schedule catastrophe with all the early warning signs: repeated schedule overruns, uncontrolled major changes in project scope, poor corrective action, and growing customer dissatisfaction.

Schedules have little value if they are too easily changed, and this was one of the main problems with the ISPR project. As in all development schedules, the lower-level milestones should have raised the alarm and provided the means of correction (see [2]).[2]

But missed milestones alone do not mean that a project is out of control. Software projects rarely or never strictly follow their detailed schedule; in fact, milestone delays often grow and shrink like an accordion throughout the project. But we are not looking at just any delay; the issue here is to identify those projects where the milestone delays are growing uncontrollably.

2.1.1   Setting a Schedule Alarm

To determine if a software project delay is out of control, we will examine the trend in all or part of the elapsed schedule and a snapshot of the delay. The basic method is as follows:

Divide the total development schedule into 12 phases, and look at each of the last three. Has the delay steadily grown in each phase, and is the total delay now greater than 25% of the total project schedule? The 25% is the threshold or alarm point beyond which the project's delay is considered severe.

For example, for a one-year schedule, we would look at the last three months.

---

[2] We differentiate between a high-level schedule that simply says that a project will be delivered in 18 months and one that lays out how it will be done (with lower-level milestones). In a detailed project schedule, it is the lower-level milestones that provide an early warning when something is seriously wrong.

1. Examine the trend of the elapsed schedule:
    - Has the total delay in relation to the elapsed schedule been growing?

      In particular:
      - – Was the delay significant two months ago?
      - – Was the delay even greater one month ago?
      - – This month, has the delay grown again?
    - Has the delay been steady (that is, not two small delays and one major delay caused by an identifiable event)?

2. Examine a snapshot of the schedule:

    Is the total delay now greater than three months (that is, 25% of the total project schedule)?

If the answer to all these questions is yes, it is probably a good idea to halt the project and reassess it.

The logic behind this method is derived from examining trends rather than just snapshots. If we only rely on snapshots to evaluate the status of a project—let's say a 12-month project—we might conclude that a three-month delay at the end of month six means the project will be three months late (and the team will be instructed to work harder to ensure there are no more delays!). But even a superficial use of trend data suggests that the project will most likely be more than three months late (possibly six months late or more) unless effective corrective action is taken.[3] This is especially true if, as is often the case, most of the delay occurred in months four to six (rather than months one to three).

We will discuss enhancements to the basic method later. But first we will demonstrate using the basic method to evaluate a late project that has just completed phase 7 of the 12 phases, using the sample data in Table 2.1.

Table 2.1 Sample Schedule Overrun Scenario

Phase (Phase = 1/12 of Schedule)	Status	Cumulative Overrun (% of One Phase)
1	On Time	0%
2	Late	50%
3	Late	110%
4	Late	160%
5	Late	160%
6	Late	165%
→ 7	Late	170%

[3] It was the oft-quoted Fred Brooks who first made us aware of trends in software project overruns. Most software project disasters are due to termites, not tornadoes, says Brooks. How does a disastrous schedule slippage happen? Brooks responds: "One day at a time." [4]

Let us look at a snapshot of the project. The cumulative overrun column tells us how late the project is in terms of phases. This is expressed as a percentage of a phase and helps highlight the relation between the delay and the elapsed schedule. This is especially true at early phases of the project when the total delay may be small relative to the total project length but large relative to the elapsed schedule, indicating a high rate of delay accumulation. The data for phase 2, for instance, tells us that the project is a half-phase late: that is, it is late by 1/24th of the overall project. But the same data also shows that the project is late by one quarter of the *elapsed* schedule (50/200).

At the end of phase 7, we see that the project has been late for six consecutive phases, and at one point (phase 4) was late by 40% of the elapsed schedule (160/400). In fact, the 40% overrun occurred while the project was just finishing the first third of its original schedule. And now, at the end of the seventh phase, the project is still late.

Now let us examine the trend. The size of the overrun has not declined since the project started and, except for phase 5, it has been steadily growing. However, the relative overrun has declined from 40% of the elapsed schedule at the end of phase 4 to 24% (170/700) at the end of phase 7. Also, the increase in the overall schedule overrun has been small in each of the past three phases (which together represent a significant part (25%) of the overall schedule).

Catastrophe: yes or no? The trend does not indicate that the project schedule is out of control. In fact, if the last three-month trend continues (and the cumulative overrun grows each month by an additional 5%), the total schedule overrun at the end of the project will be 16% (195/1200)—which, while not a great result, would rarely be considered a catastrophe.

So, in summary, we can conclude from the first seven phases of the project schedule that the schedule appears, at this point, to be under control. However, it would be wise to monitor the project closely to ensure that it doesn't slip back to a state of increasing overruns. This is especially important because the second half of a project is usually much more difficult than the first (project assets, complexity, team size, pressure—they all grow).

Let us now consider what might have been our decision if we had reviewed the project at the end of phase 4? At that point, both the snapshot and the trend did not look good; there were three consecutive phases with steeply increasing schedule overruns, the last of which is 40% of the elapsed schedule. The moderating factor here is that the overrun relative to the overall schedule is 13% (160/1200). So the project appears to be starting off rather badly, and this is definitively a warning sign, but not at this point a catastrophe.

2.1.2   Fine-Tuning the Schedule Alarm

Why have we set the overall schedule alarm point at 300% of a phase (25% of the entire project schedule)?

A 25% overrun at the *end* of a project is rarely considered a catastrophe (though it is certainly not a great success, either). However, if the accumulated delay during the development of the project, and particularly in the early phases, is already 25%, and the trend shows that the situation is getting worse, the eventual delay is likely to be much larger. Experience shows that in such cases it is very difficult to recover from an overrun of 25% without a major project overhaul.

The 25% catastrophe alarm point is a good general trigger to start with, but development organizations should fine-tune the percentage based on the characteristics of their organization, development team, and products.

Fine-tuning can also make the alarm point phase-dependent. Table 2.2 contains one possible set of phase-dependent alarm points that, for example, would declare a 12-month project to be in severe trouble (i.e., a catastrophe) if

- After four months of development, the estimated project overrun is greater than 25% of the overall schedule (that is, greater than three months).
- After seven months of development, the estimated project overrun is greater than 33% of the overall project (that is, greater than four months).
- At the end of the original schedule (12 months), the estimates indicate that more than another 40% (that is, greater than five months) is required for completion.

This example of phase-dependent alarm points is expanded in Table 2.2, where the alarm is first sounded at the end of month 7 (the actual schedule overrun is 50%, which exceeds the alarm point, which is 33%). Compare this method to the fixed 25% catastrophe alarm point where a 12-month project is considered to be in severe trouble if at any time it is estimated to take 15 months or more. The fixed alarm point approach would be appropriate when the value of the project significantly diminishes after a certain date (for example, the software to run the technology at the Olympic Games). Conversely, the phase-dependent approach is appropriate when the project continues to have full value even after a significant schedule overrun.

However, with the reality of software project overruns shown in Figures 2.1 and 2.2, a useful management method is to hold resources in reserve. This approach was formalized by Elyahu Goldratt in his acclaimed text *Critical Chain* [3], which explains the human and organizational psychology of resource reserves in improving project schedule performance. Thus, the size of the overrun (as a percentage of the overall schedule) that will trigger a schedule alarm must take into consideration the characteristics and constraints of the organization.

Table 2.2 Sample Schedule Catastrophe Alarm Points

Phase	Schedule Alarm Point (Percentage of Total Project Schedule)	Actual Schedule Overrun (Percentage of Total Project Schedule)
3	20%	0%
4	25%	5%
5	30%	10%
6	30%	25%
→ 7	33%	50%
8	35%	
9	35%	
10	40%	
11	40%	
12	40%	

Advisory: Delays early in a project, if left untreated, have a tendency to grow with time, while delays late in a project are difficult to eliminate (the later, the more difficult).

2.1.3 Monitoring an Extended Schedule

The decision to formally extend a schedule should not be taken lightly and certainly should not be done frequently. But when it becomes clear that a late project cannot recover the overrun, the unachievable schedule becomes more of a hindrance than an asset. A project plodding along with an unrealistic schedule has no realistic plan, and its progress can hardly be realistically measured.

The schedule alarm is measured in relation to the project schedule. Thus, if the schedule is totally unrealistic, the alarm will set off a warning. In fact, when a project is suspected of being in trouble, the schedule alarm mechanism is intended to provide a warning if the schedule is significantly underestimated. Then, if the schedule is not corrected (we will see in the following chapters how this is done), the alarm mechanism will continue to sound a warning every time it is applied.

Why would a development organization maintain an unrealistic schedule? One reason is that it is difficult for organizations to deal effectively with the inevitability of a software project overrun because admitting that a schedule will be missed is often perceived as admitting failure. This is especially true at the various levels of management. When a project falls significantly behind schedule, it is not uncommon for senior management to expect the project to get back on track through longer work hours and more people.

Admittedly, adding people can occasionally help a late project in the following circumstances:

- When there are open (unstaffed) project positions
- When there are additional developers available who are familiar with the project
- When the project is briefly in need of special expertise to solve a particular problem
- At peaks, such as adding testers during the test phase

But in most cases, adding people obeys the famous Brook's Law: *adding more people to a late project makes it later* [4]. This occurs because managers often fail to take into consideration the overhead of getting new team members up to speed and the added team communication and management cost. And, of course, some tasks take the same amount of time no matter how many people are assigned to them.

When an organization realizes that a project schedule is no longer realistic, and more work and more people will not solve the problem, the result is usually a new schedule. How are schedule alarms determined for this new extended schedule?

When a new schedule is produced, treat the *remaining* work to be done as if it were a new project while ignoring the past. Divide the remaining schedule into 12 phases, look at the last three, and continue with the same method described for the original schedule (see Section 2.1.1).

Consider the following example, which picks up at the point of the alarm at the end of month 7 in Table 2.2. Let us assume that following the alarm, a decision was made to halt the project and reorganize. This means that the project is in severe trouble and the 50% overrun would not be eliminated within the original schedule. As part of the project reorganization, a new more realistic schedule is prepared (we shall see in the following chapters how this is done).

The new extended schedule would then be 18 months[4] from the start of the project, but only 11 months from the time that the schedule was extended. These 11 months are the basis for the new alarm points. This is like simply monitoring an 11-month project (we are disregarding the time that has passed).

Let us see how this will work. The remaining 11-month period begins at the end of the first seven months of the original schedule. To simplify matters, we will assume that the 11 months are equal to 48 weeks, and therefore the length of each of the new 12 phases will be 4 weeks (see Table 2.3). We will use the same alarm points that we used in the original schedule.

---

[4] Of course, there is often the option to remain with the original schedule while reducing the project scope.

Table 2.3 Alarm Points in a Sample Extended Schedule

Phase of Remaining Extended Schedule	Extended Project Schedule (Elapsed Time Since the Beginning of the Project)	Schedule Alarm Point (Percentage Overrun of Extended Schedule)
1	7 months + 4 weeks	
2	7 months + 8 weeks	
3	7 months + 12 weeks	20%
4	7 months + 16 weeks	25%
5	7 months + 20 weeks	30%
6	7 months + 24 weeks	30%
7	7 months + 28 weeks	33%
8	7 months + 32 weeks	35%
9	7 months + 36 weeks	35%
10	7 months + 40 weeks	40%
11	7 months + 44 weeks	40%
12	7 months + 48 weeks	40%

The two initial phases of the remaining new schedule (8 weeks in this example) may be perceived as a form of grace period where management intervention is limited. During this initial period, the project reorganizes and is given an opportunity to demonstrate that it can adhere to the new schedule.

At the end of phase 3 (week 12), the project should be reviewed. Has the project slipped from its new schedule? If so, has the delay steadily grown in each phase, and is the total delay now greater than three phases—that is, 12 weeks or 25% of the *remaining* project schedule?

Similar schedule reviews should be performed at the end of every phase (in our example, in weeks 16, 20, 24, and so on) to determine whether (a) the project is generally on track according to the new schedule, and (b) the project schedule problems are manageable, and if not, (c) the project has again become a catastrophe.

Advisory: Projects slip their schedule when tasks are not completed on time. However, the task load of a project is usually not distributed evenly throughout the schedule; the load is usually lighter at the beginning and greater toward the end (see Figure 2.2). This is one of the reasons why schedule slippage is usually easier to recover in the early phases of a project (if treated) than in later phases.

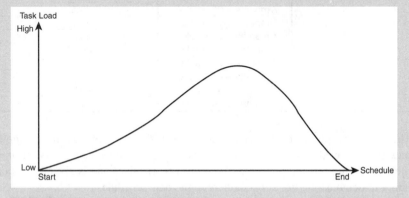

Figure 2.2 Software project task load

2.2   Budget

If we have a schedule alarm, do we also need a budget alarm? There is a belief in some business circles that budgets and schedules are interchangeable: a shortage in one can be compensated by an increase or extension of the other. This notion is occasionally true to varying degrees, but it is certainly not generally true, especially in software development.

Admittedly, though, there are some software projects where schedules can look fine due to excessive spending (such as greatly increasing the development team, contracting out parts of the project, or acquiring sophisticated development equipment and facilities). Such cases would not trigger a schedule alarm, but the cost of the project may be significantly more than the development organization is willing to pay.

Also, as we have seen, a late project may appear to be under control, especially if the original scheduled completion date is not critical and the expected overrun is acceptable. But the resulting budget overrun may not be unacceptable.

So budgets require a different catastrophe alarm mechanism than schedules. All the same, as we shall see, the techniques are not drastically different.

2.2.1   Setting a Budget Alarm

A project is a budget catastrophe if its remaining projected cost far exceeds what the development organization is willing to pay for it. In software projects, major budget overruns are often the result of schedule overruns or of attempts to reduce schedule overruns (for example, by adding staff). Consequently, schedule alarms should be evaluated before budget alarms. If the schedule has not indicated a project catastrophe, the status of the budget should be reviewed.

The budget review measures the remaining cost of the project in relation to the project's break-even point. This point is a predetermined value derived from the financial advantage to the organization. Thus, the budget alarm is triggered if the expected remaining cost of the project exceeds its break-even value.

How is the break-even value calculated? The answer greatly depends on the development organization within which the project is being developed. In a commercial organization (that is, a business), the break-even value is a function of the organization's expected *return on investment* (ROI).[5] That means that if the development of the project costs X, the revenue (or other form of value) generated by the project must be at least Y, and it must be realized within a period Z. Y is some function of X (such as $Y = 3X$), and Z depends on various financial factors (interest rates, expected life of the product, and so on), but is often between three and five years.

For non-commercial organizations (for example, the Department of Defense), the break-even value of a project is calculated based on the benefit that it produces (such as an air defense system), and it may be difficult to quantify (for example, the US F22 Stealth Fighter project cost $25 billion). In such cases, a detailed budget is established and the project is expected to stay within the boundaries of that budget (though, in reality, it is often revised).

When calculating a budget alarm, these are points to consider:

1. Does the project schedule appear to be a catastrophe? If so, project cost projections have little value at this time.

2. If the project schedule appears to be under control, then extrapolate budget overruns for the past three schedule phases up to the end of the most current updated project schedule (assume that every future phase will continue to exceed the budget at a similar rate). Is this a cost your organization can bear?

3. Have the project's customers and users recently provided feedback? Has the market research data been recently updated? Is the original cost/value and ROI analysis for this project still valid?

---

[5] For a brief overview of ROI concepts, see Wettemann [8], and for a more detailed discussion, see Denne and Cleland-Huang [9].

Let us consider the example in Table 2.4. We will assume again for simplicity that the sample project represents a 12-month schedule, and each phase is one month. The project budget is being evaluated at the end of month 6. The table shows that the monthly budget for month 6 was exceeded by 60%, while the total budget for all of the first six months was exceeded by 35%.

Table 2.4 Sample Project with Budget Overrun
(Note that the budget is not allocated equally for each phase)

Phase of Schedule	Phase Budget Overrun	Cumulative Budget Overrun
1	0%	0%
2	-3%	-2%
3	10%	4%
4	40%	19%
5	50%	28%
→ 6	60%	35%
7		
8		
9		
10		
11		
12		

The project starts off fairly well, from a budget perspective. The first two months have had no budget overruns, and the project was under budget in the second month. Month 3 begins to show a budget overrun, which consistently increases up to month 6.

We derive the rate of overrun growth (not the simple growth) from the most recent three phases in the cumulative budget column. The overrun in month 4 has grown at a rate of 375% (4% to 19%), in month 5 the rate was 47%, and in month 6 it was 25%. To predict how the project costs will continue to behave, we can fit a curve to these points.[6] The curve indicates that while the budget overrun is growing, it is doing so at diminishing rates. Thus, if we assume a similar rate trend for the remaining months of the project, we will predict that the budget overrun in month 7 will grow at roughly 21% (see Figure 2.3) and about 19%, 16%, and 14% in months 8, 9, and 10, and 12% in months 11 and 12. This simple technique produces a projection of the overall cost of the project based on the assumption that the rate of overrun growth will continue (another way of saying this is that we are assuming that problem level trend now being encountered by the development team will continue).

---

[6] This is achieved through a branch of statistics called Regression Analysis (see [5]). There are many tools that will easily fit a curve using simple (and good enough) mathematics, such as Microsoft's Excel.

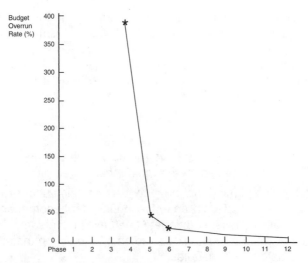

Figure 2.3 Fitting a curve to a budget overrun

Let us continue the example in Table 2.4 with some sample budgetary figures. We will assume that the budget for the sample project is two million dollars. The allocation by phase appears in Table 2.5 with the projected budget growth in the shaded cells, based on the rate trend produced by the function in Figure 2.4. This results in a projected budget overrun of $1.7 million for the whole project. At the end of month six, we expect the completion of the project to cost

$$(2,000,000 + 1,700,000) - (\$720,000 + \$254,900) = \underline{\$2,725,100}$$

This figure rightly ignores the costs already expended. Thus, the question to be answered at the end of month 6 is this: Is the completed project worth $2.7 million to the company? If not, the budget alarm is triggered.

Table 2.5 Example of Budget Overrun for a $2M Budget
(Shaded cells contain estimated values)

Schedule Phase	Allocated Budget by Phase	Cumulative Allocated Budget	Phase Budget Overrun (%)	Phase Budget Overrun ($)	Cumulative Budget Overrun (% Rounded)	Cumulative Budget Overrun ($)
1	$50,000	$50,000	0%	0	0%	0
2	$70,000	$120,000	-3%	-$2,100	-2%	-$2,100
3	$110,000	$230,000	10%	$11,000	4%	$8,900
4	$160,000	$390,000	40%	$64,000	19%	$72,900
5	$160,000	$550,000	50%	$80,000	28%	$152,900
→ 6	$170,000	$720,000	60%	$102,000	35%	$254,900
7	$180,000	$900,000			43%	$387,000
8	$200,000	$1,100,000			51%	$561,000
9	$220,000	$1,320,000			60%	$792,000
10	$250,000	$1,570,000			68%	$1,067,600
11	$250,000	$1,820,000			76%	$1,383,200
12	$180,000	$2,000,000			85%	$1,700,000

Does the triggering of a budget alarm mean that the project is no longer worth developing (and therefore should be cancelled)? Not necessarily. It is the *projected* cost that has triggered the alarm. A reduction in project scope may make the cost acceptable again, as may other reductions in development spending. As we shall see in the following chapters, this is the objective of the disentanglement process.

Advisory:

1. Re-plot the budget overrun curve every phase (month) based on the most recent three phases.

2. Keep in mind that project costs can also under-run the budget—not an entirely unusual phenomenon. This is because budgets often exhibit the same expand-and-shrink accordion phenomenon that characterizes schedules.

3. The curve should be extended to the end of the most recent schedule; if at some point the project was formally extended by three months, the budget should have been reallocated for each phase based on the updated budget plan for the extended schedule.

4. Just as a new schedule is given a form of grace period for two phases, so should the budget. Thus, budget alarms should be evaluated from the third phase after the extended schedule is put into effect.

5. Because the early phases of a project are less costly than the later phases (less staff, less equipment, less facilities, less outside support costs, and so on), the impact of actual cost deviations on the overall budget is small. In the later phases, the opposite is true.

2.2.2 Additional Budget Alarm Consideration

Budget overrun growth trends enable us to use more of the available data than just the total budget overrun. In some cases, there may be justification to look further back than three phases, but we would then lose (or greatly complicate) the ability to factor in correction. *Correction* is the change of behavior by the project team members when they recognize that the project is going off track; this results in corrective action, such as the introduction of better development methods and processes, efficiency measures, cost control, the removal of product features, and better management practices (the following chapters will discuss this in more detail).

This is also the reason that a grace period of two phases is granted after new schedules and budgets are introduced. In this period, the project team is given an opportunity to reorganize. Without a grace period, we would constantly be declaring a catastrophe while the project was getting back on track—not exactly the right atmosphere for re-motivating a team.

Another point to consider is that when determining the product's break-even cost point, it is important to take into account intangible factors, such as the morale loss and the public image cost of a halted (or cancelled) project—these factors can often be quantified. Moreover, a company may legitimately decide to develop and release a product at a loss as a marketing or strategic business investment. These factors all play a major role in determining the products break-even cost point.

2.3   Software Quality

When should a software project's poor quality raise an alarm? The problem with quality is that it is difficult to define. Schedules and budgets are easier to define, but if we are to base critical decisions on quality, we must first be clear about what it means.

Most software development organizations define software quality as a combination of customer and user satisfaction, the degree to which the software is defect free, and the degree to which it conforms to requirements [7].

The IEEE demonstrated the difficulty in defining quality when in 1982 it published its first glossary of software engineering terms [6] with four different definitions for the term "software quality." In later editions of the glossary, this was replaced with two definitions of the term "quality": (a) meeting requirements and (b) meeting customer needs or expectations.

Quality, according to the first definition, can be measured relative to a list of software requirements, though this definition can be problematic because modern requirements analysis has become a dynamic process. There are many techniques for measuring adherence to requirements, but one of the most common is the use of problem lists where each problem is a deviation from the requirements (this includes deviations from development procedures and standards). The severity and length of the problem lists then become a measure of software quality.

Quality, according to the second definition, really refers to overall customer satisfaction (as opposed to the opinion of any individual customer or user) and is not easy to measure, especially during development. One solution is to involve customers and users throughout the product development cycle by using prototypes, intermediate evaluation versions, and beta releases. The degree of satisfaction in the customer feedback then becomes a measure of the software product's quality (this is further discussed in Section 2.3.2).

Now that we have defined quality and how to measure it, we can proceed to the quality alarm mechanism.

A software project is a quality catastrophe if (a) the list of serious quality problems has been substantial for three periods and is not decreasing or if (b) customers and users who have evaluated the software while it is being developed are exceptionally critical of it.

2.3.1 The Problem List Alarm

The project problem list is a good indicator of the status of a software project. The list is commonly divided into (a) critical, (b) serious, and (c) minor problems.

Points to consider are as follows:

- Is the critical problem list growing? Are problems being resolved? How quickly are new problems being added?

- The second level of quality problems (serious) can also indicate the gravity of the situation if the list is particularly long and not getting any shorter.

- Are there objective estimates of the time needed to correct critical and serious problems (based on historical data or external expert estimates)?

- Another indicator to monitor is how well the quality problem lists are being maintained. Are problems being categorized correctly? Are problems being removed prematurely from the list? Are new problems being withheld from the list?

Severe quality problems (those that are either critical or most serious) are often difficult, if not impossible, to see in the early stages of a project. In fact, many severe quality problems emerge only toward the end of the project (and sometimes only after its release). Even the "last three phases" technique can be ineffective during the first half of the project because often problem lists have not yet been compiled or well maintained.

But project quality issues can be monitored from the outset if there is someone whose job it is to do so. This means assigning an independent *software quality assurance* (SQA) professional to every project team as soon as the project is launched. For small development teams, one SQA professional can be responsible for two or three projects, though large projects should have their own indigenous SQA team.

Consider the problem list example in Table 2.6. The project is being evaluated at the end of phase 8. How serious are the problems, and how concerned should we be?

Table 2.6 Example of a Project Problem List Summary

Phase of Schedule	Number of Minor Problems	Number of Serious Problems	Number of Critical Problems
1	0	0	0
2	18	0	0
3	14	1	0
4	10	8	1
5	25	4	3
6	45	12	2
7	25	9	5
→ 8	63	14	8
9			
10			
11			
12			

As problems are resolved, they are removed from the problem list, and the number of problems decreases. But as new problems are discovered, the number rises again. So, here too, we should consider the trend. We should also consider the actual number of critical and serious problems and apply historical data from our development organization (if available) in assessing the amount of time needed to correct the problems.

In the example in Table 2.6, the number of critical problems dropped by 1 in phase 6, then rose by 3 in phase 7, and rose again by 3 in phase 8. Because problem list activity will increase significantly toward the end of the project (phases 9–12), all we can conclude on the basis of this data is that the number of critical problems is rising, and there is a risk that the list could grow out of control. Historical data from the development organization's previous projects can help us predict how the critical problem list will grow in future phases and how long it will take to purge the list. This, in turn, will determine how concerned we should be.

The serious problem list grew by 8 in phase 6, then dropped by 3 in phase 7, and grew again by 5 in phase 8. There is no indication here of any danger that the list will grow out of control. Here, too, historical data can help us predict the behavior of the serious problem list.

In conclusion, the data in Table 2.6 does not indicate that the quality problems are growing uncontrollably. The development organization's historical data, when available, will help us determine if the number of problems should raise a quality alarm. In the absence of historical data, a review by external experts should be used to corroborate the project team's estimates of the time needed to purge the problem list. To summarize, the problem list trend alone does not raise a quality alarm, but it would be wise to reinforce this conclusion with additional corroborative data.

So, what would catastrophe alarm data look like? The second version of the example, which appears in Table 2.7, shows a software project being evaluated at the end of phase 8. At this point, we see that the problems have been increasing for the last three phases. Critical problems grew by 3 in phase 6, by 2 in phase 7, and by 3 in phase 8, while serious problems grew by 6 in phase 6, by 2 in phase 7, and by 2 in phase 8. The most significant point here is that both the critical and serious problem lists have been growing steadily for the last three phases. If this trend continues, the project may well head for disaster.

The deciding point here is the size of the project. For large projects (large development teams, long schedule, large budget), this number of critical and serious problems may not be an issue; the time and resources to correct them may be available (even within an acceptable overrun). But for smaller projects, the problem list may be overwhelming. Again, historical data can be helpful in determining if the situation is manageable or if the project is heading for disaster.

Table 2.7 Example of a Project Problem List Summary (Version 2)

Phase of Schedule	Number of Minor Problems	Number of Serious Problems	Number of Critical Problems
1	0	0	0
2	18	0	0
3	14	1	0
4	10	0	1
5	25	8	0
6	45	14	3
7	25	16	5
→ 8	63	18	8
9			
10			
11			
12			

Advisory:

1. Problem lists are often most active in the second half of the project, especially in the fourth quarter. However, they can still be useful in earlier stages, provided they are well maintained.

2. The minor problem list usually has little impact on project failure. The minor list can certainly contribute to overruns in a limited way. But by virtue of its definition, a minor problem can usually be easily and quickly corrected, have the feature in which it appears excluded from the product, or delivered in the product without being corrected.

3. Table 2.8 provides a common definition of the three
    levels of quality problems.

Table 2.8 Levels of Software Quality Problems

Critical	The software product is virtually useless if the problem is not corrected.
Serious	One or more major functions of the software product is severely impaired if the problem is not corrected.
Minor	All major functions of the software product will work correctly even if the problem is not corrected.

2.3.2 The Customer Satisfaction Alarm

Customer and user feedback are the best source for evaluating the quality of a software project. Unfortunately, it is sometimes difficult to get feedback before a project is very close to release. For large projects, it is often worth investing in prototypes and prereleases, thus getting preliminary versions of the software into the hands of users for early evaluation and feedback. This investment is like an insurance policy; it reduces the risk of major product quality issues—but at a cost.

When this cost is budgeted within the project plan, it covers the development of intermediate evaluation versions of the software product at various stages during the development cycle. The resulting customer and user feedback from these intermediate product versions can then trigger a quality alarm.

The idea of intermediate project evaluation is not new. In reality, however, most software projects do not plan for it. Under the budget and schedule crunches of modern-day market competition, insurance policy costs are often the first to be cut. And, as with all insurance, when a project becomes suspect of being in trouble, the cost of having no insurance is high. This is because it is often disruptive, time-consuming, and costly to bring a project to an acceptable state for evaluation, if it has not been planned that way. There is also the potential penalty of not evaluating a project (because there is no evaluation version), which can result in quality problems being left to exacerbate.

Clearly, customers can only provide product feedback when there is something they can be given to evaluate. In the early stages of a product, it may be a product document or a prototype. In later phases, it should be a partially functional version of the product. But when a project is suspected of being in serious trouble, and no such evaluation version exists, then one needs to be created. If none can be created within a short period (five to ten days), that itself may well be an alarm.

How is customer feedback evaluated objectively? While this is certainly not an exact science, individual customer and user response styles and mannerisms can be tempered by soliciting responses from several unrelated customers. The responses should then be combined to form a single measure of customer satisfaction. This measure will then be used to trigger the quality alarm.

> **Advisory:** In combining multiple customer responses, it is helpful to use weighted averages based on the characteristics of each customer (representative market group, familiarity with the product, area of expertise, and so on).

2.4   Keeping a Practical Perspective

The catastrophe alarm methods described here work best when combined with a healthy dose of common sense. While the alarms rely on objective qualitative measures, such measures are inherently incomplete, and common sense and subjective considerations must be added to complement them. In particular, the data-driven decision process provides a counter-balance to the notorious optimism that has long been attributed to software programmers.

All the same, the counter-balance will be effective as long as it does not become excessively arduous. There is not much practical advantage in strictly applying these methods if they result in a prolonged project evaluation. When a software project is suspected of being in deep trouble, the longer the decision process, the deeper the trouble, and the more costly the solution.

What, then, is a reasonable amount of time to spend on evaluating a software project and reaching a decision? Again, it depends on the size of the project. A six-month schedule with a team of four developers should usually be evaluated in less than a day. A two-year project with a team of 150 developers may take a week. Generally, the evaluation of any software project should rarely take more than two weeks (with the exception of especially complex or gigantic projects).

There is a fine line for the decision-maker to walk between being too hasty and too slow. On the one hand, it is obviously undesirable to incorrectly brand a project as a catastrophe, but on the other, the fear of making an incorrect decision can become very costly. The decision-maker should be ready to assume some risk. The risk can best be offset or minimized by incorporating experience and familiarity with the development organization into the decision process. Experience can fill in the gaps where project data is either lacking or inconclusive. Returning to the train allegory, train whistles are good alarms, but if you have experienced trains before, you can better recognize how close one is from the sound of its whistle.

> **Advisory:** It is always prudent to expect opposition to any tough decision and to prepare for it. Former U.S. Attorney General Robert Kennedy is quoted as saying that there will always be 30% of the people against anything. But dissent should not prevent decision (though valid counterpoints should certainly be considered). It is important to remember that *no decision* is a decision, too, even if by default.

2.5 Summary

A disastrous project, or catastrophe, is a project that is completely out of control in one or more of the following areas: schedule, budget, or quality. It is like a train coming at you; if you look, you can see it coming. In fact, with the right tools, you can see it coming from quite a distance.

Recent surveys show that software project overruns are not rare. But not every overrun or quality problem means that the project is out of control. The warning signs to look for are that the project is late and getting later, it is over-budget and getting more so, quality is poor and getting poorer, and criticism from customers is severe.

A schedule alarm mechanism evaluates the gravity of the accumulated project delay and determines whether the delay is under control. The delay is compared to both the elapsed and overall schedule. A large delay is difficult to eliminate, especially in the second half of the project, while a small delay early in the project may indicate a worrisome trend. It is important to examine the trend, because if the delay is consistently growing, the project may be entering a spin from which it will not recover and the catastrophe alarm should be triggered.

When it becomes clear that a late project cannot eliminate the overrun, a new realistic schedule should be prepared. The schedule alarm is then measured in relation to the remaining part of the new project schedule (the history is disregarded).

A project is a budget catastrophe if its remaining projected cost far exceeds what the development organization is willing to pay for it. In software projects, major budget overruns are often the result of schedule overruns or of attempts to reduce schedule overruns (for example, by adding staff). Consequently, schedule alarms should be evaluated before budget alarms. The status of the budget should be reviewed only if the schedule review has not indicated a catastrophe.

Warning Signs to Watch for in a Project
- It is late and getting later.
- It is over budget and becoming more so.
- Performance is poor and getting poorer.
- Criticism from customers/users is severe.

The budget review measures the remaining cost of the project in relation to the project's break-even point. This point is a predetermined value derived from the financial advantage to the organization. Thus, the budget alarm is triggered if the expected remaining cost of the project exceeds its break-even value.

The most popular common definition of software quality is related to adherence to requirements and the level of customer satisfaction. One method for measuring adherence to requirements is based on problem lists, where each problem is a deviation from the requirements (this also includes deviations from development procedures and standards). The severity and length of the problem lists, especially the critical and serious lists, provide a measure of software quality. If the lists are growing and problems are not being resolved, a quality alarm is triggered.

Customer satisfaction can be measured by involving customers and users throughout the product development cycle using prototypes, intermediate evaluation versions, and beta releases. The degree of satisfaction in the customer feedback then becomes a measure of the software product's quality. Highly critical customer feedback will trigger a quality alarm.

The catastrophe alarm methods described here work best when combined with a healthy dose of common sense. There is not much practical advantage in strictly applying these methods if they result in prolonged project evaluation. When a software project is suspected of being in deep trouble, the longer the decision process, the deeper the trouble, and the more costly the solution.

Exercises

1. A 25 person-year project is being developed with an 18-month schedule. The following table describes the project's schedule performance for the first seven phases:

Phase	Status	Cumulative Overrun (% of One Phase)	Overall Project Overrun
1	On Time	0%	
2	Early	-30%	
3	On Time	0%	
4	Late	40%	
5	Late	60%	
6	Late	100%	
→ 7	Late	200%	
8			
9			
10			
11			
12			

(a) What conclusions about the project can you draw from analyzing the data in the table? What can you say about months 1–7 in column 4?

(b) Make assumptions to fill in missing information about the project, including the task load distribution, and historical data about the development organization. What additional conclusions can you now draw? Should a schedule alarm be triggered?

(c) Propose phase-based schedule alarm points for this project.

If you concluded in question 1(b) that the project is not a catastrophe, what changes in the data would make it a catastrophe?

If you concluded in question 1(b) that the project is a catastrophe, what changes in the data would make it not a catastrophe?

Explain your answer.

2. A 6 person-year project is being developed with a 12-month schedule. The project is late and is being evaluated at the end of phase 12. The following table describes the project's budget performance for the 12 phases (the table is structured the same as Table 2.4):

Phase of Schedule	Phase Budget Overrun	Cumulative Budget Overrun
1	0%	0%
2	0%	0%
3	0%	0%
4	0%	0%
5	20%	7%
6	50%	22%
7	80%	40%
8	80%	55%
9	100%	70%
10	100%	80%
11	110%	95%
→ 12	120%	105%

(a) At the end of phase 12, what conclusions about the project can you draw from analyzing the data in the table? Is there any data lacking to enable this project to be described a catastrophe? Explain.

(b) Compare the way the project would be evaluated at the end of phases 3, 6, 9, and 12. What would the budget overrun curve look like at each of these four points?

(c) What data is needed for a new project plan with an extended schedule and budget? Make assumptions regarding the missing data and propose a new budget.

3. Find different definitions of software quality from three different organizations (sources may be a library, bookstore, or the Internet) and compare them. Propose quality alarms for each of these definitions and compare them.

4. Consider the following problem list for the project described in question 1:

Phase of Schedule	Number of Minor Problems	Number of Serious Problems	Number of Critical Problems
1	0	0	0
2	12	2	0
3	20	4	2
4	18	6	4
5	20	4	6
6	35	8	9
7	48	12	8
→ 8	65	20	14
9			
10			
11			
12			

(a) At the end of phase 8, what conclusions about the quality of the project can you draw from the data in the table? What data is lacking to enable you to draw a decisive conclusion? Assume any missing data, and explain why the project is or is not a catastrophe.

(b) If you concluded in question 4(a) that the project is *not* a catastrophe, what changes in the data would make it a catastrophe?

If you concluded in question 4(b) that the project *is* a catastrophe, what changes in the data would make it not a catastrophe?

Explain your answer.

(c) Consider the number of minor problems. In your opinion, can this information help substantiate your conclusions? Explain.

5. In preparation for the disentanglement discussion in the following chapters, collect data on an actual project that failed (from your company or organization, from published journals and articles, or from the Internet). Assume any missing data and analyze the project. If you were the director of development responsible for the failed project, what would you have done to save it? Provide sources for the project data, and a detailed analysis and justification of the actions that you would take.

3

Step 1—Stop

Step 10   Early Warning System

Step 9   Revise the Plan

Step 8   Risk Analysis

Step 7   Rebuild the Team

Step 6   Can Minimum Goals Be Achieved?

Step 5   Define Minimum Goals

Step 4   Evaluate the Team

Step 3   Evaluate Project Status

Step 2   Assign an Evaluator

Step 1   Stop

To stop a runaway passenger train, according to a popular survival handbook, you locate the emergency brake, pull the handle, call for help, and then make your way to the front of the train [1].[1] Dealing with a runaway software project is not much different. When you have determined that the project is indeed out of control and is unlikely to be completed with any reasonable degree of success, the next step is painful but clear: pull the brake. Then make your way to the front.

This is a difficult, controversial decision because it will always be open to harsh criticism from some circles. It is a tough decision also because, as we have seen in Chapter 2, "When Is a Project a Catastrophe?" there is really no airtight algorithm for determining that a project is a catastrophe. Ultimately, the decision is a combination of data analysis and management experience.

What are the alternatives? If you have determined that a project is headed for disaster, your options are no different from those of a traveler on a runaway train: You can hope, you can pray, and you can rely on luck. You can even try to take control of the train without stopping it, but chances are that someone has already tried this earlier and failed. So, if you cannot bring the project to a halt, all that is left is the final advice in the survival handbook: proceed calmly and quietly to the rear of the train and prepare for a crash.

It is true that businesses, development organizations, and managers occasionally survive project catastrophes without taking any special action. These are the lucky people who walk away from a crash relatively unscathed. But you cannot run a professional software development organization by relying on luck. Statistics and experience teach us that this would be a poor business strategy.

This chapter focuses on how to stop the train (a better strategy than relying on luck), discusses how to deal with opposition to the controversial step of halting the project, and explains the importance of immediately proceeding to the next step to avoid the destructive consequences of inactivity.

3.1 Stopping the Project

Stopping all development activity is the first step in the process of disentangling a seriously troubled software project. It follows an assessment of the project's condition, as discussed in Chapter 2, and it is triggered when the assessment indicates that the project is unlikely to be completed with any reasonable degree of success.

---

[1] To be accurate, the handbook offers the second and third steps (call for help, move to the front) only if the first two don't stop the train. But we want to do more than just stop the train; we want to get it under control and moving again.

3.1.1 Why Stop the Project?

Why is it necessary to stop the project? Would it not be better to have the project, which is already late, continue while the disentanglement process is being implemented?

There are several reasons why the process will not succeed if development continues in parallel. First, the process requires the full involvement of the key project players (development team members, project support staff, and stakeholders), and this will not happen if they are scrambling to keep the project going. Halting the project ensures that everyone is completely focused on the disentanglement process and thus increases the likelihood that the process will succeed.

Second, disentangling the project requires painful decisions to be made by the key stakeholders and team members (reducing goals, rebuilding the team, and so on). It is only natural that there will be resistance to these changes. Experience shows that it is highly unlikely that the necessary decisions will be made and a feasible project will be re-defined unless everyone involved fully understands that the project will not be permitted to continue in catastrophe mode. In this mode, the project continues to absorb valuable resources without ever reaching its goals (this is a situation that has been aptly documented by Keil [2] and by Nuldén [3]).

Lastly, halting the project sends a very strong message that this time "we mean business." It clearly sets the disentanglement process apart from all previous attempts to get the project back on track by conventional means (adding people, working overtime, extending the schedule, and so on).

3.1.2 Who Initiates the Project Halt?

Who makes the decision? Clearly the answer depends on the management structure of the development organization, but the leading force is usually the senior manager who initiated the disentanglement process (who henceforth will be referred to as the *initiating manager*).

The decision to halt a project should ideally be presented as a management team decision. Thus, when the decision is announced, there is a clear advantage in having as wide a range of support as possible. If possible, this should include the CEO or head of the organization, as well as other key managers.

It may also be an advantage to have other key stakeholders as part of the decision-making team because it can increase their commitment to the disentanglement process (a most desirable quality, as we shall later see). However, this can also complicate and delay the decision due to the risk of excessive politics, bias, and personal interests.

To summarize this point:

- The project halt should be initiated, at a minimum, by the initiating manager.

- There is usually an advantage in including more senior managers in the decision.
- Adding key stakeholders to the decision group can be either an advantage or a disadvantage. Decide with caution.

3.1.3 The Project Halt Procedure

The following checklist describes the procedure for halting the project. The procedure should be implemented by the initiating manager together with the project evaluator, if that person has already been appointed. The procedure is divided into four main activities: prepare, take action, follow up, and continue to the next step. (Several of the checklist items are revisited in more detail later in this chapter.)

1. **Prepare**

    - **Have a work plan for the project team.**

      When the decision is announced, ensure that a clear work plan is defined for all members of the project team (see Section 3.2). Be aware that idleness, even for a short period of time, can create additional problems (attrition, frustration, and so on).

    - **Brief key players.**

      Meet individually with the project manager and senior project team members, as well as other key stakeholders, and inform them of the intention to launch a rescue process for the project. The main goal is to alleviate concerns and to dispel rumors.

    - **Prepare for opposition.**

      Every decision, even the best and the most popular, will always have to deal with opposition from some circles. Certainly this is true of such an emotionally charged decision as halting a project. Do not be alarmed by opposition, though by all means listen to what opponents have to say (they may bring up points you have overlooked). But make it clear that the decision to halt the project is not being reopened for debate (unless you are provided with some radically new information). Emphasize that the disentanglement's goal is to save the project, if justification can be found for doing so.

      More detailed guidelines for dealing with opposition are presented in Section 3.4.

    - **Prepare to present your plan.**

      Halting a project will usually draw reaction from other members of senior management, customers, and other stakeholders, particularly if the project is large (and if the project's budget is large). Here, too, be prepared to present the overall disentanglement plan and to provide the reasoning behind the decision to launch it.

2.   Take action

- **Halt the project.**

  Formally announce that all development activity on the project is to cease. Ensure that the announcement is communicated to all relevant persons, and ensure that it is implemented.

3.   Follow up

- **Immediately meet individually with key staff.**

  Meet individually with any key staff members who were not briefed earlier, and solicit their support for the disentanglement process. For the key players who participated in the briefing that preceded the halt announcement, this meeting may be short or even unnecessary.

- **Communicate immediately the reasoning that led to the decision and the process that will follow.**

  Convene a town hall meeting to communicate information throughout the development organization about the disentanglement process and conduct a brief question and answer session. This will disperse rumors, and will help enlist support on a broad front.

4.   Continue on to the next step

- **Continue without delay to the next step of the disentanglement process.**

  If a project evaluator has not already been recruited, begin immediately to seek one. This is further discussed in Section 3.2.

In some organizations, the level of formal consultation described here may be excessive. For smaller organizations and smaller projects, many of these activities can be performed informally. However, the guiding principle should be to provide all involved parties with the feeling that they are being consulted, informed, and invited to participate in the disentanglement process. In particular, this should be well reflected in this first step.

Even in large organizations with large projects, the project halt procedure should be adapted to the organization because not all organizations and projects teams will react with the same level of intensity. Therefore, when deciding how to apply the halt procedure, it is useful to consider such factors as

- The importance of the project to the organization
- The size of the project team and the project's budget
- The emotions and sensitivities of the project team and other stakeholders
- The amount of budget already expended on the project[2]

---

[2] Although expended funds often play a part in decisions about troubled projects, in many cases, this factor is best excluded from the decision process. The funds required to *complete* the project are a much more relevant factor.

- The level of anticipation that the project will be cancelled
- The level of confidence that the project can be salvaged

How long should this step take? Theoretically, it is an instantaneous activity (zero time), but in reality this is not the case. This is because halting the project includes preparation and follow-up activities. Also, the need to quickly continue on to the next step is included in the halt procedure because of its extreme importance, though it is more a cautionary cue than an activity. Thus, the entire procedure, including preparation and follow-up, should take no more than one day.

> **Advisory:** Before making the halt announcement, review and think through all ten steps of the disentanglement process and the way they will be applied. Describe the complete process when communicating your decision. This will demonstrate that halting the project is part of a well-thought-out course of action.

3.2   Preparing for the Next Step

In some cases, the project evaluator will be already assigned and available for this first step of the process. As we have seen, this is the most desirable situation. But when this cannot be achieved, preparations to find a suitable evaluator (step 2) are performed in parallel to halting the project. In effect, preparing for step 2 becomes an integral part of step 1.

The reason for merging these two seemingly separate activities is that they are, in fact, very much connected. The link between the two is the critical need to quickly move forward with the disentanglement process after project is halted. By starting a search for candidates early, we can gain valuable extra time to find the right person for the evaluator position.

The following list of activities will help ensure that the next step follows with minimal delay:

1. **Allocate funds for the project evaluation and for the entire disentanglement process.**

    These funds must be made available before the project is halted. The cost of the evaluator, experts, office facilities, secretarial services, and other miscellaneous costs should be covered.

2. **Define the required qualifications of the evaluator.**

    Prepare a formal list of qualifications for the evaluator. If the project is complex, enlist the help of a senior technical person to assist in the definition of the evaluator's qualifications. The list should be prepared as early as possible. (This is further discussed in Chapter 4, "Step 2— Assign an Evaluator.")

3. **Begin a search for evaluator candidates.**

   The search should begin as early as possible, and the initiating manager is responsible for selecting a suitable candidate. (Chapter 4 discusses guidelines for selecting a suitable evaluator.)

4. **Allocate office facilities and services for the disentanglement process.**

   This activity is more important than it sounds. Decent facilities (office, conference room, equipment, and so on), in addition of being the tools for the job, will help establish the importance management attaches to the evaluator's activities.

Before halting the project, review these four activities. If you expect major problems in preparing for step 2 (especially in locating candidates for evaluator), consider delaying the entire process (including halting the project) for a few days until the problems are resolved. Anything beyond a few days is usually an indication the disentanglement process lacks the necessary organizational support and will therefore probably fail.

3.3 Development Team Activities

As discussed earlier, stopping a project should never leave a team idle. Apart from the fact that after the project is halted, there is still much to do, an idle team is detrimental to any attempt to rescue the project because inactivity breeds discontent, frustration, and staff attrition.

Because the risk of an idle team is a by-product of halting the project, its resolution is considered part of the project halt step and is included in the "prepare" stage of the halt procedure (see Section 3.1.3). This means that a work plan for the project team should be prepared before the project is halted.

After the project is halted, the initiating manager together with the project manager should ensure that all team members understand the work they need to perform in preparing the project for assessment. This includes the following tasks:

1. **Collecting and updating project documentation and data**

   All project document items should be collected, and all project team members should update the items relevant to their areas of responsibility (individual progress reports, error reports, unit test results, and other development documentation items). Support personnel (testers, and so on) should also prepare updated plans and status reports.

All team members should participate in updating high-level project documents, such as project requirements and design specifications. The project manager should divide these responsibilities among the project team members. Then the project manager should review the documents and reports to ensure their accuracy.

2. **Preparing status reports**

In addition to the project documentation, each team member should prepare an individual status report that should include the following:

- Tasks completed
- Status of tasks being developed
- Personal work schedule to the end of the project
- Problems

3. **Bringing the project software to the nearest point for demonstration**

The objective of this activity is to demonstrate the status of the project, if possible, with a live demonstration, and if this is not possible, with a passive prototype or graphic presentation. The project should be brought to the nearest demonstration point backward, but not forward. This means that, except for minor exceptions, no new code should be written, no new features should be added or integrated, and no defects should be corrected (otherwise, there is a risk that the demonstration will take much too long to prepare).

4. **Assisting the project evaluator**

As soon as the evaluator is assigned to the project, the team members will be expected to assist the evaluator throughout the disentanglement process.

5. **Additional activities**

In addition, other activities should be prepared and held in reserve, such as training and assistance to other projects.

Advisory: Though additional reserve team activities, such as training, temporary reassignment, and even vacation, are sometimes justified, it is important to ensure that all team members remain available or can easily be recalled should they be required to assist during the disentanglement process.

3.4   Dealing with Opposition

We have seen that the decision to halt a software project can generate significant opposition, particularly if it is a high-profile project. While this opposition may be based on issues of substance, it can also be the result of the high emotions, deep concerns, and significant political undercurrents that characterize projects that are in deep trouble.[3]

Following are some points to consider in dealing with opposition:

- Prepare a broad level of management support. Start at the top: brief the highest levels of management in the organization and stress that you expect opposition. Have these levels of management make their support known. They should also make public that you have been assigned the authority to make the decisions related to the disentanglement process.

- Be ready to provide to the opponents an overview of the disentanglement process. Stress that the project is only halted for two weeks while an attempt is being made to save it.

- Make sure your decision is perceived as being professional and resolute. Prepare a brief explanation of the reasoning behind your decision. Make it clear that the decision is no longer open to debate (though you should always be prepared to listen to new information if it is really new and of substance).

- Ensure that opponents understand that the alternative to the process may be canceling the project. Be prepared to present examples of projects (from your organization or from others) that were not salvaged in time and were subsequently cancelled. Then present examples of projects that were successfully saved by using this or similar processes.

- Be prepared for the suggestion that you should launch the disentanglement process without halting the project. This is rarely a good strategy. Halting the project ensures that everyone is completely focused on the disentanglement process and increases the likelihood that the process will succeed.

Generally speaking, it is best to operate with broad agreement among all parties involved in the project. This is best served by discussing decisions with the relevant stakeholders before they are made. However, common management wisdom maintains that there comes a time when too much reconsideration and reevaluation can paralyze an organization. Thus, you should strike a reasonable balance between the need to enlist broad support and the need to act swiftly.

---

[3] In reality, these are also issues of substance, but emotional issues require a more temperate approach (compared to the brisk pragmatic approach to business issues).

As a final point, a good way to deal with significant opposition to the disentanglement process without creating excessive delay is to debate the disentanglement decision in parallel to the preparations to implement it. So, for example, the search for an evaluator can (and should) proceed in parallel to the debate. However, it is important to be aware that this parallel approach makes it difficult to control the flow of early information to all involved parties. This is not necessarily a bad thing, provided the information is provided authoritatively and accurately (this will ensure that what flows is information rather than rumor).

3.5   What Can Go Wrong (and What to Do About It)

Halting a project is the first active step in the disentanglement process. It almost, though not quite, makes the process irreversible. It is therefore important to ensure that the process is indeed ready to be launched before proceeding with this first step.

Here or some problems that can occur and suggestions on how to deal with them:

- **Funding problems**

  The disentanglement process itself is not a costly activity, though the halting of the project for two weeks can be perceived as costly (of course, the alternative is usually more costly!).

  In most cases, the necessary funds can be allocated from within existing budgets. If the initiating manager cannot find the required funding for the process, either (a) the organization is not sufficiently dedicated to the process or (b) the process should be launched by a more senior manager.

  Action: The disentanglement process has little or no chances of success without a supportive organization and should not be attempted without it.

  If the person who initiated the process does not have the necessary authority, there are three options:

  1. Convince a more senior manager to become the initiating manager.

  2. Lobby the organization's management for the necessary authority.

  3. Abandon the disentanglement process.

  Of the three options, option 1 is most probably the best. This is because the emotions, politics, and concerns that usually accompany failing projects will inevitably produce problems during the disentanglement process that will require the involvement of a senior sponsor, and it is best if the initiating manager has the authority and the status to fill that role.

- **Severe opposition**

  We have seen that the politics, emotions, and concerns that characterize a failing project can generate significant opposition to halting the project and, in fact, to the entire disentanglement process.

  Action: Suitable responses to this problem are discussed in Section 3.4.

- **Weak management support**

  Many of the problems that will inevitably arise during the disentanglement process will require support from the highest levels of the organization's management (see, for example, Section 3.4). Problems arise when senior management appears unaware of the extent of the crisis, does not allocate enough time to resolve the problems, or generally provides limited or no support. Without this support, the process will have limited or no prospect of success.

  Action: The organizational status of the initiating manager must be sufficient to be able to lobby and convince the organization's top-level management to support the disentanglement process. Otherwise, a similar approach to the solutions in problem 1 listed previously should be pursued (convince, lobby, or abandon).

  Lobbying and convincing top-management requires much preparation. This should include documented case studies: examples of projects that failed because they were permitted to run their course without applying an orderly rescue process, as well as projects that were successfully rescued.

- **Unprepared for the next step**

  As we have seen, a smooth and seamless transition to step 2 of the disentanglement process is important. Being unprepared usually means that either insufficient effort was invested or, despite the considerable efforts, no suitable candidates for evaluator were located.

  Action: If insufficient effort has been invested in preparations for step 2, (a) increase the awareness of the importance of this activity and (b) postpone halting the project at least until two potential candidates are located.

  If, despite all efforts, no candidates have been located, postpone the halting of the project and refer to the "What Can Go Wrong" section in Chapter 4 for appropriate action.

It is important to remember that it is rare for all the problems discussed in this chapter to occur in a single project. A continual lack of cooperation is uncommon, and when it does occur, it is usually displayed by no more than a few individuals. In fact, most project personnel know very well when a project is in danger of cancellation and will cooperate with the disentanglement process, often quite willingly, because ultimately it is in their interest to do so.

Advisory: If the disentanglement process appears to be ill-pre-
pared (no evaluator candidates, insufficient funding, no
support), it is probably a good idea to postpone the first
step until the process is better prepared. Otherwise, in
the runaway train allegory, it would be like pulling the
emergency brake at the wrong time and derailing the
train over a cliff.

3.6 Summary

Stopping all development activity is the first step in the process of disentangling
a seriously troubled software project. The decision to halt the project will usually be made by the senior manager who initiated the disentanglement process
(referred to as the *initiating manager*).

The following checklist describes the procedure for halting the project:

1. Prepare
    - Have a work plan for the project team.
    - Brief key players.
    - Prepare for opposition.
    - Prepare to present your plan.

2. Take action
    - Halt the project.

3. Follow up
    - Immediately meet individually with key staff.
    - Communicate immediately the reasoning that led to the decision and
      the process that will follow.

4. Continue on to the next step
    - Continue without delay to the next step of the disentanglement
      process.

Not all teams will react to halting the project with the same level of intensity.
Therefore, when deciding how to apply the halt procedure, it is useful to consider
factors such as

- The importance of the project to the organization
- The amount of budget already expended on the project

- The size of the project team and the project's budget
- The emotions and sensitivities of the project team and other stakeholders
- The level of anticipation that the project will be halted
- The level of confidence that the project can be salvaged

Theoretically, halting a project is an instantaneous activity (zero time), but in reality this is not the case. The entire procedure, including preparation and follow-up, should take no more than one day.

Preparations to find a suitable evaluator (step 2) are performed in parallel to halting the project and, in effect, preparing for step 2 becomes an integral part of step 1. This is because of the critical need to quickly move forward with the disentanglement process after project is halted. These preparations include

1. Allocation of funds for the project evaluation and for the entire disentanglement process
2. Definition of the required qualifications of the evaluator
3. Beginning a search for evaluator candidates
4. Allocation of office facilities and services for the disentanglement process

If you expect major problems in preparing for step 2 (especially in locating candidates for evaluator), consider delaying the entire process (including halting the project) for a few days until the problems are resolved. Anything beyond a few days is usually an indication that the disentanglement process lacks the necessary organizational support and would therefore probably fail.

After the project is halted, the initiating manager together with the project manager should ensure that all team members understand the work they need to perform in preparing the project for assessment.

The decision to halt a software project can generate significant opposition, particular if it is a high-profile project. While this opposition may be based on issues of substance, it can also be the result of the high emotions, the deep concerns, and the significant political undercurrents that characterize projects that are in deep trouble.

Exercises

1. Razor Car Rental Inc. has quickly grown from a small, local company with 12 rental locations to a nationwide company with 180 locations. Razor is losing new business because of its antiquated rental system, and so Razor has hired Western Administrative Software Engineers (WASTE) to quickly develop a Fleet And Reservation Management system (FARM). WASTE committed to developing the FARM in 14 months at a cost of $2.6 million.

    It is now 22 months since the WASTE started working on the FARM (they are eight months late and they have spent $4.2 million), and they now say they will complete the FARM in another six months and the total cost will be $5 million.

    You are Razor's initiating manager, and you have decided to halt the project as part of the disentanglement process. Prepare a documented plan of all the tasks you will need to complete before and directly after the project is halted. What problems specific to the FARM do you expect and how are your preparing to deal with them?

2. Review the FARM project described in exercise 1. As Razor's initiating manager, consider two alternate strategies: (1) Halt the WASTE team and start evaluating the FARM, and (2) Let the WASTE team continue development, and evaluate the FARM in parallel.

    Compare the two strategies specifically for the FARM. Identify the positive and negative aspects of each and list any assumptions that you make. Are there any conditions under which you would choose strategy 2 (explain)?

3. Class project: Review the FARM project described in exercise 1. Designate a class debate moderator. Divide the class (less the moderator) into two groups, one representing Razor and one representing WASTE.

    The Razor team should designate key players of the company, including the initiating manager. The WASTE team should also designate their key players including the FARM manager and the senior WASTE managers.

    The WASTE position is that Razor should permit the FARM to continue for another six months at which time it will be completed, and that halting the project will only make the problem worse. The Razor position is that the WASTE must be halted and re-assessed; otherwise, it may never end. Hold a moderated class debate between the two teams on why the project should or should not be halted, and have the moderator keep notes of the key arguments and the counter-positions that are presented. After the debate, review the key points that were brought up.

4

Step 2—Assign an Evaluator

Step 10   Early Warning System
Step 9   Revise the Plan
Step 8   Risk Analysis
Step 7   Rebuild the Team
Step 6   Can Minimum Goals Be Achieved?
Step 5   Define Minimum Goals
Step 4   Evaluate the Team
Step 3   Evaluate Project Status
Step 2   Assign an Evaluator
Step 1   Stop

In Sun Tzu's *Manual for War*, the famed strategist declares that "emotions have no place in military decisions" [4]. In the nineties, Sun Tzu became required reading for senior managers throughout corporate America, though his strategies were subject to quite a bit of cherry picking. One example is his statement about emotions, which is often questioned because some emotions clearly do have a place in business management (and probably in battle too), as in the case of excitement and enthusiasm.

But it is also true that some emotions, such as anger and despair, can have a negative effect on decision making, clouding one's judgment and fostering bias. Assumedly, this is the context in which Sun Tzu made his statement.

When software projects are in trouble, it is not uncommon for decisions to be driven by emotion, producing passionate advocates and opponents. Thus, when a failing project is being evaluated, anyone even remotely associated with it will, to some extent, be influenced, or suspected of being influenced, by its emotional overtones. This makes difficult decisions even more difficult, which in turn can result in the project sinking ever deeper into trouble. So paradoxically, the project's strongest supporters can inadvertently end up contributing to its demise.

How can this paradox be avoided? Can emotions be put aside so the development organization can concentrate on the business of saving the troubled project? In reality, it is often difficult for anyone close to the project to disregard emotions and make an objective evaluation. Let us see how the issue is dealt with in a case study (from Steve McConnell's book, *Rapid Development* [1]):

> An inventory-control system, ICS 2.0, had been almost finished for quite a while with repeated requests for "another few weeks." After many extensions (due to ostensibly minor setbacks), it became clear that no one really knew when the project would be finished.

> Eventually, a senior manager cancelled the project but later revived it, this time with the help of an external evaluator (McConnell calls him a "project-recovery expert"). The evaluator spent a few weeks learning the project and its problems and preparing a new schedule together with the project team. The main goal was redefined as "finishing the project," not "delivering all the requirements," and several features were removed and targeted for later releases. (These are called "win conditions," which form a minimized achievable goal—the "win" condition.)

> According to the new schedule, which was worked out jointly by the evaluator and the team, the project would be completed in another ten weeks. The difference this time was that the project had been reduced in scope, and it was now reasonable to fit it into the new schedule (this reasonableness had been one of the missing ingredients in the original schedule). Another difference was that the team had mapped out all the required work tasks and had identified risks and dealt with them—something they had not done before.

> McConnell states that the reduced ICS 2.0 project was completed in nine weeks, and that everyone considered the modified project a "win."

One of the central points of the ICS 2.0 story is that repeated attempts to get the project back on track failed until the assignment of an external evaluator who was free of any preconceptions. The need to reduce project functionality, as well as other necessary project changes, was easier to recognize with fresh unemotional thinking. In the new project plan, inflexibility was replaced with realistic pragmatism (*the main goal was redefined as "finishing the project," not "delivering all the requirements"*). It is especially interesting that the project, after all its delays and problems, was still considered a "win."

For another example, let us return to the troubled Canadian government software project mentioned in Chapter 2, "When Is a Project a Catastrophe?" After concluding that they could no longer determine when the project would be completed, the Canadian government contracted an external company to independently assess the project and to recommend a course of action. This was a wise decision because it would have been almost impossible for an *internal* evaluator to function effectively due to the considerable political fallout generated by the troubled project.

Recruiting an outsider as a project evaluator increases the likelihood of getting an unbiased and unemotional evaluation. But admittedly, not all organizations with a troubled project need to go as far as an external company to find a suitable evaluator. However, as a general rule, the more distant the evaluator from the project, the better.

While the use of an external evaluator to help eliminate emotions and bias is important, this tactic alone will not, of course, guarantee a successful project evaluation. But a good candidate can increase the likelihood of success because the evaluator is a critical factor in the success of the entire disentanglement process.

This chapter reviews the desirable qualities of an effective project evaluator and provides guidelines for selecting the most effective candidate for the job. The chapter also discusses the measures required for the evaluator's success. Though the discussion is geared primarily toward the initiating manager and the project evaluator, other project stakeholders will find the discussion helpful too.

4.1   Whom Should You Choose—Qualities of an Effective Evaluator

The project evaluator is the person who leads the disentanglement process and is responsible for the project rescue plan. Whom should you choose? We have already seen that the person should be external, or at least as distant from the project as possible. In addition, you should ideally assign a reliable, pragmatic, experienced, and successful project manager who (a) understands the project technology, (b) has good social skills, and (c) can reprioritize other responsibilities to allow sufficient time for the evaluation. We will discuss each of these qualities in more detail.

Choosing a Project Evaluator
- External (this might be the time to use a good consultant)
- Reliable, pragmatic, and experienced
- Understands the project technology
- Has good social skills
- Can devote sufficient time

Reliability: When a troubled project's future is wavering, reliability and dependability are often in short supply. At such times, an infusion of reliability will often be like a breath of fresh air. Anything less will only serve to demoralize the project team further and increase management's conviction that the project is unsalvageable.

Pragmatism: This is no time for a perfectionist. Disentangling a catastrophe requires compromising on things that would normally not be put in question. A pragmatic planned approach to the various conflicting budget, quality, functional, and schedule requirements is vital for an evaluator to be able to redefine a feasible project that delivers a small set of goals that is still acceptable to the project's stakeholders.

Social Skills: Dealing well with people is a necessary skill for any key team role, but it is especially needed when the team members are overcome with anxiety about their project, their future, and possibly their jobs. Good social skills will especially help promote the necessary trust with the project team members as well as with the other stakeholders.

Experience: When the problems are severe, experience becomes a vital asset. Thus, an effective evaluator will ideally have met and resolved similar problems before. This does not mean that we are looking for someone who has led many project failures (we certainly are not!), but rather someone who has successfully tackled similar problems before (such as effectively realigning unrealistic expectations).

Technological Expertise: Though an understanding of the project technology is desirable, it is not always essential. Many aspects of the project's problems in areas of project management, planning, and management of stakeholder expectations (and this is where many of the problems are usually found) can be tackled without a thorough familiarity with the project technology. However, occasionally, in complex technological projects, when the main problems are closely related to the project's technology, an evaluator may be unable to work effectively without sufficient technical expertise (we will discuss this subject in more detail later).

Availability: Getting a failing project back on track is not a spare-time activity. It is essential that the project evaluator devote as much time as needed to the process. For most projects, this activity is full time.

> **Advisory:** Strike a reasonable balance between the search for a good project evaluator and the need to act swiftly. As a rule of thumb: Plan to find the right person within a week.

4.2   Initial Briefing

Whose responsibility is it to select and brief the project evaluator? Organizational structures differ among companies, but generally the responsibility lies with the initiating manager. This management level will usually have the advantage of a broader perspective without being too distant from the project.

Project managers will often argue that the selection responsibility is theirs, but their affinity to their project and their close involvement with its problems make it extremely difficult for them to be sufficiently dispassionate and objective.

This section suggests some of the topics to be covered by the initiating manager and the project evaluator during the initial briefing session. It also discusses the important issue of commitment, which is an essential part of the briefing. This includes commitment from the organization to the evaluator (primarily to provide all necessary support) and commitment from the evaluator to the organization (to devote all necessary time and energy to the process).

4.2.1   Topics to Be Covered

Initially, start the evaluator's briefing with an overview of the project's position within the broader organizational picture. This should cover the following areas:

- **The importance of the project to the organization:**

    The consequences to the organization if the project is cancelled

    The consequences of continuing to fund the project if it is unsalvageable

    The effect and cost of overruns

    The significance of the organization's image (internal and external)

    Legal and marketing considerations

- **The main stakeholders:**

  Senior management

  Customers and users

  Marketing and sales staff

  Partners and investors

- **The effect on other internal organizations:**

  Quality assurance

  Testing group

  Maintenance and support

  Field installation

  Other projects

- **Political pressures and sensitivities:**

  Pressure groups

  Alliances

  Personal interests

  Internal and external competition

  Biases

  Individual preferences

The next stage of the briefing session should cover the narrower project perspective:

- **An overview of the project:**

  The software product being developed

  Legacy and off-the-shelf product components

  The project team members, project functions, and responsibilities

  Customer and user issues

  The project's development process and tools

  Training issues

- **A review of the project's main problems:**

  The presumed reasons for the project failure

  The presumed source of the problems

  Experience within the organization dealing with similar problems

- **Action by management in dealing with the failing project up to now:**

  How senior management responded as the project's problems began to unfold

  The actions that were taken and the results that followed

- **How and why the project was designated a catastrophe:**

  An overview of the decision process described in Chapter 2 and how it was implemented

- **The major project team players:**

  An overview of the team's strengths

  The project manager

  Team leaders

  Main project team members

  Team sensitivity issues

4.2.2   The Basic Commitment

The evaluator's goal is to try and save a failing project from cancellation, if reasonable justification can be established for doing so (not all projects can or should be saved). This is a tough assignment, which has little chance of success without a clear commitment[1] from the evaluator and from the initiating manager.

Commitment to the process starts with management providing all necessary support to the evaluator. In fact, management's full commitment should be evident from the start of the initial briefing session, which, in turn, will reinforce the evaluator's commitment (the reverse is also true: a weak commitment is similarly contagious).

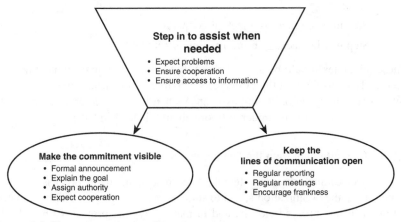

Figure 4.1 Management commitment

---

[1] According to one widely respected definition, when you make a commitment, you are, in effect, mentally binding yourself to a course of action [3]. The higher your commitment, the less deterred you will be by problems, hardships, and other unwelcome situations related to the course of action. Thus, when people make a commitment, you expect them to *stay the course in the face of difficulties.* Many would add that if you are committed to something, you are also committed to its success, and they would therefore include: *...to achieve the best possible outcome.*

In practical terms, management support means making the commitment visible, keeping the lines of communication open, and providing assistance to the evaluator should the process stall. The following guidelines for the initiating manager deal with the application of these three basic principles:

1. **Make the commitment visible.**

   Get the message out through a formal verbal and written organizational announcement.

   Provide a brief explanation for the action taken and the objectives of the disentanglement process.

   Clarify the evaluator's authority and responsibilities.

   Announce that full cooperation is expected.

2. **Keep the lines of communications open.**

   Establish a regular reporting schedule between senior management and the evaluator.

   Encourage bluntness and frankness.

   Hold the meetings regularly even at times when there is little to report. Some meetings can be brief (when there is little to report or discuss), but none should be skipped.

3. **Be prepared to provide active assistance.**

   Provide assistance to the evaluator to resolve problems that will inevitably occur.

   Step in when there is a lack of cooperation.

   Step in when access to information is withheld.

These principles should be applied carefully to assure that management does not needlessly interfere with the evaluator's activities. This means striking a reasonable balance between providing assistance when it is needed and permitting the evaluator to do the job unhindered (more about this later in Chapter 5).

4.2.3 Commitments from the Evaluator

The project evaluator's commitment to the disentanglement process is just as important as the organization's, and to some extent even more so. The evaluator's actions will be observed closely, and in many ways the project team and other project players will take their cue from the level of commitment that they see.

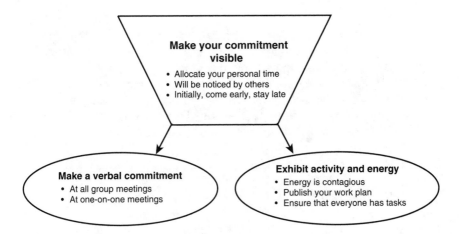

Figure 4.2 The project evaluator's commitment

The following guidelines for the project evaluator will help establish the commitment to the process:

1.   **Make your commitment visible.**

     Allocate plenty of your personal time.

     This is the first indication of commitment that will be noticed by the project team.

     Initially, start early and stay late.

2.   **Make a verbal commitment.**

     Through a general project team meeting.

     Through brief one-on-one meetings with the key players.

3.   **Exhibit activity and energy.**

     Energy is contagious.

     Publish your own work plan.

     Ensure that all team members have tasks to perform.

Generally, people like working with a committed and dedicated person, provided they don't see the person's goals as being contrary to their own. Thus, it is important to ensure that the goal of the disentanglement process (trying to save the project) is understood by the project team and the other key players. Getting this message across clearly should be the first task of the process.

Advisory: The initial briefing is not the first meeting between the initiating manager and the evaluator; it is the first *formal* meeting as part of the disentanglement process. It serves as an information baseline for the evaluator. As such, it is important during the briefing to reiterate the essentials from all previous informal meetings and to re-establish joint commitments to the process.

4.3   Large Software Projects

Large software projects, especially very large projects, may require a team of two or more evaluators, though with a clearly designated chief evaluator. The process for selecting the chief evaluator is the same as for a single evaluator, except that in this case, experience in large projects is essential. The selection of the other members of the team should then be left to the chief evaluator. This selection process is less stringent than for the chief evaluator; for example, the other team members do not have to be external (this is further discussed in Chapter 5, "Step 3—Evaluate the Project").

What is a large software project? The simple answer is that any project is large, in our context, if a single evaluator cannot review it within two weeks. When in doubt, it is usually best to err on the side of caution and assign a second (or third evaluator). It is important, though, to be aware of the overhead of team-work in comparison to the work of a single person, and this overhead must be taken into consideration by the chief evaluator when mapping out the tasks within the team.

As the initiating manager, if you know or suspect that the project will need an evaluation team, should your selection criteria for the evaluator be any different? The answer is obviously yes. In addition to the previously discussed qualities of an evaluator, you will be looking for a candidate who can run a small team and who has a good understanding of the additional complexities posed by large projects. Following are some additional points that you should consider:

- Large projects usually mean large budgets and often large doses of politics, especially when the project is in deep trouble. Ensure that the evaluator you choose is capable of handling the politics and rebuffing any excessive interference. As the initiating manager, be prepared to offer assistance, if necessary.

- It is important to select an evaluator who has experience leading a group (someone with experience as a project manager, team leader, and so on). The candidate should have the ability to quickly select between one and three team members (this should take no more than one to two days). Here too, be prepared to offer assistance.

- The evaluator must have demonstrable experience in large successful software development projects. This should include a good understanding of planning of large projects, as well as team management, development, and interfacing with stakeholders.

- If it is difficult to quickly find an evaluator with all the necessary skills, forgo technological skills in favor of large project qualities (technological skills can be provided by other evaluation team members).

To summarize, the differences between the evaluation of small and large projects are similar to the differences between the development of small and large projects: large means more politics, more people, and more complexity. It is important to remember, though, that the project evaluation schedule should be no longer than about two weeks regardless of the project size and, unlike regular projects, this schedule cannot be extended. This is because it will be almost impossible to continue the suspension of all project development activities beyond the designated two weeks, and this is especially true in large projects. (We discussed the need for project suspension during the disentanglement process in Chapter 3, "Step 1—Stop.")

4.4   What Can Go Wrong (and What to Do About It)

Most of the problems that emerge during the assignment of a project evaluator are in one way or another derived from a few basic problems, such as a poor choice or a hostile response. Virtually all problems can be dealt with, especially if they are discovered early.

The following list provides some of the more common problems in the selection of a project evaluator (or the evaluator team) and proposes ways for dealing with them:

- **No suitable candidates for project evaluator.**

  There really is no such thing as *no* suitable candidates for any position, so when a problem like this arises, we are usually dealing with some form of a bad selection process. In reality, the problem is usually caused by one or more of the following:

- Low prioritization of the task of finding candidates, and possibly low prioritization of the entire disentanglement process. Examples are
    - Insufficient budget/funds allocated to adequately compensate the evaluator.
    - Insufficient effort dedicated to locating candidates.
- A lack of expertise/knowledge on the part of the initiating manager to locate suitable candidates.

Action: In most cases, half of the solution is accepting that "no suitable candidates" is a pretext for the real problem. When the real problem emerges, the solution becomes obvious: allocate more funds, dedicate more time/effort, reprioritize the search, and get technical assistance (see the "initiating manager lacks expertise" point discussed next).

- **Initiating manager lacks expertise to select a project evaluator.**

  This problem can occur when the initiating manager does not have a technical background or when the failing project is technically complex. In such cases, the initiating manager may not be able to quickly assess the technical abilities of the project evaluator candidates.

  Action: Enlist the assistance of a senior technical manager from another project to work with the initiating manager in the selection the project evaluator.

- **Inadequate or ineffective project evaluator.**

  Selecting a suitable evaluator is essential for a successful evaluation process, and, in contrast, a poor choice makes success unlikely. Two common causes of a poor choice are (a) a lack of time to select well and (b) the natural inclination to prefer an insider (not independent or objective).

  Here are some signs of a poor choice: An evaluator who appears unable to handle the delicate human-relations of a failing project and seems to be creating unnecessary friction or an evaluator who appears unable to handle the complexities of a large project.

  Generally, if the points in Section 4.1 appear severely lacking, re-examine your choice of evaluator.

  Action: Strike a balance between the following two guiding principles: (1) replacing the evaluator is a drastic measure that can have negative repercussions on the disentanglement process, and (2) when an evaluator needs to be replaced, the earlier this is done the better. Here is how to balance these two principles:

  1. Ensure that the problem is indeed with the evaluator and is not due to a lack of support from the initiating manager or from other members of senior management. Otherwise, move on to the next solution.

2. Consider whether the problem can be resolved quickly by drawing the evaluator's attention to it and providing specific guidance on how to proceed. Do not repeat this option more than once. If you do not perceive an immediate improvement, move on to the next solution.

3. Find a new evaluator quickly, but, if possible, keep the current one on the job while you search. In fact, start looking for a replacement in parallel to solution 2.

In cases where the current evaluator cannot be kept on the job while locating a replacement, ensure that the project team is kept gainfully occupied in the interim. See Chapter 3 for a list of tasks to be carried out by the team during the evaluation.

- **Inadequate or ineffective evaluation team members (for a large project).**

  The chief project evaluator is responsible for selecting the evaluation team members. Many problems can arise with the selection of team members, some due to the fact that they are usually not subject to the same stringent selection criteria as is the chief evaluator (such as the need to be external).

  Action: The chief evaluator should replace unsuitable team members immediately. This is especially true when a team member exhibits weak social skills. Unlike the similar case with the chief evaluator, in this case it is better to proceed short-handed than to risk unnecessary friction with project team members and other stakeholders.

  The evaluator should enlist the assistance of the initiating manager to help free up potential replacement candidates and, if necessary, to expand the evaluation budget so that a replacement can be found within two days (ideally within one).

- **Rejection of or hostility to an external project evaluator.**

  This is not uncommon in a situation where emotions and job security concerns run high.

  Action: The resolution of this problem must come from senior management, and especially from the initiating manager. Senior management's full support for the disentanglement process and for the evaluator needs to be made perfectly clear to all involved parties through written announcements and town hall meetings. In cases where specific individuals are the source of the problem, it is useful to hold a brief meeting between the initiating manager, the evaluator, and the specific individual.

As mentioned earlier, most problems are variations or derivations of the ones in the previous list. For example, problems of commitment or allocation of personal time by the evaluator are possible early warnings of a badly chosen evaluator.

> **Advisory:** When the initiating manager lacks sufficient technical expertise, it is often wise to have a senior technical manager involved throughout the disentanglement process. While the two senior managers will together fulfill the role of initiating manager, it is important that one of the two will be in the lead role.
>
> Adding a technical expert is an especially good practice when disentangling large projects.

4.5 Summary

When a failing project is being evaluated, anyone even remotely associated with it will, to some extent, be influenced, or suspected of being influenced, by its emotional overtones. Using an outsider as a project evaluator increases the likelihood of getting an unbiased and unemotional evaluation. The more distant the evaluator from the project, the better.

Generally, the responsibility to select and brief the project evaluator lies with the senior manager who initiated the disentanglement process, referred to as the initiating manager. In choosing an effective evaluator, the initiating manager should seek a reliable, pragmatic, experienced, and successful project manager who (a) understands the project technology, (b) has good social skills, and (c) can reprioritize other responsibilities to allow sufficient time for the evaluation.

The evaluator's goal is to try and save a failing project from cancellation, if reasonable justification can be established for doing so. This is a tough assignment, which requires clear commitment from the evaluator and the full support of the initiating manager. In practical terms, support means making the commitment visible, keeping the lines of communication open, and providing assistance to the evaluator should the process stall. However, these principles should be applied carefully to assure that management does not needlessly interfere with the evaluator's activities.

Large software projects may require a team of two or more evaluators with a clearly designated chief evaluator. The process for selecting the chief evaluator is the same as for a single evaluator, except that in this case, experience in large projects is essential. The selection of the other members of the team should then be left to the chief evaluator.

In selecting an evaluator for a large project, the initiating manager should consider candidates who have experience with large budgets and subsequently increased politics, leading teams, and developing large projects. These skills are more important than technological expertise.

Most of the problems that emerge during the assignment of a project evaluator are in one way or another derivations of being unable to find suitable candidates, a lack of expertise on the part of the initiating manager, making a bad choice for evaluator, poorly selected evaluation team members, and hostility to the external evaluator.

Exercises

1. Search the Internet or your local library and find detailed reports of two failed software projects: one that was successfully saved and one that was terminated. Concentrate especially on details that can provide insight into the qualities of the evaluators. From the facts of the two cases, draw additional conclusions about the qualities and suitability of the evaluators (provide the reasoning that led to your conclusions).

    Compare the two project evaluators and show how their selection influenced the attempt to save the projects. Discuss how the outcomes would have been different if different candidates had been chosen as evaluators.

2. Consider three different projects of varying size and complexity: small, medium, and large. The projects may be real or conceptualized (prepare a short description of each project).

    Using a comparison table, discuss the advantages and disadvantages of establishing an evaluation team (of more than one evaluator) for each of the three projects. Propose criteria for deciding the point at which it is advantageous to add an additional evaluator, and explain the reasoning behind your proposal.

3. Class debate subject: Given the choice between a suitable evaluator candidate who cannot devote full time to the disentanglement process and a partially suitable candidate who can devote full time to the process, whom would you choose? Make several sets of assumptions about the degree of suitability, the amount of time dedicated to the process, and the characteristics of the project; how would your choice differ under each set of circumstances?

5

Step 3—Evaluate the Project

Step 10   Early Warning System
Step 9   Revise the Plan
Step 8   Risk Analysis
Step 7   Rebuild the Team
Step 6   Can Minimum Goals Be Achieved?
Step 5   Define Minimum Goals
Step 4   Evaluate the Team
Step 3   Evaluate Project Status
Step 2   Assign an Evaluator
Step 1   Stop

Software projects can sometimes seem like a train traveling through a tunnel. We know how it went in, but we are not sure how it will come out, at least not until it finally emerges on the other side. In the meantime, all we hear are the muffled rumblings of the wheels on the track. And if we peer through a tunnel porthole, all we will see are dark shadows.

Most anyone involved in software development, from team member to senior manager, will easily recall observing, or even experiencing, a software project chugging through a dark tunnel. These are the projects where nobody really knows the true status: on time or late, on budget or over budget, high quality or poor quality, or somewhere in-between. But while not all software projects are dark mysteries, experience shows that the ones that are will often emerge from the tunnel in a rather dismal state—if at all.

What is it about software projects that makes them so difficult to track? Is poor status reporting ingrained in the nature of software development; is it a management problem, a matter of ethics, or maybe a combination of all three?

One view is that the dark tunnel syndrome is essentially a problem of ethics because people simply do not report truthfully. Penn State University professor Effy Oz examined professional ethics and standards in his review of a failed reservations software project, which was cancelled after three and a half years and with a 125 million dollar development bill [1]. A senior executive at American Airlines, one of the project's main stakeholders, reported that people in the development organization had not been reporting the true status of the project. Apparently, Oz concludes, the project's clients were misled into continuing to invest in an operation that was, in reality, plagued with problems.

Oz goes on to describe a web of inaccurate status reporting by the development organization, including schedule manipulations and totally unrealistic optimism (regarding the developers' ability to recover lost time), and opines that the failed project seemed to be a case of miscommunication at best, and grand deception at worst. He concludes that software organizations need a code of conduct for both managers and employees that governs their behavior when projects do not proceed as expected.

But some of us who have been both down in the software trenches and in the senior management seat may see things a little differently. Often, software developers sincerely believe their excessively optimistic reports. In fact, many would probably pass a polygraph test with flying colors. And there is nothing new about this observation; the oft-quoted software engineering pioneer Fred Brooks stated decades ago that programmers are notorious optimists who believe in happy endings and fairy godmothers [2]. Even today, this groundless optimism continues to be a common problem in software development and is one of the main causes of the dark tunnel syndrome.

While Oz implies that failing projects result in poor status reporting, more recently Snow and Keil went as far as suggesting that the opposite is true: software project failures are *caused* by poor status reporting. They also conclude that while most projects, software or otherwise, suffer from poor status reporting, the situation is worse in software projects.

> Although this [poor status reporting] is a general problem that can occur with any type of project, the literature suggests that information technology may be particularly challenging in this regard. The intangible nature of software makes it difficult to obtain accurate estimates of the proportion of work completed, which may promote misperceptions regarding project status [3].

Realistically, all the previous factors probably play a part in creating the problem: the overly optimistic nature of software developers (when it relates to schedules), objective difficulties stemming from the intangibility of software, and issues of professional ethics.[1] But no matter what the actual mix of reasons, the situation undoubtedly becomes yet more difficult when dealing with a project that is in deep trouble.

This is the scenario that greets the project evaluator at the beginning of the disentanglement process. Not only is the project halted and its status unknown, but the practical value of the available project information is unknown; it may be excellent and accurate or, as just mentioned, it may be much less than that. It follows, therefore, that one of the first orders of business in evaluating a failing project must be a critical review of all available information. It is, in essence, akin to turning on the lights in the tunnel so we can see the train.

This chapter presents a set of practices, principles, and guidelines for evaluating a failing project and determining its true status. It also discusses the sources of project information to be reviewed and how to identify and locate missing information, deal with large projects, and fit the pieces of the puzzle together.

The guidelines are mainly geared toward the project evaluator, whose principal objective, at this stage of the disentanglement process, is to get up to speed as quickly as possible. Because the discussion covers a broad range of project status issues, most project stakeholders will find the discussion generally useful, not least as a vehicle for re-examining their own pre-perceptions of the project.

5.1   The Evaluation Review

The goal of the evaluation review is to help the project evaluator determine the true status of the project. It involves a series of meetings with key team members and project stakeholders, the collection and review of relevant project documents, and the review and evaluation of the product being developed (that is, a product demo).

---

[1] Are software developers really different (compared to other fields of technology)? There is a respectable school of thought that claims they are. See, for example, the chapter "Principles of Managing Software Engineers: Are They Really Any Different?" in [7].

The project evaluator should follow the basic concepts that apply to any good project review but should also adapt them to the specific characteristics of a failing project. Accordingly, this section is divided into two parts:

- **A brief overview of the basic concepts of software project reviews**

  This overview includes a list of guidelines and activities based upon a standard process for conducting software project reviews.

- **Adapting a review for a failing project**

  This section revisits several of the key features of a project review and shows how to adapt them to the specific characteristics of a failing project.

5.1.1   An Overview of Software Project Reviews

The following points cover some of the key principles for conducting software project reviews:

- **Follow a process.**

  Adopt an orderly process and adapt it to the needs of your project. Almost any orderly review process will do, just as long as the review is not ad hoc. See Table 5.1 for a checklist of some of the items to be reviewed (not all items are always required).

- **Ensure team participation.**

  A successful project review is not a detached activity; it must have input and active participation from the project development team, as well as other major players related to the product being developed.

- **Evaluate results, not effort.**

  The basic purpose of a project review is to determine the facts and establish the exact status of the project. This means concentrating primarily on results and achievements. Dedication and effort are important, but they are not factors in determining the project's status. (They *are* factors in explaining the reasons for the status.)

- **Document the findings.**

  The results of any formal project activity need to be documented; otherwise, there is a high risk that they will be lost, forgotten, confused, or disputed, and this often leads to the activity having to be repeated. This is especially true of project reviews.

- **Revise.**

  Correct and revise the review findings based on feedback from stakeholders, team members, and other key project players. Ensure that any revision of findings is based on new or corrected data or on the correction of errors in analyzing the data.

- **Follow-up on the findings.**

  Virtually all effective project reviews uncover issues that require follow-up action by the project team members and others. This should include updated plans, milestones, estimates, and risk analysis. A formal follow-up process greatly increases the likelihood that the action items get implemented. (In the evaluation of a failing project, the follow-up is included in the subsequent steps of the disentanglement process.)

Table 5.1 Example of Software Project Items Subject to Management Review

Item #	Item to Be Reviewed	Priority
1	Anomaly reports	3
2	Audit reports	1
3	Backup and recovery plans	2
4	Contingency plans	1
5	Customer or user representative complaints	1
6	Disaster plans	2
7	Hardware performance plans	1
8	Installation plans	2
9	Maintenance plans	2
10	Procurement and contracting methods	2
11	Progress reports	1
12	Risk management plans	1
13	Software configuration management plans	2
14	Software project management plans	1
15	Software quality assurance plans	1
16	Software safety plans	3
17	Software verification and validation plans	2
18	Technical reviews reports	1
19	Software product analysis	2
20	Verification and validation report	2

Advisory: There are several excellent standards and guides for conducting software project reviews; one of the more comprehensive, flexible, and useful sets of guidelines is the IEEE Std 1028 Standard for Software Reviews [6]. This IEEE guide covers considerably more than is necessary or even practical for the evaluation of a failing project. However, a refresher reading of the relevant sections, particularly the four-page section on management reviews, will help maintain an awareness of the essentials.

5.1.2 Reviewing Failing Projects

Failing projects are characterized by heightened concerns, and their reviews are by nature critically decisive. This produces special sensitivities, which require a swift, unprejudiced, and systematic approach. Following are some guidelines:

- **Plan the review.**

  In the short time frame that characterizes the evaluation, efficient use of the review time is important. There will be limited opportunity to return to activities that were missed or not entirely completed. This requires an orderly plan.

  The plan should cover the people to be interviewed (starting with the initiating manager and the project manager), the documents to be reviewed, an evaluation of the product, and the decisions to be made, all within a detailed target schedule. It is useful to review the plan with the initiating manager to ensure that it is complete.

- **Adapt the review.**

  The evaluation of a failing project does not require all the items and activities of a full formal project review. Keep the review on a sufficiently high level to get a reliable perception of the project while still remaining within the time constraints of the disentanglement process.

  As an example, consider the items in Table 5.1. It is not necessary, or even possible, to review all the items in the table within the constraints of the disentanglement process (refer to the priorities in the table to help decide what to implement).

- **Make a concentrated effort.**

  Start the process with a blaze and keep the pace reasonably vigorous. In a dispirited situation, there are few things more refreshing than energy. Also, a concentrated effort will help prevent an unduly drawn-out process.

- **Don't let problems deteriorate.**

  Prepare a prioritized list of problems and update it daily. Don't wait too long to request assistance.

- **Enlist the help of experts.**

  The evaluation of large or complex projects may require the project evaluator to decide between conflicting views in technical- and business-related areas. These conflicts can result in a drawn-out evaluation, especially when they require expertise beyond the scope of the evaluator's knowledge. The use of objective expertise is a good way to resolve these conflicts. Experts can be external or internal to the organization as long as they can provide a reasonably objective opinion.

- **Work closely with the team.**

  Plan to include the project team in the evaluation process from the outset. Avoid secrecy or behind-closed-doors discussions. Request input from the team on all major issues. Present your evaluation to the team before finalizing it and consider their responses. Look for details and facts that you overlooked or misunderstood, while resisting undue pressure to amend your findings.

- **Work closely with management.**

  Update management regularly on your progress, especially regarding problems, even if you are dealing with them effectively. Generate intermediate reports and get feedback from management before finalizing your recommendations.

- **Work closely with the stakeholders.**

  The list of project stakeholders (beyond management and the project team) includes customers, users, marketing personnel, and other involved parties (for example, investors, partner organizations, and product support groups). Expect these groups to take an active interest in the disentanglement process.

  Identify the key stakeholders and include them in the process: interview them and collect any relevant material they may have (for example, market research information, product cost analysis, competitive analysis, and other relevant documents).

- **Maintain objectivity.**

  It is important that all project stakeholders perceive the evaluation process as being objective. The evaluator should not appear to have a personal bias in favor of anyone. The results of the evaluation review should be perceived as being professional and not personal.

An external evaluator can be helpful by "calling a spade a spade"—saying things as they are. Here is an example:

> Often in a failing project, there is a web of fictions that is upheld and that no one has the courage to say is ridiculous. At one project being developed for the military, there used to be an absurd decree by management that after a module was released, the users were strictly limited in the number of changes they could request. There is logic to this as long as it isn't taken to an extreme, and it was. The users had some important requests that were rejected, but were not unreasonable to request. An objective external evaluator would have been able to say, "Guys, this is ridiculous. The users have some important changes that they want and they need to be done, even if it is not fun for your programmers to implement them."

Often an entangled project requires these types of tough decisions. The evaluator's job is to present an unflattering, realistic picture of the project so that subsequent decisions needed to save the project can be based on fact rather than fiction.

It is important to remember that these are not rigid rules but rather guidelines to be adapted to the characteristics of the project and the organization. Adapt them based on the size and importance of the project, the amount of development progress that has ostensibly been made, the level of cooperation from the team and the stakeholders, and, most importantly, the state of available project status information.

> **Advisory:** Formally agree with management on an essential ground rule before you start the evaluation process: if you are to prepare an objective, balanced project evaluation (and maintain your integrity with the main players), you must be free of undue pressure from all sources, including from management. Refer back to this agreed-upon ground rule whenever you feel that your independence is at risk of being compromised.

5.2 Sources of Project Status Information

Now that we have revisited some of the common practices for successfully reviewing software projects and several additional guidelines for evaluating those that are in severe trouble, we can move on to more practical issues of implementation. In this section, we will discuss specific methods and techniques related to the collection of project information in various ways from various sources.

In most cases, the project status information exists; the main problem is finding it and collecting it. This information will come from three main sources (see Figure 5.1):

1. Verbal sources, through interviews with team members and stakeholders.

2. Operational sources, through evaluating product demos, visual representations, and preliminary versions of the software product.

3. Documented sources, through project development specifications, status reports, meeting minutes, and other project documents.

The collection of project information may appear to be a rather straightforward effort, but in reality it is not always so. The status of a failing project cannot be evaluated in the same way as the status of a project that is progressing well. This is because the collection of information must overcome the conflicts, concerns, and sensitivities that characterize a failing project. This we will see in the following sections.

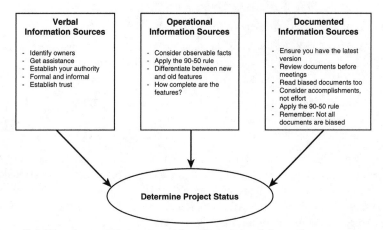

Figure 5.1 The three main sources of project status information

5.2.1   Verbal Status Information

The collection of verbal information usually starts out with a concentrated effort at the beginning of the process (though interviews, meetings, and so on) and continues at varying levels throughout the evaluation. Because time is critical, the bulk of the most important interviews should be completed within a day or two. Many of the potential problems usually stem from the fact that the evaluator is external to the organization (an outsider).

As the project evaluator, you should consider the following points:

- **Identify the owners of critical project information.**

  If you have come from outside of the development organization, you are unfamiliar with the project, the team, and the other main players. Obtain the names of the persons who have project status information from senior management, from the project manager, and from the people you interview (they should direct you to others).

- **Request assistance.**

  During interviews and discussions, some of your co-conversationalists will not have the information you request, but often they will know better than you where and how to get it.

- **Establish your authority.**

  As an outsider, you need to quickly establish that you have the authority to conduct the evaluation. Initially, enlist the help of senior management to establish your authority and refer back to management whenever serious questions of authority arise (try not to call on management too often; you should be able to overcome minor problems yourself).

- **Don't restrict yourself to formal methods.**

  Seek one-on-one informal discussions and conversations to get a better understanding of the background of the project's problems.

- **Overcome any issues of trust.**

  Develop an environment of trust by explaining the reasons for your assignment and establishing that you are trying to save the project from cancellation (that is, you are on the project team's side).

The main problem with verbal information is that its accuracy, completeness, and reliability is uncertain (more so than the more easily substantiated operational and written information). This is because people are naturally less accurate in conversation than in formal writing. After key interviews and conversations, it is sometimes helpful to summarize the main points that you have heard and request the provider of the information to confirm that the summary is accurate.

5.2.2 Operational Status Information

Often even a failing project will have some type of operational or visual representation. It may be as much as a partially functioning version of the product that is being developed, or as little as a set of user screen layouts that illustrate the design. Regardless of their level of sophistication, these representations are usually well worth reviewing, especially if they have been kept updated, because they can provide a useful hands-on (or eyes-on) sense of the actual project status that is difficult to grasp from written reports or interviews.

The types of issues that you will need to deal with are as follows:

- Discrepancies between what you hear and what you see. Consider only observable facts (for example, not "this feature used to work well but something has gone wrong").
- Evaluation of partially complete features. Assign limited value to features that are almost finished; remember the 90-50 rule (*It takes 50% of the time to do 90% of the work and another 50% to do the remaining 10%*).
- Evaluation of actual progress from visual representations. In reviewing progress, ensure that you are able to differentiate between legacy and commercial off-the-shelf (COTS) features on the one hand and newly developed features on the other hand.
- Evaluation of completed features: Are they really complete? Determine how advanced they are. Are they approved or signed off? How much have they been tested?

5.2.3 Documented Information

Documented project status information will usually come from such sources as meeting summaries, test reports, previous project reviews, and of course, status reports. They are often among the most easily accessible sources of information. On their own it may be difficult to establish their objectivity and accuracy, but even so, they can be used to quickly get a general grasp of the project and its problems.

When reviewing written status information, consider the following:

- Ensure you are reading the latest version of the written material.

- Make notes from the written materials, and refer to them at key verbal interviews, conversations, and meetings.

- Despite concerns about objectivity, review existing status reports; don't discard them. They can save time, even if they are not accurate.

- Consider accomplishments, not effort.

- Here again, apply the 90-50 rule for almost completed tasks,

- Don't assume that reports *have* to be inaccurate, they may be correct—and in many cases, they are!

At the beginning of the project evaluation, it is often a good strategy to request that team members and other key players produce reports specifically for your review. This can help you plan and use your time more efficiently.

5.3 Evaluating Large Software Projects

Is there a difference between the evaluation of small and large software projects—apart from the obvious differences in the size of the team and the amount of information to be reviewed? While these two obvious differences certainly mean that the amount of work is greater for the evaluation of larger projects, they also generate a higher level of interest (due to higher costs), more politics, and they generally result in a more complicated assignment.

So larger projects both amplify the problems we discussed in the previous sections and add new ones. In the following discussion, we will examine these problems and we will look at some of the solutions.

5.3.1 How Are Large Projects Different?

"Software project failures are common," says Carnegie Mellon Software Engineering Institute's Watts Humphrey, "and the biggest projects fail most often." Humphrey continues: "On small projects, some uncertainty about each team member's status is tolerable. However, as projects get bigger and communications lines extend, precise status information becomes more important. Without hard data on project status, people communicate opinions, and their opinions can be biased or even wrong." [5]

Humphrey's remarks apply to any large project, but we have seen that they are especially true in failing projects where biased information and uncertainty are especially severe. So what will you need to deal with when evaluating a large project?

As illustrated in Figure 5.2, the evaluation of a large project is characterized by the following:

- Many evaluation activities will take longer. This means simply that there is more work to do in the evaluation of large projects and you need to prepare for it (we will discuss how to prepare shortly).

- Determining the project status will be more difficult. This is because the lines of communications are extended, the interfaces are more difficult to understand, and each problem is affected by a very large number of parameters.

- More people will be involved in the evaluation process. Apart from the fact that more people increase the evaluation workload, they also extend the communication lines between the people involved in the project, as mentioned by Humphrey. This is one of the reasons for increased project complexity.

- Personal interests and political pressure will be greater.

- The project has greater importance to the organization, the budget is large, and generally everyone will take a greater interest in the project.

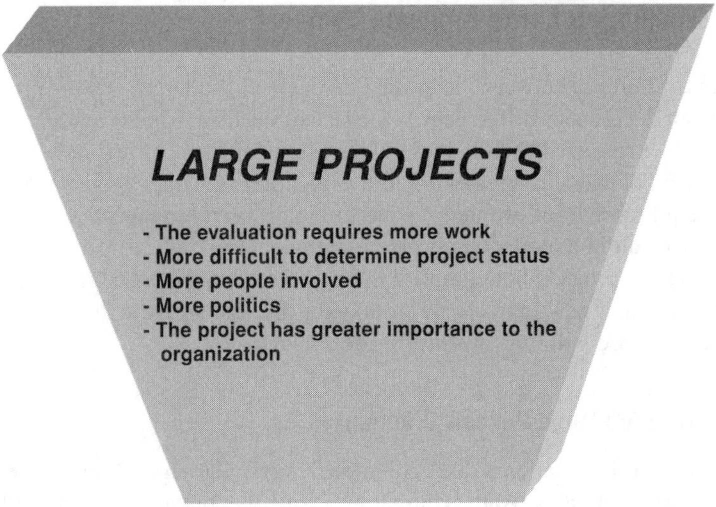

LARGE PROJECTS

- The evaluation requires more work
- More difficult to determine project status
- More people involved
- More politics
- The project has greater importance to the organization

Figure 5.2 Evaluating large projects

In summary, larger projects involve more work. And experience shows that more work is usually resolved in one of three ways:

1. Reduced scope (limit the evaluation)
2. More time (extend the evaluation)
3. More people (expand the evaluation team)

Regarding the first option, the evaluation process cannot be limited—there can be no shortcuts if such a critical process is to succeed.

As for the second option, the reasons for keeping the review process short are even more valid for large projects: the high cost of halting the project, declining team motivation, and stakeholder pressure from management, users, customers, marketing, and investors.

All of which leaves one option: more evaluators.

5.3.2   The Evaluation Team

When evaluating a large, seriously troubled project, the only practical way to deal with the higher workload is to establish a team of evaluators. The objective is to create a small, well-chosen team whose members will work exceptionally well together for approximately two weeks. The size of the team is obviously a function of the size of the project, but in most cases a team of between two and four evaluators will suffice.

Following are some points to consider when establishing the team:

1. An evaluation team should always have a clearly designated chief evaluator who leads the team.
2. The chief evaluator should be the one to select the evaluation team members.
3. While individual personality is an important factor when establishing any functional team, it is especially important in a project evaluation team due to the heightened sensitivities of the failing project and the very short timeframe.
4. This is not the time to establish a democratic team, but it is the time for a team of experts (see Chapter 5 in [7]).

5.3.3   Guidelines for Evaluating Large Projects

While the following list of guidelines is primarily intended for the chief evaluator, they are also useful for all members of the evaluation team:

- **Set up the team quickly.**

  Time is critical. Give high priority to the task of staffing the evaluation team. Your goal should be to staff the team within two days.

- **Do not delay the evaluation.**

  Start the evaluation immediately; don't wait for the full team to be in place.

- **External is good, but not essential.**

  The more removed the other evaluation team members are from the project the better, but they do not need to be external; there is not always time to look outside the organization. However, do not select the other evaluators from within the project or from among the main stakeholders. As the evaluation leader, you are external, so you are responsible for keeping the team independent and objective.

- **Choose experts as team members.**

  One of the advantages of establishing a review team is that it provides an opportunity to select one or two experts as team members. Review the technical, product, and business aspects of the project and determine whether the evaluation could benefit from specific expertise in these areas.

- **Keep overhead to a minimum. Minimize formalities.**

  This is a small team with a very short schedule. Keep the overhead and formalities to the minimum necessary for the team to work in an orderly manner.

- **General team guidelines apply.**

  The review team is subject to the same rules as most other teams, including the following:

  Establish your leadership of the team (this is not the time for a democratic team structure).

  Keep each evaluator's tasks independent. To the extent possible, avoid duplication or overlap.

  Work as a team; keep everyone informed and updated.

Advisory: As we have seen, a large project means that project expenses are high and that each evaluation day is costly to the organization (all development activity has been halted). High costs usually attract considerable attention from senior management and other major stakeholders, and this can significantly stretch the evaluation process (which, in turn, produces even higher costs).

This issue should be discussed during the initial briefing session (see Section 4.2). The problem can usually be resolved through three or four prescheduled formal briefing sessions of up to two hours each, where senior management can monitor the project evaluation without undue intervention in the daily working of the evaluation.

5.4   Fitting the Pieces Together

We have seen that the evaluation of a failing software project involves the collection and evaluation of verbal, operational, and written project information. What problems can we expect when merging this information together to form a complete picture? The problems are the same ones that we might expect when assembling pieces of any picture (a jigsaw puzzle, for example), and not surprisingly, the solutions are similar too.

1. **Contradicting information (the pieces don't fit together)**

   This problem arises, for example, when a project requirement is presented very differently at two different interviews or when a status report states that a feature has been completed but the feature is missing from the latest version of the software product.

   The simplest way to resolve the contradiction is to have a brief joint meeting with all parties involved: those who provided the conflicting information and anyone who shares responsibility for it (the project manager, the customer, the representative of marketing, and so on).

2. **Missing information (pieces of the puzzle are missing)**

   The good news here is that knowing that information is missing is, in itself, half of the solution. This reduces the problem to one of discovery: who has the information?

   Start from the bottom up in the management chain, from persons who are responsible for close-by pieces of the puzzle, to the team leader who owns the general area with the missing piece, to the project manager, marketing manager, or customer, and, if the piece is still missing, to the initiating manager. Somewhere along the chain, someone will likely produce the missing piece.

3. Ambiguous information (some pieces seem to fit in more than one place)

This is a variant of the contradiction problem, when an item of information seems to represent two different possible situations. The information requires clarification. One example is a project development plan that specifies a two-year project, when it is unclear if it was intended to be a two person-year or a two calendar-year project. Another example is when a project schedule is extended, say, by three months, and then reported to be three months late: Is it three months late according to the new extended schedule or according to the original schedule?

The resolution of this problem is fairly straightforward: Identify the original owner of the general area that contains the ambiguous item of information. In the case of ambiguous requirements, consult with the customer, marketing, or management; for ambiguous project plans, consult with the project manager, or senior management, and so forth.

4. Vague information (the shape of some of the pieces is not well defined)

This problem arises when an item of information seems to be important, but it's meaning is not clear. In contrast to ambiguous information, which has a double meaning, vague information has too many or none.

An example would be a statement that 65% of the project has been completed. On the face of it, this certainly appears to be a valuable piece of information, but after further consideration the statement is virtually meaningless. What does the 65% refer to? Is it the percentage of programming tasks or function points completed, the percentage of user features that have been delivered, the percentage of the schedule that has passed, the percentage of budget that has been used, or the percentage of lines of code that have been programmed? It is unclear whether the statement refers to any of these. (Besides, all these are questionable measures of progress.)

Vague information is usually information that is missing some important details (without which it has little or no value). The first step in resolving the problem is to determine whether the information is worth the time and effort needed to clarify it. For example, information on the percentage of the project that has been completed has much less value than information on the amount of work that remains in order to complete the project. If the vague information is worth pursuing, clarify it, similarly to the procedure for ambiguous information (see 3).

5. Misleading information (some pieces appear to fit, but the picture seems wrong)

During the project evaluation, most information from team members and project stakeholders is usually provided both honestly and sincerely, and any bias is typically introduced unintentionally. However, in rare cases, you may deliberately be given misleading information.

Whenever you suspect that you are being given misleading information, enlist the help of the initiating manager. This is a serious ethical problem, which is beyond the scope of the evaluator's responsibilities (see the Effy Oz example discussed earlier [1]).

6. **Irrelevant information (we seem to have pieces from another puzzle)**

   Here, too, the good news is that knowing that information is irrelevant is, in itself, half of the solution. This reduces the problem to one of re-appraisal before excluding the information: Is the information indeed irrelevant? (An example is a description of a feature that was originally considered for the project but, in the final count, was excluded.)

   If there is any doubt about the irrelevancy of the information, consult with the project's main players (either the project manager, the representative of marketing, the customer, or the initiating manager) before excluding it. However, do not discard irrelevant information; you may change your mind about its value later.

Generally, most problems related to ill-fitting pieces of the picture can be resolved and clarified verbally. Usually, the main challenge is to locate the person who has the correct or missing information. It is helpful to start the process with a prepared list of the main owners of project information; compile it with the help of key project players (senior manager, project manager, customer representative, marketing representative, and so on).

5.5   What Can Go Wrong (and What to Do About It)

While the intent of the guidelines described in this chapter is to increase the probability of a successful evaluation, obviously things can still go wrong. When they do, it is a good policy to have a prepared plan of action. In fact, preparation is one of the best forms of prevention.

The following list discusses some of the more common causes of a breakdown in the evaluation process and proposes responses to deal with them:

- **Lack of cooperation**

  A lack of cooperation is not uncommon when dealing with a project in trouble, especially during the first few days of the evaluation. This can be due to hostility or suspicion toward an outsider, job security concerns, or even declining interest in the failing project.

  Action: The response must come from senior management through strong visible support for the disentanglement process. An effective solution is a three-way meeting between the initiating manager, the evaluator, and the uncooperative person or party.

- **Project complexity**

  A project may be too complex for an external evaluator to adequately comprehend, especially within the limited time available. The problem can become especially severe if an expert advisor cannot be found within a reasonable time (usually two to three days).

  Action: This is usually a question of priorities. Raise the priority for finding an expert: Increase the compensation (pay) for the expert, or free up an expert from another project. The cost of the expert should be compared with the costs of failing to disentangle the project.

- **Prolonged evaluation process**

  When the evaluation process takes too long, there is often a tendency not to seek the cause of the slow pace (that is, not to solve it) because that too takes time. But if it appears that the evaluation will delay the entire disentanglement process by more than a few days, the cause needs to be found immediately. Note that this is not a concession that a delay of a few days is tolerable; in fact, such a delay puts the disentanglement process at risk.

  The cause of the delay may be one of the two problems mentioned previously (a lack of cooperation or project complexity), or it may be a badly chosen evaluator.

  Action: If the slow pace is the result of one of the first two problems mentioned here, apply the appropriate solution provided. If the problem is related to the evaluator, the initiating manager needs to take action, which may entail replacing the evaluator. If the slow pace is due to some other cause, senior management should get involved in the resolution.

- **Excessive interference**

  It is reasonable to expect many of the project stakeholders to show keen interest in the disentanglement process. But excessive interest becomes interference, which disrupts the process.

  Action: Preventing interference starts at the very beginning of the evaluation and should be part of the support message put out by the initiating manager. If interference becomes a problem despite the support message, the evaluator will have to enlist the support of senior management to eliminate the problem. If, however, it is members of senior management who are excessively interfering, the evaluator must convene a formal and candid meeting with the initiating manager and explain the consequences of the interference. Usually, a reasonable solution can be found that will satisfy management's need to monitor the process and the evaluator's need to operate unhindered.

- **Inconclusive results**

  In most cases, inconclusive results should be avoidable. If the process and guidelines are followed, the danger of an inconclusive result situation should emerge as the evaluation proceeds. Indications of the looming problem are usually evident during the evaluator's update sessions with senior management (this is the time for the initiating manager to ask pointed questions).

  Action: As soon as either management or the evaluator detects indications that the process is not converging, an urgent special review meeting should be convened and dedicated to resolving the problem. Possible courses of action include public reinforcement of management support for the process, additional funding to hire an expert, or assigning an additional evaluator. It is also possible that the problem is a by-product of the other problems discussed previously, and, if so, the appropriate solution provided here should be applied.

Though there are several other things that can go wrong in the evaluation process, they are all mostly variations or consequences of the problems discussed here. Thus, most solutions involve either the close monitoring of progress, the hiring of experts, resolving evaluator unsuitability, preventing stakeholder interference, or a combination of all these.

> **Advisory:** Of all the standards, recommendations, and guidelines discussed in this chapter, three factors, more than any others, are essential for the success of the evaluation of a failing project:
>
> The successful selection of an evaluator
>
> Senior management support
>
> Compiling and following a good plan
>
> All the other guidelines and recommendations just serve to improve the odds of success.

5.6 Summary

This chapter presents a set of practices, principles, and guidelines for evaluating a failing software project and determining its true status.

The evaluation of a failing software project is, for the most part, an intensive, critical project review. As such, it is subject to the same general principles as any other type of software project review. These principles include the need to follow a process, enlisting team participation, concentrating on results rather than effort, and documenting and following up on the findings.

Other principles that are specific to failing software projects include the importance of starting the review with a concentrated effort and keeping the pace reasonably vigorous; ensuring that problems do not deteriorate; enlisting the help of experts; working closely with the team, with management, and with other project stakeholders; and making a special effort to maintain objectivity. These are not rigid rules, but rather guidelines to be adapted to the characteristics of the project and the organization.

The first key goal of the evaluation process is to establish the true status of the project. The first step is the collection of existing project status information from three main sources: verbal, operational, and documented (written).

When large software projects fail, you can expect that many evaluation activities will take longer, project status will be more difficult to determine, more people will be involved in the evaluation process, political pressure will be greater, and the importance of the project to the organization will be greater. This leads to a heavier evaluation workload, which can only be resolved by establishing a team of evaluators led by a chief evaluator.

When evaluating a large, seriously troubled project, it is important to set up the team quickly—but do not wait to start until the full team is in place. Try to recruit team members externally (though this is not a firm requirement).

When assembling the pieces of the evaluation together to get a clear project status picture, most problems can be resolved verbally. Usually, the main challenge will be to locate the person who has the correct or missing information. It is therefore helpful to start the process with a prepared list of the main owners of project information.

Despite the project evaluation guidelines provided here, things can still go wrong. The most common causes of a breakdown in the evaluation process are a lack of cooperation, project complexity beyond the abilities of the evaluator, a slowly moving evaluation, excessive external interference, and inconclusive evaluation results. Most things that go wrong in the evaluation and disentanglement process are generally variations or consequences of these problems.

Exercises

1. Search the Internet or your local library for a relatively detailed, recent case of a failed software project. Review the attempt to rescue it; did it succeed? You may make assumptions about missing details, but if you do so, list them. Compare the evaluation process used in the failed project to the process described here.

    What were the main problems during the evaluation of the project? Why did the rescue process succeed or fail?

2. For the project described in Exercise 1, what mistakes were made and what could have been done better (refer in particular to the project evaluation)?

    If the rescue failed, what could have been done differently to save the project?

    If the rescue succeeded, why did it succeed and what lessons can be learned and applied to other troubled projects?

3. Class project: Review the case of the inventory-control system, ICS 2.0, at the beginning of Chapter 4, "Step 2—Assign an Evaluator." Make assumptions regarding the missing details of the project and divide the project tasks among three or four project teams. Assign the students to each of the teams.

    Select one student to represent the initiating manager. Select two or three students for the evaluation team (one will be the chief evaluator). Conduct a simulated evaluation of the ICS 2.0 project with at least one instance of each of the problems described in Section 5.5, and document the discussion, problems, solutions, and recommendations.

    3.1   For each project team: Prepare a new plan of action for your area of responsibility. Concentrate on what you will be doing differently when the evaluation process has been launched (refer also to step 1 in Chapter 3, "Step 1—Stop").

    3.2   Evaluation team: Prepare a summary of the evaluation process.

    3.3   Initiating manager: Prepare a report of the main problems that required management intervention and how they were resolved.

4. Consider the problem of added overhead in an evaluation team of a large project (compared with a single evaluator). Are there cases where the overhead exceeds the benefit of the additional evaluators? Consider examples where the decision to establish a team is (a) beneficial, (b) questionable, and (c) detrimental. Explain your answers.

6

Step 4—Evaluate the Team

Step 10   Early Warning System

Step 9   Revise the Plan

Step 8   Risk Analysis

Step 7   Rebuild the Team

Step 6   Can Minimum Goals Be Achieved?

Step 5   Define Minimum Goals

Step 4   Evaluate the Team

Step 3   Evaluate Project Status

Step 2   Assign an Evaluator

Step 1   Stop

How important are development teams to the success of a software project? Does team structure really matter? To a varying degree, most of us believe it does. DeMarco and Lister [1] showed almost two decades ago that most issues that arise in technology projects are people issues, not technical ones, and successful projects consistently give significant weight to the human factor.

But it seems that many development organizations do not know that. Recent research has shown that a large percentage of software development organizations do not perceive their teams to be their most important asset for the success of their projects, and some do not see them as important at all (see Figure 6.1). When projects fail in these organizations, it is usually a good idea to start the rescue procedure by looking at the team. In fact, according to DeMarco and Lister, it is probably always a good idea to start with the team.

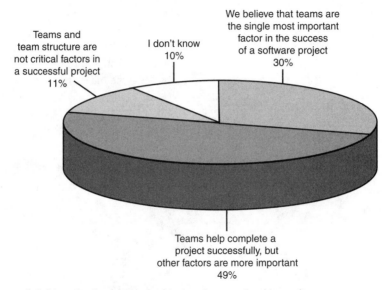

Figure 6.1 How the importance of teams is perceived by software organizations [2]

When reviewing a team, for what should the evaluator be looking? The simple answer, of course, is anything that might be hindering the success of the project. This is often easier said than done because team problems are not always easy to perceive due, in part, to the complexities of human relationships. However, the evaluator, as an outsider, is often at an advantage to detect such problems.

For example, it is not rare to hear a senior manager say, "We put together a great team; the problem can't be there." But the problem may indeed be there, as the following case illustrates:

Several years ago, a Florida-based software company won a key contract for the improvement of an airborne defense sub-system. A large part of the software was to be completely rewritten based on state-of-the-art hardware technology, which at that time had not yet been operationally implemented. In fact, the company concluded that one of the main project risks was the difficulty implementing the new software technology.

The company chose a multi-faceted strategy for dealing with the high software technology risk, which included close supervision of the project and the creation of an expert team of developers. The budget was increased to reflect the higher staff costs, and a strong team of experts was assembled.

Despite its high-profile team, the project was plagued with problems almost from its first day. The project manager found it difficult to manage the team, and the team members were constantly at odds with each other over the many problems that inevitably arose. Six months into the eighteen-month project schedule, the project manager was already forecasting a twelve-month overrun.

An external consultant concluded that the main problem with the project was the team, and the main problem with the team was that it wasn't one. In short, the project developers were functioning as a group of individuals—there was no team spirit. For such a complex project, a weak team spelled disaster.

The lesson here is that team problems are often located beneath the surface. While a team may appear strong at first glance, a closer look can reveal poor internal relationships and poor team spirit. And these may be the result of an incompatible team (as in the case of the airborne sub-system project), a lack of skills, bad planning (for example, impossible schedules resulting in impossible pressure), understaffing, or poor project management.

This chapter discusses methods for evaluating the development team of a failing software project and is mainly addressed to the project evaluator who conducts the team evaluation with the objective of identifying team problems that may have contributed to the failure. The main questions to be considered during the evaluation are as follows:

1. Can the team, as a unit, successfully deliver the project?

2. Does the project manager have the required leadership, technical skills, and personality necessary to lead the project team, and does he or she command the respect of the team members?

3. Do the project team members have the technical skills needed to do their job? Are all positions filled with the right people?

This step in the disentanglement process does not yet deal with finding solutions to the problems, nor does it deal with the restructuring of the team; that all comes in a later step (this is explained in Section 1.1.3). But the evaluation of the team, together with the conclusions on the status of the project (from the previous step 3), is essential input for the decisive steps to follow.

6.1   General Guidelines

In general, you should approach the team evaluation both resolutely and tactfully. Aim to strike a reasonable balance between an open, straightforward approach and the confidentiality that is always required when evaluating people. Here are some general guidelines:

1. You will be reviewing the team on three levels:

    Team performance

    Project management

    Team members

    These are not three separate reviews, but rather three overlapping perspectives of the team, which are part of a single review. While a substantial part of the interviewing can be performed concurrently, information from the review of team performance will provide input to the project management review, which will then provide input for the team member reviews. This will be discussed in detail in the following sections of the chapter.

2. Before proceeding, prepare for the evaluation by having the initiating manager first brief you about the team and any major team-related problems. Then conduct interviews with the team members and with key project players.

    a. Review the team as a unit. Interview the project manager and other key project players to learn about team performance and general team issues.

    b. Review project management. Interview the project manager and other key project players.

    c. Interview the individual team members.

    d. Finally, meet with any remaining key project players with whom you have not met and who can help fill in information and complete the picture.

3. Though your time is limited, try not to unduly rush the evaluation of the team. Allocate between one and two days for the team evaluation.

4. As the project evaluator, it is important that you be aware of the sensitivities involved in evaluating the development team of a failing software project. There will be job security and career concerns as well as the tension that always accompanies any type of personal review. In most cases, these concerns cannot be eliminated, but they can be alleviated.

    a. At the beginning of each interview, explain briefly the objective of the evaluation and of the overall process. Emphasize that your goal is to save the project.

    b. Clarify to the team that this step is purely part of the evaluation process and will not, at this point, result in any restructuring of the team.

    c. Rebuff politicking, defamation, and lobbying. It will help establish you as an unbiased professional.

5. The evaluation of the team can begin early by overlapping parts of the project evaluation (step 3). This can be more efficient and can save time by reducing the number of interviews (many of the same people will need to be interviewed for both steps 3 and 4). For example, the one-on-one team member interviews can often cover both the individual progress report and the individual team member review. Do not, however, finalize your conclusions about the team before you have finalized the findings for the previous step (the project). This concept is illustrated in Figure 6.2.

Adapt these guidelines to the specifics of the organization, the project, and the team that you are evaluating. They are not rigid rules; use them more as a reference list. Bear in mind that not all project teams of failing software projects will exhibit the same level of concern, and not all team members will be equally sensitive to the disentanglement process. But when a project fails, there will always be some level of concern because people will always be concerned about how the failure will reflect on them.

In the following sections, the three levels of the team evaluation (team unit, project management, and team members) are discussed in detail.

Advisory: It is sometimes necessary to interview all team members (especially in very small projects). However, this is not always the case. In the interest of efficiency, consider carefully the need for each interview before you schedule it. For example, it will probably not be necessary to interview a new team recruit.

This advisory is equally applicable to the team unit review (Section 6.2) and the individual team members' reviews (Section 6.4).

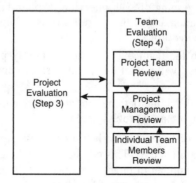

Figure 6.2 Project and team evaluations—concurrent reviews

6.2   Reviewing the Team Unit

In the previously discussed airborne subsystem example, this phase would have immediately homed in on the main problem (the project had no team, just a collection of expert individuals). While many major problems can be recognized at the team level, others will only surface during lower-level discussions (this is discussed in detail in Sections 6.3 and 6.4). The team review provides a general overview of the project team and raises issues for later discussion on the individual level.

Start with a review of the project team and focus on the performance of the team as a unit. Interview the initiating manager to get a general perspective of the team, and then meet with the project manager and other parties who interface regularly with the team (interviews can be conducted with multiple participants).

The following list covers several key issues that should be considered during the interviews:

1.   **General team performance**

Consider the team as a single unit: How well does the team perform? Are team activities well coordinated, and do team members cooperate well with each other? Consider the team's accomplishments: Were they due to teamwork, or would individual team members working on their own have achieved them in any case? Consider the team's setbacks: Could better teamwork have prevented them? How has the team performed over time? Has performance improved or declined?

2.   Skill set

Consider the skill set necessary to deliver the project: Does the team have these skills? Does the team have the necessary experience? Are the team member's skills up to date? Does the development organization have a training program for software developers, and if so, is the team taking advantage of the program?

3.   Unstaffed positions

At this point, we are not yet considering understaffing (budgeting for a team that is too small to deliver the project); rather, we are looking at budgeted team positions that have not been filled.

Are all approved team positions staffed? If not, for how long have unstaffed positions been empty? Is the project manager constantly looking for new people to fill empty positions? Are the right people in the right team positions? Are some positions only partially staffed (are people working part time when they are needed full time)?

4.   Size of team

Consider the size of the team that has been budgeted in relation to the amount of work to be done. Is the team understaffed (too small)? Is the team overstaffed (too big)? Note that in some cases, overstaffing can be a problem (redundancy, overlapping responsibilities, greater management burden, over-budgeting, and so on). How severe is the understaffing or overstaffing?

5.   Development facilities

Consider the facilities and tools available to the team. Does the team have the necessary development tools to deliver the project? Do team members have appropriate workspace, desks, offices, labs, and meeting rooms? Does the team have the necessary communications facilities (such as computer networks, or voice and data services)? Does the team have the necessary office services (administration, technical support, and so on)?

6.   Distributed teams

Is the project software being developed at a single location, or is it a distributed software development (DSD) project (parts of the team are at distant locations)? If it is a DSD project, how well does the distributed team work? Does the project have the necessary infrastructure for DSD? Is the project suited for DSD (can it be divided into independent sub-systems or tasks)?

7. **Team spirit and morale**

Clearly, the failure of a project will affect the morale and spirit of the team. But is there anything else that is causing low morale (if so, what is it)? Is there a lack of team commitment to the project? Is team attrition high?

8. **Relationships with other groups and teams**

Consider the project team's relationships with other external groups and teams. How well does the team work with the software quality assurance (SQA) team, the independent test team, the field support team, hardware development teams, other stakeholders, and other projects?

9. **Conflicts**

Are there any internal or external team conflicts or tensions that could disrupt the project? How long have they existed? How severe are they? Have there been attempts to resolve them?

10. **Management**

How good is the relationship between the team and management (the project manager and senior management)? Is senior management aware of the team problems? Have there been any attempts to resolve the problems? Have the managers responsible for the project been changed recently or frequently? If so, does management still support the project and its team?

These ten points are not distinct, meaning that they do not need to be covered separately (they are not a checklist in the sense that you finish one and move on to the next). The interviews and meetings can cover a broad range of topics at a single session, and some of the topics can be discussed concurrently. Whenever necessary, the topics can be followed through at meetings with individuals, as discussed in the following sections.

> **Advisory:** Use the input from the team unit review to prioritize the later interviews with the individual team members and the other project players. This way you will be able to put the main pieces of the picture in place more quickly. Reevaluate the priorities after each interview or meeting, and be prepared to repeat interviews with people whenever you become newly aware of a missing piece of critical information.

6.3   Reviewing Project Management

The project management review focuses mainly on the leadership (not the administrative[1]) aspects of the project and considers the main problems confronting the project manager and the way they are handled. In the airborne subsystem case discussed earlier, this phase would have uncovered the management problems in leading a team of mavericks.

Very often, project managers are the first to be imputed for a failed project. It is important, however, to remember that projects fail for many reasons, several of which are unrelated to the qualities of the project manager. The evaluator should approach the review with no preconceptions. Although senior management may sometimes instinctively blame project management, it is the evaluator's responsibility, after examining the facts, to independently determine if there are any major incompatibilities between the qualities of the project manager and the needs of the project. This is especially important because of the career-related impact of the evaluation results.

The following list contains several key management review points to be considered by the project evaluator:

1. **Skills**

    Consider the *main* skills required for the management of the project (avoid a comprehensive wish list for an ideal project manager). Concentrate on core skills without which it is clear that the project manager will not be able to successfully lead the project. Does the project manager have these skills? (See [3] for a discussion of software project management skills and responsibilities.)

2. **Relationships**

    How do others perceive the project manager's ability to successfully lead the project? Consider the quality of the project manager's relationships with the following groups:

    The team—Consider individual relationships, respect as a leader, and loyalty. Have there been any severe conflicts?

    Senior management—Consider individual relationships with key managers, issues of respect, and confidence in the project manager's required capabilities. Have there been any severe conflicts?

    Other groups—Consider the working relationship with project support groups, such as the test group, quality assurance, field support, marketing, other projects, and so on.

---

[1] That is not to say that administrative project tasks are unimportant.

Other project stakeholders—In addition to senior management and marketing, consider the relationship with customers, users, investors, subcontractors, partners, and so on.

Have any of these relationships contributed to the failure of the project? If so, how severe is the problem? If other project problems are resolved, will the relationship problem still endanger the successful completion of the project?

3. **Confidence in the project (can it be saved?)**

    Is the project manager confident that the project can be saved? Is saving the project worth the effort?[2] In the project manager's opinion, what are the top three well-defined activities that will salvage the project? How reasonable are these expectations?

4. **Spirit, motivation, commitment**

    How committed is the project manager to the success of the project? Consider the project manager's personal identification with the project, the amount of time invested in the project (full time, part time, and so on), loyalty to the project team, and more generally the level of enthusiasm in making the project a success. (Clearly, spirit and commitment are very much dependent on the previous point: confidence in the project.)

5. **Other problems**

    What other problems related to the project manager may have contributed to the failure of the project? Consider, for example, personal problems that may be affecting the project manager's work.

6. **General capabilities**

    Based on the previous points (1 to 5), consider the project manager's overall ability to successfully manage the project (leadership, personality, competence, and so on). Concentrate only on major points (remember that this is not a performance review).

    Consider the following question: If the other project problems (that are unrelated to the project manager's performance) are corrected, will the project manager be capable of successfully leading the project?

As part of the overall project evaluation, the review of project management will have considerable prior information to draw upon. Hence, many of the project's problems will likely be known to the evaluator before the review meeting with the project manager. This prior information will help focus on any potential project management problem areas.

---

[2] The importance of confidence is illustrated in the famous maxim, "If you believe you can do it, you are probably right. And if you believe you can't do it, you are probably right too."

> **Advisory:** When dealing with team members, you are dealing with the development organization's most valuable asset. In times of stress, this can be a delicate and sensitive task. When team issues become particularly complicated, it is wise to enlist assistance from a professional in the field (for example, the organization's human research manager). There are also several excellent reference texts on the subject (see, for example, Allcorn and Diamond [4] and Moorhead [5]).

6.4   Reviewing Individual Team Members

This review identifies team member problems that can prevent the project from being successfully completed. This is achieved through individual interviews that focus on the team problems identified during the team unit review. It is important to remember that this is not a performance review for the team members, and it is not concerned with problems that will not affect the overall success of the project.

If the team is large, there may not be sufficient time to meet with all team members individually—in such cases, select the ones relevant to the main team problems that have already been uncovered.

The following list includes several key points to be considered during the individual team member interviews:

1. **Job function**

   Determine the team member's job function and compare it with the job function described by the project manager. Are there significant discrepancies?

2. **Skills**

   Does the team member have the skills necessary to perform the job function (avoid a comprehensive wish list and concentrate only on the main skills)?

3. **Achievements and contributions**

   Consider the results (not effort) of the team member's work on the project so far. What have been the main contributions to the project? Have the team member's activities been a factor in the failure of the project? If so, how severe is this factor?

4. **Relationships**

Consider the team member's relationship with other persons involved in the project, including

- Other team members
- The project manager
- Members of other groups/teams
- The project stakeholders

Are any of these relationships problematic? If so, how serious are the problems and how do they affect the project?

5. **Morale and commitment issues**

Does the team member have any morale issues that go beyond the failure of the project? How committed is the team member to the project and especially to the attempt to rescue it? Can the team member be expected to stay with the project if a disentanglement plan is implemented?

6. **Other problems**

What other problems have affected the team member's work on the project? Consider such issues as work environment, tools and facilities, training, and personal problems.

7. **Capabilities**

Based on the previous points (1 to 6), consider the team member's overall ability to successfully perform the job function tasks. Concentrate only on major points.

Consider the following question: If a new, feasible project plan is implemented, will the team member be capable of successfully fulfilling the requirements of the job description?

Here again it is important to remember that this is not a team member's performance review. While the list of team member review points covers a wide range of issues, only those that are relevant should be used.

6.5 Consolidate Your Findings

As we have seen, there are several sources of information for the evaluation of the project team. The goal of consolidation is to combine the information together to form a single picture.

However, it is not uncommon for the team evaluation to produce parts of a picture that are not entirely compatible. In many of these cases, the pieces will fit well enough together and the incompatibilities will not substantially distort the overall picture. While this is usually sufficient for the evaluation of the team, occasionally it is not. In these cases, fundamental incompatibles that cannot be easily reconciled may require repeat interviews or a re-analysis of the project data. (This problem is further discussed in Section 6.6.)

Before consolidating the findings, ensure the availability of all documented information that was collected during the reviews. Then proceed with the following guidelines for finalizing the team evaluation:

1. **Complete the picture.**

    Combine the main findings of the reviews, and clarify, reconcile, or eliminate incompatibles.

2. **Archive all information.**

    Archive copies of all interviews and team information that were collected during the evaluation. This will save substantial time if the findings ever need to be re-examined.

3. **Prepare a short team overview document.**

    The document should be no more than 3–6 pages (depending on the size and complexity of the team) and should take between two and four hours to prepare. Include the main sources of information, the list of interviews, the reasoning that led to any significant findings, and any problems or incompatibles that arose during the evaluation.

4. **Review the overview with the initiating manager.**

    Review a draft of the document with the initiating manager. Expand any key points that are unclear and correct any factual errors.

5. **Adjust the evaluation.**

    Additional information about the team may well continue to emerge throughout the disentanglement process. If any of the new information affects your main findings, be prepared to adjust your conclusions. However, avoid frequent changes to your findings, especially when the new data does not significantly affect your key conclusions.

Due to the findings on individual team members, the team overview document cannot be considered a public document. However, a summary of the findings should be available to the team and to the project stakeholders (consult with the initiating manager regarding any business reasons to limit distribution).

Advisory: Do not permit incompatibilities on team issues to delay the disentanglement process. If the problem cannot be resolved within one day, make your best judgment based on the information that is available to you. Briefly review your judgment again at the end of the process.

6.6   What Can Go Wrong (and What to Do About It)

As noted at the beginning of this chapter, most issues that arise in technology projects are people issues, not technical ones, and this is no less true when dealing with the people aspect of a failed project. So it would not be surprising to find that the same is true of the *evaluation* of a failing project, which means that most of what can go wrong is people-related.

Here are some of the problems that can occur and the responses to help deal with them:

- **Lack of cooperation**

  During the evaluation of the team, there are several reasons why team members and other key project players may withhold cooperation: career and job security concerns, hostility or suspicion toward an outsider (the evaluator), and an exaggerated sense of team loyalty.

  Action: If the problem exists with just one or two team members, enlist the project manager's help in dealing with them—assuming that the project manager is not part of the problem. Otherwise, the solution will need the help of senior management by making their support clearly visible.

  If the problem is with the project manager, a three-way meeting between the initiating manager, the evaluator, and the project manager may be the best solution.

- **Excessive politics**

  In any large organization, it is not unusual for personal interests, lobbying, and corporate politicking to influence employee behavior. This is especially true when dealing with team issues, and the result is a degree of bias in the reviews.

  Action: Whenever possible, the problem should be resolved directly with the biased individual through repeat interviews. If the information is particularly important, consider including the project manager or the initiating manager in the repeat interview.

  Bias due to politics and personal interests is often detectable, especially when there are other sources for the same information. By comparing information, bias can often be filtered out, which demonstrates that knowing that bias exists is often just as important as eliminating it.

- **Protracted team evaluation**

  As mentioned earlier, team evaluation should take between one and two days. When the evaluation takes longer, it is usually for one of the following reasons:

1. Poor team cooperation.

2. The team is large.

3. Severe team performance issues.

If the problem is not resolved, the result will be a delay of the disentanglement process.

Action: Poor team cooperation should be resolved as described previously (in "Lack of cooperation"). If the team is too large, prioritize the interviewees—it is not always essential to interview all team members. If the team performance problems are severe, concentrate on the main problems—remember that the intent, at this stage, is not to resolve all the problems, but rather to identify them.

- **Incompatible information**

  It is natural, when collecting information from many human sources, to find incompatibilities in the way the information is reported. This is certainly true of the evaluation of a development team. If the inconsistencies are significant and if they appear within critical items of information, they can produce an ambiguous or distorted picture of the project team.

  Action: This problem is discussed in Section 6.5. Fundamental incompatibles that cannot be easily reconciled may require repeat interviews or a re-analysis of the project data. If the incompatibilities remain, but they do not substantially distort the overall picture, they can be disregarded. Otherwise, use your best judgment to reconcile the differences.

> **Advisory:** Remember that the evaluation of the team is not a detailed performance review. The objective of this step is to identify team problems that may have contributed to the project's failure. Restrict yourself to this objective alone.

6.7   Summary

Most issues that arise in technology projects are people issues, not technical ones, and successful projects consistently give significant weight to the human factor. So when projects fail, it is usually a good idea to start the rescue procedure by looking at the team. This objective of this step in the disentanglement process is to identify team problems that may have contributed to the failure.

In general, aim to strike a reasonable balance between an open, straightforward approach and the confidentiality that is always required when evaluating people.

1. Prepare for the evaluation by having the initiating manager brief you about the team.

2. Allocate between one and two days for the evaluation.

3. Explain briefly the objective of the evaluation and of the overall process.

4. Clarify to the team that this step does not, at this point, result in any restructuring of the team.

5. Discourage politicking, defamation, and lobbying.

The team evaluation consists of three overlapping reviews, which address the following questions:

1. Can the team, as a unit, successfully deliver the project?

   This includes a review of the general team performance, the team's skill set, the size of team, unstaffed positions, the development facilities, distributed teams, team spirit and morale, relationships with other groups and teams, conflicts, and other team issues.

2. Does the project manager have the required leadership, technical skills, and the personality necessary to lead the project team?

   This includes the review of following points: skills, confidence in the project (can it be saved?), relationships, spirit, motivation and commitment, and general capabilities.

3. Do the project team members have the technical skills needed to do their job?

   This includes the review of following points: job function, skills, achievements and contributions to the project, relationships, morale and commitment issues, and general capabilities.

After the reviews are complete, the information needs to be consolidated to form a single picture. In many cases, the pieces will fit together well enough. However, if significant incompatibilities exist, it may be necessary to repeat parts of the interviews.

The following guidelines describe the main points for finalizing the team evaluation:

1. Complete the picture. Combine the main findings of the reviews.

2. Archive interviews and information collected during the evaluation.

3. Prepare a short team overview document. The document should be no more than 3–6 pages long and should take between two and four hours to prepare.

4. Review a draft of the document with the initiating manager.

5. Adjust the evaluation based on additional information about the team that will emerge throughout the disentanglement process.

Following are some of the problems that can occur:

- Lack of cooperation: Resolve with the project manager or initiating manager.

- Excessive politics: Resolve directly with the biased individual through repeat interviews. By comparing information, bias can often be filtered out.

- Protracted team evaluation: This is usually due to poor team cooperation, a large team, or severe team performance issues.

- Incompatible information: May require repeat interviews or a re-analysis of the project data. Otherwise, use your best judgment to reconcile the differences.

Exercises

1. Review the airborne subsystem case at the beginning of the chapter. Discuss the way the team of experts was established. Considering the technology risks, what other team options could management have chosen? In your opinion, can the team of experts be made effective? Explain.

    What is the role of the project manager in solving team spirit problems? Explain.

2. Consider the airborne subsystem case at the beginning of the chapter and plan the project team evaluation. Document any assumptions that you need to make about the project.

    Create a list of people to be interviewed. Based on the description of the project's problems, consider the responses that you would most likely get from the reviews of the overall team performance, the project manager, and the individual team members. Prepare a summary of your findings.

3. Review examples of failed software projects by searching your local library, the Internet, or other sources. Find at least one project where the team functioned poorly. Summarize the team problems based on the discussion in this chapter.

4. Class project, based on exercise 2: Choose a project evaluator. Divide the class into three groups:

- One group will review the overall team.
- One group will review the project manager.
- One group will review the individual team members.

Each group should then merge the findings of their group members (from the solutions to exercise 2) into a single set of findings (but only for the review that was assigned to them—team, project manager, or individual team members).

The project evaluator, with the help of the class, should now consolidate the three reviews into a single team evaluation. Discuss incompatibilities with the class, and decide how to resolve them. Which incompatibilities can be disregarded? Explain why.

7

Step 5—Define Minimum Goals

Step 10   Early Warning System
Step 9   Revise the Plan
Step 8   Risk Analysis
Step 7   Rebuild the Team
Step 6   Can Minimum Goals Be Achieved?
Step 5   Define Minimum Goals
Step 4   Evaluate the Team
Step 3   Evaluate Project Status
Step 2   Assign an Evaluator
Step 1   Stop

There is a surprising answer to a problem often given to students of operations research. The problem involves a city bus company that provides poor service. Passengers are required to wait a long time for a slow-moving bus to pick them up. The students are given the statistical parameters of the problem and are asked to provide the bus company with recommendations on how to improve its service. The solution is surprising because it involves *removing* buses rather than adding them or increasing their capacity. Apparently, fewer busses reduce traffic congestion, allowing them to move faster.

This is a variation of the famous "hand in the cookie jar" dilemma, where in order to get some cookies out, you first have to let some go (you can dip in again later for more).[1] This principle is widely used in business, politics, and military strategy, and anywhere optimization is associated with compromise.[2]

Software development has its own version of the dilemma. By trying to provide too many features, software projects often end up providing less, and sometimes none, as in the case of a failed project. More often than not, overloaded projects end up with fewer features rather than none (they deliver whatever fits into the remaining schedule). But the problem is that when software projects deliver fewer features than originally planned, customers rarely end up with the features that they would have chosen. It takes a combination of foresight and courage to methodically cut back an overloaded feature list (rather than just letting it eventuate), and the earlier the list is cut back, the better.

The problem of unachievable goals is by no means new. The Cutter Consortium, which has been analyzing data on software projects for many years, has found that an overloaded feature list is the second most common reason for software project overruns (the first is changing requirements) [1]. A more compelling notion has come from The Standish Group, which has declared that the reduction of requirements to the bare minimum is a key ingredient of a successful software project [2]. In effect, The Standish Group is simply saying that if a feature is not absolutely necessary, it should be discarded. Although it is arguable whether this approach is valid for all projects, it is essential for rescuing failing projects.

Reducing project goals is a key step in the disentanglement process. This chapter describes the method for defining minimum goals and discusses how to overcome opposition and gain acceptance for a more modest project. The emphasis is on the word *minimum*, and the objective is to reduce the project to the smallest size that achieves only the most essential goals. It is a process that determines

---

[1] We should note that in the cookie jar anecdote, the goal (cookies) is reduced, while in the bus company story, it is the means (busses) that is reduced. The basic idea, though, is similar: By making do with less, you end up with more.

[2] See, for example, Sun Tzu's *Manual for War*, in which the legendary strategist states, "The best way to achieve the goal of a military campaign and hold down costs is to plan on a short campaign—the shorter the better, so long as we achieve victory over the enemy." [3]

which cookies should remain in your hand while still being able to remove it from the cookie jar.

This step does not, as yet, include a rigorous feasibility analysis of the over-all project with reduced goals (that comes later in step 6). But the reduction of goals is obviously performed with feasibility in mind. There is, after all, no sense in releasing just one or two cookies if it is obvious that releasing five or six is required.

The discussion and the recommended guidelines in the chapter are mainly directed toward the project evaluator. However, this step, more than any other, cannot succeed without the involvement and support of the key project players.

7.1   Project Goals and the Disentanglement Process

Goals are related to action, and they define the desired outcome after the action has been completed, such as "I will study hard and become a famous scientist." An extravagant goal is often referred to as a *mission*; the Starship Enterprise had a mission statement: "To boldly go where no man has gone before."

Goals can be extravagant, modest, or overloaded (they can aim for too much). In some cases, goals can be severely lacking, as in the alleged story that President Kennedy's famous goal statement originally went "By the end of this decade, I will put a man on the surface of the moon," and only later was it amend-ed to include "and bring him safely back to earth."

But anecdotes aside, one of the problems with goals is that the term is not sufficiently well defined. The IEEE glossary of software engineering terminolo-gy [4], for example, does not include the term, though it does describe related terms, such as "requirements," "features," and "specifications." So before dis-cussing how to reduce goals, we will first clarify what we mean when we talk about software project goals and how they relate to the disentanglement process.

7.1.1   Sorting Out Goals, Objectives, Requirements, and Deliverables

The problem with the definition of a goal given at the beginning of this section ("the desired outcome after an action has been completed") is that it fits several related but non-identical terms; for example, *goal, mission, objective* all define a desired outcome. Then there are *requirements*, which are certainly related to the desired outcome of a project, and *deliverables*, which are the items to be provid-ed at the end of a project (not to mention *features* and *specifications*). All these goal terms are in some way related to a desired outcome.

In order to provide here a level of consistency, Figure 7.1 illustrates the overlapping of goal terms, and the following overview describes their usage within the context of the project disentanglement discussion.

Project Goal

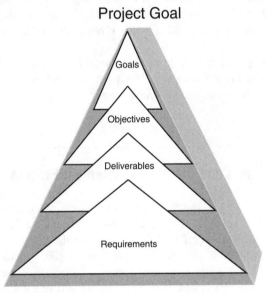

Figure 7.1 Overlapping goal terms

1. **The goal/mission statement**

   The description of a goal is often presented in a top-down manner starting with a brief summary of the desired outcome, followed by more detailed descriptions. It is common to refer to the brief summary as the *goal statement* or the *mission statement.*

2. **Goal**

   A set of related goals is often referred to simply as a "goal," as in: "to complete a project on time, within budget, according to requirements, and with high customer satisfaction." This goal actually includes four related goals. When generalizing, the plural term "goals" is more detailed and can be used to cover all items to be delivered by a project team during and at the completion of development (the "project goals"). Thus, the goal/mission statement is executed by taking action to achieve the project goals.

3. **Objectives**

   The usage of "objectives" overlaps goals to a large extent; any differences will be disregarded in the following discussion.

4. **Deliverables**

The term "deliverables" covers the tangible items to be provided when the project is completed. This commonly covers the required product features and can also include documentation, training, field support, and forms of maintenance. Providing the deliverables is part of the project's goals.

5. **Requirements**

The term "requirements" usually refers to a signed-off, formal, documented list of items to be delivered at the end of a project. It is sometimes part of a legally binding contract. However, occasionally there may also be requirements that refer to the way the project is developed, its design, and even the program language in which the software is to be written. Requirements usually define the project's deliverables, and they may also describe how the deliverables are to be produced.

In the context of the disentanglement process discussion, we shall mainly use the generalized term "goals" as described in item 2 of the previous list.

7.1.2   Who Sets the Project Goals?

As part of the initial groundwork toward the reduction of project goals, it is essential to know who is responsible for setting them. This is because any changes to the project goals as part of the disentanglement process will need the approval of those who originally set them. Thus, it is mainly from among the goal-setters that the evaluator will need to enlist support and recruit allies.

So who are the goal setters? Software project goals are set by parties that have a vested interest in the results of the project, such as members of senior management, marketing staff, customers, investors, or any combination of these. Occasionally, goal setters are familiar with the development process that produces their product, but not always. When goal setters lack a basic understanding of software development, it can lead to the setting of unachievable or overloaded goals. In fact, development naïveté is one of the main reasons software project goals rarely conform to the Standish Group's rule of bare minimum.

To successfully negotiate achievable project goals, it is therefore useful to know the parties involved in setting project goals, particularly the following:

- **Their stake in the project**

  What is their investment and their risk? How will they benefit from success, and what is their cost of failure or partial failure? For business-oriented organizations: What is their expected *return on investment* (ROI)? (See Section 2.2.1 for an additional discussion of the subject.)

- **Their alternatives**

  Do they have backup or alternative plans if the project does not deliver all its goals?

- **Their familiarity with the development process costs**

  What are the features and functionality costs in terms of time, budget, and complexity?

- **Their two or three critical needs (in relation to the product being developed)**

  Of all the project's major deliverables, which are the most essential (the ones without which the project will have little or no value)?

- **Their schedule constraints**

  How quickly do they really need the functionality?

The initiating manager and the project manager are often good sources for this information, and studying it is usually well worth the project evaluator's time. In fact, being familiar with the goal setters and the other project stakeholders is a good strategy in any software project (for project managers). But for the project evaluator, it is especially valuable in disentangling a failing project when significant concessions on the part of the goal setters will probably be needed.

7.1.3 Goal Monitors Make Good Allies

When a software project is in severe trouble, the need to negotiate new goals should not come as a surprise. But in reality, it often does. The reason is that not all project stakeholders closely monitor the project, nor, as noted previously, do they necessarily know the consequences of the goals that they have set for the project development team. In terms of the cookie jar allegory, some stakeholders may perceive that the hand cannot be removed from the jar, but they do not necessarily make the connection with the number of cookies that were grasped.

Ideally, the principle project stakeholders (senior management, marketing, and the customer) should continually monitor the project as it is being developed. But in reality, troubled software projects are usually monitored neither often nor effectively. Nevertheless, the more information stakeholders have about the true state of the project, the better allies they will make for the evaluator in negotiating new goals. So look for allies among those most knowledgeable about the project.

Here's how this should be done:

- **Who has shown interest in development?**

  If the project has had orderly status reviews, identify the main participants. If no orderly reviews have been held, find out who has taken an active interest in the project development procedure.

- **Are any of the project stakeholders goal setters?**

  Seek out the project goal setters who have been monitoring the project to any degree. The more familiar they are with the project problems, the better. These may be good allies in renegotiating goals.

- **Those who aren't goal setters can also help.**

  Seek other stakeholders (those who aren't goal setters) who have been involved in monitoring the project. These can also provide support in renegotiating goals.

- **Identify a small team of potential allies.**

  Select the three or four best potential allies. Meet with them individually to hear their views about the status of the project and the importance of the goals.

The initial groundwork of identifying the project goals, the goal setters, and potential allies from among the project goal monitors should take about a half-day but no more than one day. The investment in the groundwork is always worthwhile, as it can potentially make the remainder of this disentanglement step easier.

> **Advisory:** Recruit allies early in the disentanglement process.
> They will be a valuable asset throughout the process.

7.2 Guidelines for Minimizing Goals

As noted previously, the emphasis in this step of the process is on the word *minimum*; the project should be reduced to the smallest size that achieves only the most essential goals, as illustrated in Figure 7.2. The intent is to re-plan the project so that it delivers a smaller product of adequate value but with a high probability of success.

The main problem, of course, is determining which goals are most essential, because many of the parties involved in the project will have conflicting ideas of what is necessary. This is why the recruitment of allies and supporters is so important, and the most valuable allies come from (a) senior (executive) management and (b) the customer.[3]

---

[3] The term "customer" here refers to the entity that requested the project or that will use the product being developed or, more generally, for whom the project is being developed.

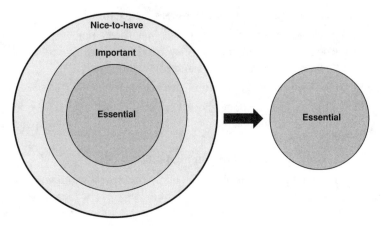

Figure 7.2 The goal reduction procedure

Obviously, allies alone will not eliminate the conflicting views of the project's goals. Though agreement can often be established about the top features, there is usually less agreement about where to draw the line. This problem can usually be solved with the help of a simple technique, described next.

7.2.1 The Goal Reduction Process

To minimize project goals, work with the key project stakeholders to divide the project requirements (functionality, features, and performance criteria) into three sets:

Set 1: Essential requirements without which the project will have no appreciable value. This set includes the requirements without which the product will be unable to perform its most essential functions. This set also includes the correction of high-priority software defects for which there is no work-around. When in doubt about whether a requirement belongs in this set, do not include it.

Set 2: Important requirements that greatly improve the project but are not essential. These are the product features that add significant value to the product but are not required for the product to perform its most essential functions. This includes the correction of mid-level software defects, as well as high-level defects for which there is a work-around.

Set 3: Nice-to-have requirements that add to the project but are not especially important. These are the requirements that add spit and polish to the final product. They may include ease-of-use requirements, an attractive user interface, low-level defect correction, and important features that are not immediately required when the product is first released.

Start by retaining the requirements from Set 1 and eliminating Sets 2 and 3 from the project (see Figure 7.2). This will often create tremendous opposition, but remember—we are dealing with a project that was totally out of control and may otherwise be cancelled. Occasionally, some elements from Set 2 can be added, but this should be rare. All remaining requirements (from Sets 2 and 3) should be targeted for subsequent releases of the software.

> **Advisory:** A word of caution: Be prepared to forestall the ploy by some stakeholders to second-guess the whole categorization process by their insistence on listing all (or most) requirements in Set 1.

7.2.2 Goal Reduction—A Case Study

Software projects become overloaded because they either started out with an over-ambitious set of goals or because their goals became unachievable due to development problems. But in either case, leaving the problem unresolved is one of the key causes of project failure. Consider, for example, the following case of a business-critical project struggling with overloaded goals.

Several years ago, CCSI,[4] a large New York-based marketing promotion company that deals with customer loyalty, designed a sophisticated computer-based system that would offer incentives to consumers based on their individual preferences and purchasing patterns. Consumers would be encouraged to enlist in the program after which information about their buying habits would be collected at participating stores when their membership card was electronically read at the checkout register. Thus, for example, new parents would be offered promotions on baby products, and photography enthusiasts would be offered discounts on camera equipment and supplies.

CCSI launched a nationwide drive to enlist hundreds of thousands of consumers in the program, and they invested several million dollars in an intensive advertising campaign. The problem was that the software to drive their computer system was in serious trouble and would not be ready in time for the advertised launch date of the program. This problem, if left unsolved, would generate significant losses for CCSI in dwindling interest by consumers, in lost revenue, and in penalties to be paid to participating retail stores.

---

[4] Though the details of the case are essentially accurate, the name of the company is an anonym.

The situation continued to deteriorate, due in no small way to CCSI's unre-lenting demand that their developers deliver everything that they had com-mitted. Eventually, the CEO of CCSI realized that unless some of the cook-ies were released, the hand would never emerge from the jar.

The software functionality was then divided into the following categories:

1. **Essential:**

    System operator console

    Collecting and storing membership information

    Collecting and storing retailer and store information

    Collecting customer purchasing data after a membership card is elec-tronically read

    Rudimentary display of collected information

2. **Important:**

    Collection and storage of product promotion information

    Analysis of consumer membership data

    Production of product promotion notices for individual consumers

    Backup and recovery

3. **Nice-to-have:**

    Formatted system reports

    Sophisticated graphics user interface

    Remote system query access

    Effectiveness analysis (to what extent does the system increase business?)

A first release of the system with the essential features enabled the pro-gram to be launched on schedule while the rest of the system's features were still being developed. After further consideration, the backup and recovery functionality was also added to the first release. Subsequent releases added the remaining features from the important and the nice-to-have categories.

Though it was extremely difficult for the CCSI management and marketing per-sonnel to accept the reduction in goals (the system was intended to be part of a new flagship service), it was fortunate that they realized the necessity in time. Had they realized the need earlier, they could have ended up with more functionality in their first release (see Figure 7.3), but had they waited longer, they would prob-ably have been unable to produce on time even a minimal-goal first release.

A key point of the CCSI case is that the project team was able to significantly reduce the project goals while still delivering the product's critical functionality. While admittedly this is not always possible, it can be done in more cases than one might think. In fact, it is not the unfeasibility of reducing goals that usually prevents companies from salvaging a small but still useful product; it is the unwillingness to come to terms with the necessity to do so (until it is too late).

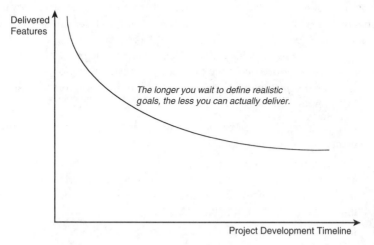

Figure 7.3 Delivered features as a function of the time when a realistic feature load is set

7.2.3 Dealing with Opposition

Expect opposition to the changing of project goals; it's both common and natural. In fact, among most stakeholders, forgoing committed product features is perceived as being contrary to their interests. But as we have seen, it may well be in their interest to do so when projects are in serious trouble.

Opposition is often strong when key stakeholders (customers, senior management, and marketing representatives) believe that their interests conflict with those of the project development team: for example, the stakeholders are trying to get as much as possible while the developers are trying to deliver as little as possible. In their eyes, the developers are intentionally painting an exaggerated, grim picture of the project to avoid their obligations. Stakeholders who think this way will continuously argue over each attempt to reduce the project goals.

But even though a desire for comfortable goals and schedules surely constitutes some of the developers' motivation, professional pride and integrity are much stronger factors, and the development team usually has a keen interest in the success of the project. (These lines of thought roughly coincide with the "theory-X versus theory-Y" approach to management.)[5]

In reality, a project team's success usually does coincide with the success of the project and the satisfaction of the customer (and of course the satisfaction of management), so that ideally there should be significant overlap between the interests of the key stakeholders and those of the project development team.[6]

But opposition to reducing goals is a fact, so how can the project evaluator effectively deal with it? In Sections 7.1.2 and 7.1.3, we discussed the importance of seeking out allies and we reviewed the steps for doing so. We also noted that the best allies are those who have a significant stake in the project and who have generally stayed informed about the project's progress.

The following list summarizes the key points for the project evaluator in dealing with opposition:

- Recruit allies. If allies cannot be found, enlist the help of the initiating manager.
- Be ready for opposition and prepare your response. Work with your allies and with the project development team to collect the facts. Summarize the impact and cost of the project's requirements, and divide them into the three sets (as defined in Section 7.2.1).
- Review the plan for reducing the project goals with your allies.
- Meet with the project's key stakeholders:

  Present the goal reduction plan to the key stakeholders.

  Be prepared to negotiate, and demonstrate some flexibility, but beware the ploy discussed earlier, where all (or most) goals are presented as being essential.

  If necessary, use your ultimate argument: There is little sense continuing with the disentanglement process unless the project goals are significantly reduced.

---

[5] According to Douglas McGregor's [5] Theory X (the authoritarian management style), the average person dislikes work and will avoid it whenever possible. Therefore, most people must be forced with the threat of punishment to work toward organizational objectives; also, the average person prefers to be directed, avoids responsibility, is relatively unambitious, and wants security above all else.

Conversely, according to McGregor's Theory Y (the participative management style), effort in work is as natural as work and play, people will apply self-control and self-direction in the pursuit of organizational objectives, without external control or the threat of punishment, commitment to objectives is a function of rewards associated with their achievement. Also, people usually accept and often seek responsibility, and the capacity to use a high degree of imagination, ingenuity. Furthermore, creativity in solving organizational problems is widely, not narrowly, distributed in the population. Furthermore, in industry the intellectual potential of the average person is only partly utilized.

[6] Admittedly, it would be naïve to assume that this is always so, but all the same the interests of the two parties often do coincide to a considerable degree.

- After agreement, prepare a summary document (between one and three pages) with the new (reduced) project goals.

Project goal minimization is a key step in the disentanglement process and should take between one and two days. Strong allies and good groundwork together with a resolute project evaluator can help ease and shorten the step. Whenever the negotiation gets mired, remind the stakeholders that the project is in serious trouble and the alternative to reducing goals may well be the cancellation of the project.

7.3   Minimum Goals for Large Projects

Large software projects with large sets of goals are complex to manage and usually run a much higher risk than small projects. The Software Engineering Institute's Watts Humphrey observes that large software projects are produced by large organizations, which "affects their ability to operate and to produce high-quality products for predictable costs and schedules."[6] Humphrey apparently sees largeness in itself as a potential cause of project failure.

But largeness is also self-preserving. Because wrong decisions can be very costly in large projects, there is a tendency for management "not to meddle with the project." Thus, large organization complexity, project complexity, significant project risk, and fear of the consequences of making major decisions all serve to make the minimization of goals for large projects more difficult than for small ones.

But there is another perspective for stakeholders to consider. The added difficulty of large projects goes hand in hand with the added benefits of success; disentangling a large project usually reaps far greater rewards than rescuing a small one. In fact, it is the high stakes of large projects that ultimately convince key project stakeholders to accept a reduction of goals. Indeed, the dire consequences of total project failure are the project evaluator's ultimate argument.

The following guidelines cover several of the main points in reducing large project goals:

1. Large projects usually mean large budgets and increased interest from the highest levels of management within the organization. Preparation and groundwork are essential for gaining support from senior management.

2. Is the project so large or complex that it has produced management paralysis? If so, discuss the problem with a higher level (even the highest level) of management (enlist the help of the initiating manager). Make it clear that if the project is not changed, the results will not change either.

3. Estimate the cost of failure (in most large projects, it will be significant). What is at stake? Quantify the value of the rescued project.

4. Would the project have better been developed in an evolutionary process? If so, present the goal reduction as a correction of the initial process.

5. Large projects mean large problems. Concentrate on the top two, and explain how they will be resolved by minimizing goals.

6. Large projects often have one or more requirements that carry a heavy burden in terms of cost (for example, schedule and development resources). Do all key stakeholders understand the cost of these heavy requirements? Opposition to their removal or postponement may be reduced or eliminated by explaining their cost and their impact on the project.

The reduction of goals for large projects should not consume more than the recommended time for this step of the process (between one and two days). Do not get involved in the lowest levels of requirements. Review project goals on a high-to-medium level. Leave the lower-level details to be completed by the project team after the minimized project is resumed.

> **Advisory:** For large projects, stay on schedule by working in parallel. The project evaluation is probably being conducted by an evaluation team (more than one evaluator), so parallel work is practicable.
>
> Examples of candidate tasks for parallel work in this step include preparation groundwork, coordinating with allies, prioritization and categorization of requirements, and the calculation of requirement costs.

7.4 What Can Go Wrong (and What to Do About It)

Reducing software project goals is a sensitive activity. Opposition is not always based on rationale; it is often driven by emotions, bias, and by a lack of information and understanding regarding the development process. Consequently, the effort can become mired and even stall.

Here are some of the problems that may stall the process and the responses to help the evaluator deal with them:

- **Opposition is unyielding.**

  Despite explanations regarding the inevitability of total project failure if goals are not reduced, the key stakeholders continue to oppose any significant changes to the project scope.

  Action: This is the time to use allies. Meet with them before meeting with the opposition and plan their support. Also, enlist the help of the initiating manager in order to prepare senior management for this step in the process. In general, prepare well for the confrontation and make every effort to position yourself on the side of the stakeholders (make it clear that you are working to achieve *their* best interests).

  As a last resort, explain that the disentanglement process cannot proceed without a significant reduction in the project's goals.

- **The essential list is too long.**

  This is the materialization of the caution advisory in Section 7.2.1. The project goals (or requirements) were too easily classified as essential without sufficient thought or consideration. This totally defeats the purpose of the classification process.

  Action: If the essential list cannot be negotiated down, follow this procedure:

  1. Identify up to 30 of the project's key requirements.
  2. Work with the stakeholders to list the requirements according to priority. Do not permit requirements to have the same priority (if no other criteria can be found, list similar priority requirements according to their cost in terms of schedule and resources).
  3. Any requirement that would potentially consume 10% or more of the project's development resources should be broken up into smaller requirements.
  4. Define a new provisional essential list from the highest-priority requirements. The new essential list should include as many high-priority requirements as will fit into a new target project schedule.
  5. Negotiate this new provisional essential list with the project stakeholders. The rule is that any requirements that are added to the list must replace other requirements of similar cost in time and resources that are removed from the list.

- **There is a lack of allies.**

  When there are no allies for reducing project goals, all key players expect to continue doing things more or less the way they did before. This is clearly a recipe for failure, unless at least one influential stakeholder can be won over.

Action: Sections 7.1.2 and 7.1.3 describe the method for identifying possible allies. There are always allies to some extent; not all stakeholders oppose the reduction of goals to the same degree. Work with those whose opposition is lowest.

If there is no other support, work with the initiating manager to convince other key stakeholders to become allies.

- **There is a lack of support in identifying requirements and costs.**

The identification of project requirements should ideally come from project documentation. If requirements documentation is non-existent (or greatly outdated), you will need to rely on the project manager, the project team, and the stakeholders. If their support is lacking, this step in the process becomes extremely difficult or even impossible to implement. This is similarly true if there is no cooperation in determining the requirements' development costs.

Action: The resolution of this problem must come from senior management, and especially from the initiating manager. Senior management's full support for the disentanglement process and for the evaluator needs to be made perfectly clear to all involved parties, through written announcements, group meetings, and town hall meetings. In cases where specific individuals are the source of the problem, it is useful to hold a brief meeting between the initiating manager, the evaluator, and the specific individual.

- **Goals are vague (it is unclear what to reduce).**

Vague goals are difficult to reduce (consider a business manager stating that "we are going to build a product for less than our competitors"; it only has meaning if his developers know or can find out the competitors' costs). In fact, vague goals are often one of the causes of project failure because the development team members do not have a clear understanding of what they are expected to deliver.

Action: A failing project with vague goals presents an opportunity to clarify the goals and set clear direction for the development team. First, demonstrate that the goals are vague; provide examples and show that the team can interpret the goals in many ways. Establish a team of three (the evaluator, the project manager, and a representative of the stakeholders) to clarify the goals on a high level. Do not spend more than one day on this effort. Further clarification of the goals, on a more detailed level, should be one of the project team's first tasks after the reduced project is resumed.

- **Goals are overwhelming (even after reduction, there are too many).**

This is a similar situation to the essential list being too long (discussed previously). The main difference is that the essential list may be a genuine reduction of the original project scope, and the stakeholders may truly be trying to cooperate in the goal reduction effort. The problem stems from the fact that the goals were so unrealistic to start with that even after being reduced, they remain so.

Action: Follow the procedure for the case where the essential list is too long (described previously). Also, review the next step (Chapter 8, "Step 6—Can Minimal Goals Be Achieved?").

- **Goals are already minimal; further reduction makes the project valueless.**

There are several variants of this problem: (1) The problem is really due to unyielding opposition; (2) It is really a problem of the essential list being too long; and (3) All project requirements are genuinely necessary.

Action: If this is a case of versions (1) or (2), revert to the actions described above. However, if the product will truly have no value if it is significantly reduced, unless there is a glaring project problem elsewhere that is causing project failure, there may be no option other than to cancel the project entirely.

In some cases, it may still be effective to generate a first minimal release even though its value would be questionable. Then the next release with more features may be able to provide the essential functionality. If acceptable, this approach is similar to an extension of the project schedule but with the advantage of taking an initial smaller step with less risk and a higher likelihood of success.

- **Evolutionary development (a series of product releases) is unfeasible.**

This problem usually occurs when the project is time-dependent; its value is related to it being available at a specific time (for example, an income tax return software application or election analysis software).

Action: Can a minimal product release provide enough essential functionality to make the project worthwhile? If the answer is yes, obviously this is the course of action to follow. If the answer is no, it may be necessary to cancel the project entirely unless there is a glaring project problem elsewhere that is causing project failure.

If the product is not time-dependent, the unfeasibility of evolutionary development is questionable and should be reassessed. The situation may be similar to generating a first minimal release for the "goals are already minimal" problem (see previous). To recap, this means that it may still be effective to generate a first minimal release and a later release with more features that may be able to provide the essential functionality.

As we can see, most of the problems are related to either projects that are not conducive with goal reduction or non-cooperative stakeholders. In most project disentanglement efforts, the goal reduction step is key to the success of the entire process, so stakeholder cooperation is vital for success. However, when projects cannot be reduced due to their characteristics, the only hope for a successful project rescue effort is when the cause of the failure is evident elsewhere (for example, a completely unsuitable project team, exceptionally poor project management, or a lack of adequate development facilities).

> **Advisory:** Do not over-use the threat of withdrawing from the disentanglement process and conceding to project cancellation. In fact, the measure should be used rarely and only when all other attempts to convince the stakeholders have failed.

7.5 Summary

Reducing project goals is a key step in the disentanglement process. This chapter describes the method for defining minimum goals and discusses how to overcome opposition and gain acceptance for a more modest project. The emphasis is on the word *minimum* and the objective is to reduce the project to the smallest size that achieves only the most essential goals.

Goals are related to action, and they define the desired outcome after the action has been completed. A set of related goals is often referred to simply as a "goal." When generalizing, the plural term "goals" can be used to cover all items to be delivered by a project team during and at the completion of development (the "project goals").

As part of the initial groundwork toward the reduction of project goals, it is essential to know who is responsible for setting them. This is because any changes to the project goals as part of the disentanglement process will need the approval of those who originally set them.

Software project goals are set by parties that have a vested interest in the results of the project, such as members of senior management, marketing staff, customers, investors, or any combination of these. To successfully negotiate achievable project goals, it is useful to know the goal setters' stake in the project, and their alternatives, technical familiarity with the development process, two or three critical project needs, and their schedule constraints.

The more information stakeholders have about the true state of the project, the better allies they will make for the evaluator in negotiating new goals. Establish a small team of potential allies from among the stakeholders who have shown interest in development of the project.

To minimize project goals, work with the stakeholders to categorize the project requirements (functionality, features, performance criteria) into three sets:

Set 1: Essential requirements without which the project will have no appreciable value.

Set 2: Important requirements that greatly improve the project but are not essential.

Set 3: Nice-to-have requirements that add to the project but are not especially important.

Start by retaining the requirements from Set 1 and eliminating Sets 2 and 3 from the project. Occasionally, some elements from Set 2 can be added, but this should be rare. All remaining requirements (from Sets 2 and 3) should be targeted for subsequent releases of the software.

Expect opposition to the changing of project goals and deal with it by recruiting and working with allies. Negotiate with the project stakeholders and be prepared to demonstrate some flexibility.

The minimization of goals for large projects is more difficult than for small ones. Key project stakeholders may become fearful of the project risk and complexity and take a strong position against any change and against the removal of any functionality. It is usually the high stakes of large projects that ultimately convince key project stakeholders to accept a reduction of goals.

Following are some of the problems encountered in minimizing project goals:

- Opposition is unyielding. This is the time to use allies.
- The essential list is too long. Prioritize the project requirements and use the top of the list as the new minimum goals.
- There is a lack of allies. Work with the initiating manager.
- There is a lack of support in identifying requirements and costs. Senior management's full support for the process needs to be re-clarified to all parties involved in the project.
- Goals are vague. Establish a team (evaluator, project manager, and a stakeholder) to clarify the goals on a high level.
- Goals are overwhelming. Prioritize the project requirements.
- Goals are already minimal. In some cases, it may still be effective to generate a first minimal release even though its value would be questionable.
- Evolutionary development is unfeasible. If the product is not time-dependent, the unfeasibility should be reassessed. Phased releases may, in fact, be possible.

Exercises

1. Review the case described in Section 7.2.2. Make and document additional assumptions about the project. Who, in your opinion, are the main stakeholders in this project? Where would you expect the main opposition to come from and where would you expect to find allies? Explain your answers.

2. Review the case described in Section 7.2.2. In your opinion, should this project have been developed from the start in a phased (evolutionary) manner? What are the arguments in favor and what are the arguments against? Make and document any additional required assumptions about the project.

3. Find an example of a failed software project by searching the Internet, professional journals, or your local library. List all the failed projects' main goals, and propose a minimized set of goals. Discuss the attitude of the project's main stakeholders, and explain how you, as the project evaluator, would have dealt with them.

4. Search the Internet, professional journals, or your local library and find two examples of failed or rescued software projects: one small and one large. Compare the problems that led to the two projects failing, and compare the initial and final project scopes.

5. Class project: Review the case study described in Section 7.2.2. Select a project evaluator. Divide the rest of the class into two groups: allies and opponents of the minimized project. Have the evaluator present the minimized project (that was adopted in the case study), and have the two groups debate the solution. Assign one person to take notes of the main arguments for and against, and review the merits of the entries in the list at the end of the debate.

8

Step 6—Can Minimum Goals Be Achieved?

Step 10   Early Warning System
Step 9   Revise the Plan
Step 8   Risk Analysis
Step 7   Rebuild the Team
Step 6   Can Minimum Goals Be Achieved?
Step 5   Define Minimum Goals
Step 4   Evaluate the Team
Step 3   Evaluate Project Status
Step 2   Assign an Evaluator
Step 1   Stop

Put a person who is five feet ten inches tall into six feet three inches of water, and the odds are he'll learn to swim, says noted business pundit Tom Peters. He may sputter and spit a bit, but he can always hop up off the bottom and get air. But, continues Peters, put the same person in seven feet four inches of water, and you may have a dead body on your hands [1].

Peters' point is that stretch goals are fine as long as they are of the six feet three inches variety and not the seven feet four inches kind.

When is a goal high, but not too high? Or in swimming pool terms, if the person is drowning, how much should you lower the water level? You can drain the pool completely and the person will not drown, but then it is unlikely that he will learn to swim (assuming that is your goal). In fact, it is unlikely that you will achieve your goal even if you reduce the water level to three feet. But the same is true if you reduce it to seven feet. The point is that if you reduce requirements too much, the goal you achieve may have no value. But if you reduce requirements too little, you may still be risking failure (a failed project or a drowned person).

At this point in the disentanglement process, we have already determined that the project is failing (the person is drowning), and in the previous step we ensured that the goals were genuinely reduced (the water level was lowered).[1] Now we need to determine whether the new goals are achievable (whether the person can now learn to swim without drowning).

This chapter discusses how to determine whether the minimum goals are achievable and what to do if they are not. The proposed methods are directed primarily toward the project evaluator, though project developers, stakeholders, and many of the other involved parties will have a keen interest in this step, too.

8.1 Achievable Goals

One of the problems with achievable goals is that until the project ends, it is difficult to know whether they are indeed achievable. This is because of the unknown elements that define the risk associated with all software projects. If there was no risk, and goals were deterministic, this step in the disentanglement process would be easy—almost like determining how many cookies we can carry away in a jar. If we know the dimensions of a cookie and of the jar, some basic arithmetic is all we need.

---

[1] Remember that the term *goals* here includes project requirements. Refer to Chapter 7, "Step 5—Define Minimal Goals," for an explanation of how various goal terms are used in this discussion.

But goals are not deterministic, so deciding whether they are achievable is not easy. The problem is that even the risk is difficult to quantify (at least with any great degree of precision), so there is really no shortage of grounds for disagreement. Those who want broader goals and those who want narrower goals can each make a case for their position.

Add to this the project stakeholders' diverse interests, biases, and varying levels of technical understanding, and it becomes clear why serious disagreements exist about what is and is not achievable.

In order to reduce the disagreements (there is no sure way of eliminating them), it is helpful to examine the project against a list of criteria. These criteria describe a set of project-dependent tests that helps establish whether the goals can *reasonably be expected to be achieved*. The criteria are essentially part of the same feasibility process that every development organization should ideally apply at the beginning of every project.

If the development organization has an effective project feasibility process, that process should be used to determine whether the minimized goals are now achievable. Otherwise, the sample process described in the following section should be used.

8.1.1 A Feasibility Process

In this section, we briefly outline the main elements of a feasibility process. The discussion here is in the context of *any* project, not only a failing project, and is intended for completeness.[2] The section that follows focuses on adapting the approach prescribed here in the context of a failing project.

A formal project feasibility process requires at least the following criteria to be met. Note that when applying the process to a project in progress, some of the criteria may have already been satisfied because the analysis performed at the beginning of the project may still be valid.

1. **The goals have been properly documented.**

   Documenting goals has a dual purpose. It ensures that all parties have a similar understanding of the goals. It also ensures that the full extent of the work involved is understood, and nothing is overlooked.

   There are software development methods where project requirements are developed as the project proceeds (for example, agile software development methods). This does not mean that goals are completely unspecified or boundless (see [3]). In these cases, too, the project goals can and should be documented. Then, if they undergo significant changes during the project, the feasibility process may need to be repeated.

---

[2] See McConnell [2] for a broader overview of software project feasibility analysis.

2. **The goals have been estimated.**

    In order to establish the feasibility of a project, all work needs to be properly identified and estimated in terms of schedule and development resources. Any effective formal method that makes good use of historical data[3] can be used (see, for example, [5] and [6]).

3. **The technical feasibility has been established.**

    The objective here is to ensure that the project is not being given a technically impossible assignment (the team is not expected to convert coal into diamonds, so to speak). Feasibility should be determined by experienced professionals (not managers, customers, or marketing personnel) after performing a technical evaluation of the main project requirements.

4. **Available schedule and development resources are compatible with the new estimates.**

    This is where goals, schedules, resources, and dependencies are compared. The objective is to ensure that sufficient development time and resources are being made available for the project.

5. **A development team is available.**

    It is critical to ensure that a team is available to develop the project and that its members believe in the feasibility of the project (goals, schedule, and resources).

    Most feasibility processes involve these five factors, at the very least. They vary mainly in the way they are applied in such areas as standards, estimation techniques, risk analysis (spare, contingencies, and so on), and roles and responsibilities.

Remember that the entire feasibility process (which can take quite a while to implement) is not required at this step of the disentanglement process. The next section discusses how to adapt it for a disentangled project.

8.1.2 Achievable Goals for a Disentangled Project

We now focus on how to use the feasibility process to determine whether the reduced project goals are achievable.

If feasibility analysis was competently implemented at the beginning of the project, its results will be a valuable asset during the disentanglement process. Not only can some of the work be reused, the results can help identify problems in the way the original goals were evaluated (and prevent their repetition). Catastrophic projects, however, usually became so because they did not follow an

---

[3] Using historical data (that is, learning from experience) is one of the best ways to handle risk (refer to the earlier discussion about risk). This is true in software development and virtually everywhere else.

orderly process. This means that a feasibility analysis dating back to the beginning of the project may well not exist, or if it does, may be of questionable value. Nonetheless, it is always worthwhile to check; if a competent analysis exists, it will save both time and effort.

The following five points are based on the generic feasibility process outlined in Section 8.1.1, but they are adapted specifically for the evaluation of the reduced goals of a project that is being disentangled:

1. Ensure that the reduced goals are documented and agreed to by all key stakeholders. The document does not need to be rewritten if one already exists; an updated version of the existing project document can be used.

2. Prepare preliminary estimates for the new goals for the work that is required to deliver them. This is also an initial sanity check to ensure that the goals have been significantly reduced.

   • Consider whether the new set of goals is a genuine and significant reduction of the project scope. If not, there is no sense continuing with the feasibility analysis (because there will be no significant difference between the achievability of the original goals and the new goals).

   • Is there a single requirement in the new set of goals that adds an order of magnitude to the complexity of the project? If so, are members of management aware of this and will they reconsider its inclusion?[4] This may be the difference between achievable and non-achievable goals.

3. Re-evaluate the technical feasibility of the project. If the project is technically complex, enlist the help of technical experts with the evaluation.

   Consider the completeness and robustness of the reduced project. For example, does a feature remain that is dependent on a feature that was removed?

4. Prepare a high-level schedule to help establish the achievability of goals (in the context of redefining the project scope). The final schedule will be prepared in step 9 after the scope has been agreed upon, the team has been rebuilt, and the project risks have been identified.

   Compare the amount of work required to deliver the goals (from point 2 of this list) to the length of the high-level schedule. Is there now a reasonable chance that the team will be able to deliver the project requirements within an acceptable schedule, within a reasonable budget, and with an

---

[4] Fred Brooks (of *The Mythical Man Month* fame) tells the story of a senior naval officer's last-minute requirement after many months of negotiating features, schedule, and cost for a new Navy helicopter. "It must be able to fly across the Atlantic," he stated. Only after laboriously explaining to him the enormous complexity that it added to the project was the officer willing to drop the requirement.

acceptable quality level? "Acceptable," in this context, means acceptable to the key project stakeholders. "Reasonable" means that the estimated work fits comfortably into the schedule, leaving 20% spare.[5]

5. Consider how genuinely confident the team members are (and especially the project manager) in their ability to achieve the new set of goals. This is discussed in more detail in Chapter 9, "Step 7—Rebuild the Team."

Full project feasibility analysis can be a lengthy activity. As noted earlier, however, a comprehensive feasibility analysis is not required during this step of the disentanglement process. At this stage, the activity should take between one and two days to complete. The following guidelines explain how this is achieved:

- Do not go into detail if detail is not required. Whenever possible, stay on a high level and leave low-level details to be completed by the project manager and the team after the project resumes. For example, in the project plan, the low-level tasks that are assigned to individual developers need to be estimated and scheduled so that each team member can have an individual work plan. But for the disentanglement process, it is sufficient to estimate and schedule these tasks together as a major feature or high-level software module.

- Do not repeat work that has already been done. Even though existing estimates, requirements specifications, schedules, and so on may be not be complete, current, or even accurate, some of the information may be reusable (lists of requirements, support tasks, and so on). Check to see if they can be used.

- Work with the development team members and divide the work with them.

- Estimates can be prepared at different confidence levels (see [6]). The difference between the efforts to prepare a 90% and a 95% confidence level estimate may be very substantial (the amount of extra detail that is required as you approach 100% grows exponentially). A very high confidence level is not required at this point. Remember, you will have another opportunity to check the feasibility after performing steps 7, 8, and 9, when the team has been rebuilt, the risks have been analyzed, and a new plan has been prepared (though the team will still have to deal with many of the low-level details later).

- Locate a technical expert early in the disentanglement process (you may require him at several steps in addition to this one). The expert should start evaluating the feasibility of the new goals during step 5 ("Define new minimal goals") even before they are finalized.

---

[5] The amount of spare (or buffer time) that should be included in a project schedule is debatable (recommendations vary between 10% and 33%). What is not debatable is that a project schedule requires spare.

> **Advisory:** It is important to remember that achievable goals alone do not guarantee that the reduced project is achievable (or feasible). Other factors within the project plan will have to be evaluated before the feasibility can be established (for example, risks and resources).

8.1.3   If the Goals Are Not Achievable

What if after all the effort in defining and negotiating the new goals, the feasibility process indicates that they are still not achievable? This problem, which is briefly discussed in Chapter 7, "Step 5—Define Minimum Goals," may be the result of any of the following conditions:

1. Key stakeholders are unwilling to genuinely reduce the scope of the project.
2. Goals were so unrealistic to start with that even after being reduced, they remain unrealistic.
3. There is no reasonable chance that the team will be able to deliver the requirements within an acceptable timeframe, within a reasonable budget, or with an acceptable quality level.
4. The goal minimization process (see Chapter 7) was implemented poorly.

In cases 1, 2, and 3, if the schedule and resources are inflexible, use the process described in Section 7.4. In case 4, it may be necessary to repeat the goal minimization process (steps 5 and 6), though this could extend the disentanglement process by an extra one to two days.

The ultimate case to be made is that without achievable goals, the disentanglement process cannot succeed and cannot continue. However, this argument should be used sparingly.

8.2   The Midway Report

The minimization of project goals is one of the key steps in the disentanglement process. Because it is a difficult and contentious activity, it is certainly not one that the project evaluator would eagerly choose to repeat. It is therefore important to capture and document all major decisions, evaluations, and conclusions that produced the new reduced-scope project. It is also important to document summaries of the discussion that led to agreement among the key stakeholders.

This key step also occurs about midway through the disentanglement process, and its success provides good reason for optimism about the success of the project rescue effort. Therefore, before proceeding, it is often helpful to distribute to key stakeholders a midway report on the status of the disentanglement process. The objective of the report is to reduce concern among stakeholders about the future of the project by keeping the process transparent and open.

This midway report should include the following:

- **A summary of the first six steps of the disentanglement process**

  This should include a brief overview of the decisions, changes, and accomplishments of the first six steps (it is not necessary to list them with their respective steps).

- **An overview of the reduced project goals**

  The successful negotiation of new achievable goals is a key accomplishment. The report should include a summary of the new project goals and a description of the main changes that were deemed necessary.

- **A brief review of the project feasibility analysis showing that the new goals can now be achieved**

  One of the main stakeholder concerns will be that the project may slip back into catastrophe mode after it is restarted. This concern can be partially alleviated by including an overview of the analysis showing why the project goals are now achievable. However, it is important to remind the stakeholders that the final determination will be made after the new estimates are completed (this will also serve as a call for further cooperation in the following disentanglement steps).

- **A brief description of the next four steps**

  This should explain how the process will proceed and conclude and may exhibit a cautiously optimistic tone provided that the minimized goal steps were concluded successfully. By demonstrating that the process is proceeding well, stakeholders will be encouraged to support the remaining disentanglement steps (after all, everyone likes to be associated with success [7]).

The midway report should contain only information that has already been produced by the process (nothing new should be generated specifically for the report). The report should be no more than two to three pages long and should take about two hours to prepare (the effort should require only the summarizing and formulating of existing information).

Advisory: The midway report is intended for informational purposes only. It includes a report of the disentanglement tasks that have been completed and the decisions and agreements that have been reached. Therefore, nothing in the report should be reopened for debate (except in rare cases when significant *new* information has become available).

8.3   What Can Go Wrong (and What to Do About It)

Many of the problems and solutions discussed in Chapter 7 are applicable to the current step, too. Here are some additional problems that may occur and their suggested solutions:

- **The schedule is unachievable.**

    This problem occurs when there is a deadline for the project that cannot be moved, and even a reduced version of the project cannot fit into the fixed schedule.

    Action: Step 9 of the disentanglement process produces a revised project plan. Begin that discussion now, even though some of the proceeding steps have not been completed.

    Start with a general discussion of the project schedule. There is little sense proceeding with the disentanglement process if it has become clear that the project cannot be rescued (there is a critical deadline that we now know cannot be achieved).

    Convene a meeting with the evaluator, the initiating manager, the project manager, and two or three of the main unyielding stakeholders. Devote as much time as necessary to this meeting, and have all participants ready to thrash out all preconceptions about the project's rigid schedule. The objective is to agree either on an evolutionary delivery of the project (a partial version of the software on time, followed by a more functional version later), or an extension of the deadline. If neither option can be agreed upon at this meeting, the disentanglement process cannot proceed.

- **Insufficient development resources exist.**

    This is the counterpart of the unachievable schedule problem (resources and schedule are to some degree interchangeable). This problem occurs when the development resources required to support the goals and the schedule are grossly inadequate (point 4 in Section 8.1.2 cannot not succeed). This problem most commonly occurs as a lack of human resources.

Action: Here, too, move the discussion of the project resources forward and hold a broad discussion at this point (the fine points can be left to be completed in step 9). Follow a similar course of action to the one described for the unachievable schedule problem.

- **The midway report re-opens agreements.**

  Generally, the benefit of distributing the midway report outweighs the risk of regressing in the disentanglement process. The problem occurs when stakeholders review the report with their staff and colleagues and hear renewed arguments about the wisdom of the project changes. This leads to second thoughts about issues that have been agreed upon and can set the process back significantly.[6]

  Action: Prepare for the problem—speak to all key stakeholders before the report is distributed and discuss your concerns with them. Before they receive the report, request the stakeholders' support in ensuring that it does not cause the disentanglement process to regress. Enlist the help of the initiating manager to reinforce this request.

- **The goals are not achievable.**

  This problem is discussed in Section 8.1.3 and is mentioned here again for completeness.

  Action: Follow the course of action discussed in Section 8.1.3.

As noted earlier, reducing the project to achievable goals is a key step in the disentanglement process and, in most cases, the success of the step is vital to the overall success of the effort. It is therefore often helpful to lay the groundwork for the reduction of goals at the very beginning of the disentanglement effort. This should be part of the opening message conveyed by the initiating manager to all project stakeholders and developers (for example, "Be aware that it is likely that we will need to reduce the scope of this project. It is vital that we get your support should this become necessary."). Reiterate the message from time to time as the process moves forward.

The objective of the groundwork is to ensure that the stakeholders have time to get used to the need to change the project scope and to raise any general objections well before the decision needs to be made (this is similar to raising the level of water in the pool slowly rather than throwing the person directly into six feet three inches of water).

---

[6] Bear in mind that occasionally new arguments may justifiably reopen points that have previously been agreed upon. Tread this ground carefully, however, and resist baseless attempts to reopen agreements.

Advisory: It is entirely appropriate to perform parts of later disentanglement steps earlier in the process, if circumstances require it. Thus, as we have seen, estimation (which is part of step 9) can be moved forward to help resolve problems in reducing the project's scope (steps 5 and 6). This is especially true of risk analysis (step 8) in cases where a specific risk event overshadows attempts to rescue the project.

8.4 Summary

This chapter discusses how to determine whether the minimum goals are achievable and what to do if they are not. The proposed methods are directed primarily toward the project evaluator.

In order to bridge the disagreements about what is and what is not achievable, it is helpful to follow a formal project feasibility process. If the development organization has such a process, it should be used to determine whether the minimized goals are now achievable. Otherwise, use the following process:

1. Ensure that the reduced goals are documented and agreed upon by all key stakeholders.

2. Prepare preliminary estimates for the new goals.

3. Re-evaluate the technical feasibility of the project. If the project is technically complex, enlist the help of people who have the necessary technical expertise.

4. Consider whether there is a reasonable chance to deliver the requirements within an acceptable timeframe, within a reasonable budget, and with an acceptable quality level.

5. Consider the confidence of the team members in their ability to achieve the new set of goals.

The feasibility process should be applied on a high level and should take between one and two days to complete.

If the feasibility process indicates that the goals are not achievable, it may be due to the following:

1. Key stakeholders are unwilling to genuinely reduce the scope of the project.

2.   Goals were so unrealistic to start with that they remain unrealistic even after being reduced.

3.   There is no reasonable chance that the team will be able to deliver the requirements within an acceptable time frame, within a reasonable budget, or with an acceptable quality level.

4.   The goal minimization process (see Chapter 7) was implemented poorly.

In cases 1, 2, and 3, use the process described in Section 7.4 and in case 4, consider repeating the goal minimization process (this could extend the entire disentanglement process by one to two days).

This goal minimization step occurs about midway through the disentanglement process. Therefore, before proceeding, it is helpful to distribute to key stakeholders a midway report on the status of the disentanglement process.

Many of the problems and solutions discussed in Chapter 7 are also applicable to the current step. Some additional problems that may occur are

- The project's deadline is unachievable: Begin the revision of the project plan (step 9) now. Convene a general discussion with the initiating manager, the project evaluator, the project manager, and two or three of the main unyielding stakeholders to thrash out all preconceptions about the project's rigid schedule.

- Insufficient development resources: Follow a similar course of action to the one described for the unachievable schedule problem.

- The midway report reopens agreements: Prepare for the problem. Speak to all key stakeholders before the report is distributed and discuss your concerns with them.

Reducing the project to achievable goals is a key step in the disentanglement process. It is therefore often helpful to lay the groundwork for the reduction of goals at the very beginning of the disentanglement effort.

Exercises

1. Review the case described in Section 7.2.2. Apply the feasibility process described in Sections 8.1.1 and 8.1.2 to the minimized goals in the case. Document any assumptions that you need to make about the case. Summarize the results of the feasibility process and explain your conclusions.

2. Review the case described in Section 7.2.2. Consider the options available to the project evaluator if the backup and recovery feature cannot be included in the first release due to (a) technical complexity, (b) an inflexible deadline, or (c) a lack of hardware resources to support the backup and recovery feature.

   As the project evaluator, how would you handle these problems? Explain.

3. Find an example of a failed software project by searching the Internet, professional journals, or your local library. Assume that you are the project evaluator, and compose a midway report based on your conception of the first six disentanglement steps. Include an overview of the failed project.

9

Step 7—Rebuild the Team

Step 10 Early Warning System
Step 9 Revise the Plan
Step 8 Risk Analysis
Step 7 Rebuild the Team
Step 6 Can Minimum Goals Be Achieved?
Step 5 Define Minimum Goals
Step 4 Evaluate the Team
Step 3 Evaluate Project Status
Step 2 Assign an Evaluator
Step 1 Stop

How do you strengthen a weak team? Some development organizations will look to see if there are enough superstars on the team. Others will look at size and add more people or more work hours [1]. But these areas are rarely where the main problem lies. In fact, having too many superstars is not always a good thing [2], and some of the best teams are small and agile [3]. More than anything else, it is the level of enthusiasm and teamwork that usually makes a team successful.

Harvard professor Richard Hackman puts teamwork at the top of his list of successful team factors ("It must be a real team") [4]. He emphasizes the importance of focusing team members' talents in a way that strengthens the team itself as a performing unit. Though this may seem like a universally held principle, it is not. We saw an example in the defense contractor case described in Chapter 6. When confronted with severe project problems, the company believed that the solution would come from a team of experts. But as the project began to fail, an external consultant concluded that "the main problem with the team was that it wasn't one."

Hackman notes that organizations have traditionally been designed and managed to support and control work performed by individuals rather than teams. That is why many organizations, when confronted with a failing project, opt for a group of strong individuals, rather than a group of competent team players (see Figure 9.1). As we have seen, this can produce a dysfunctional team, which in turn can be a mortal blow to the project.

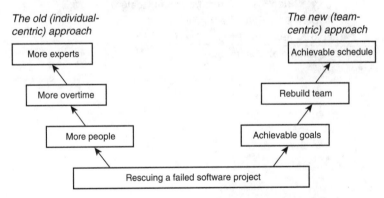

Figure 9.1 The individual and team approaches to rescuing a failed
software project

Of course, this is not to say that when a project fails, the team is always to blame. As we have seen, there can be many reasons for a project to fail (unachievable goals, for example) that have little or nothing to do with the team. Still, experience shows that when rescuing a failing project, there is always some team rebuilding to do. There may be individual members of the team who simply do not have the necessary skills, while the rest of the team has the potential to function well. But even if the team members do fit well together and have all the necessary skills and abilities to do their job, their enthusiasm will be deflated and team spirit will be low when their project fails. After all, nothing dampens enthusiasm more than being associated with failure.

Rebuilding a competent team is a key step in the disentanglement process. It involves resolving the main team problems on both the overall team level and the individual team member level. This step is a sensitive stage in the disentanglement process for the project evaluator, one that requires a combination of tact and resolve. This is a central theme, which is reflected throughout the guidelines and recommendations in this chapter.

This chapter discusses how to rebuild a competent project team in preparation for restarting the project. The discussion covers a broad range of areas related to teams and individual team members, including team management, team structure, the team's relationship with other groups, and team spirit and morale. The approach builds upon the results of the team evaluation (step 4) and the new project goals (steps 5 and 6).

For the project team members, this chapter will help explain the team problems that need to be resolved and the changes that will be required. This is particularly important because rebuilding a team is not a cloistered activity; its successful implementation is greatly dependent on the cooperation and support of management, the team, and other key project players.

9.1   Review the Team Evaluation

As discussed previously, this step of the disentanglement process is closely linked to the evaluation of the project team (step 4).[1] Before proceeding with the current step, review the team overview document, which was prepared at the end of the team evaluation.

The key subjects of the team evaluation are an excellent resource for identifying potential team problem areas. They are used in the next section for exactly that purpose, so they are reproduced here as a checklist:

1. **The project team**

     General team performance

     Skill set

     Unstaffed positions

     Size of team

     Development facilities

---

[1] The reason for the separation of these two steps is explained in Section 1.1.3.

Distributed teams

Team spirit and morale

Relationships with other groups and teams

Conflicts

Management

2.   **Project management**

Skills

Confidence in the project (can it be saved?)

Relationships

Spirit, motivation, commitment

Other problems

General capabilities

3.   **Individual team members**

Job function

Skills

Achievements and contributions

Relationships

Morale and commitment issues

Other problems (beyond the failure of the project)

Capabilities

As a project evaluator, this is also a good time to re-familiarize yourself with the internal politics of the organization, especially as it relates to the team and the team members. Also, because several days will have elapsed since the completion of the team evaluation step, this may be a good opportunity to incorporate any additional team information that may have emerged since the evaluation was completed.

> **Advisory:** Even though the team evaluation was completed just a few days before the current step, do not skip the review of the team overview document. This will ensure that you have all the key findings and issues fresh in your mind before proceeding to resolve problems and rebuild the team.

9.2 Identify Problems

Are there always team problems to be resolved? We have seen that not all project failures are caused by development team problems. In fact, even when projects are in serious trouble, the project team may be functioning well (all things considered).

But there will always be team problems to be resolved, no matter how good the team is. This is because when projects fail, team spirit usually plummets. The disentanglement process is designed to restore the team's enthusiasm. In most cases, it does so by redefining a project that is achievable and by rebuilding a team that has the ability to deliver the project's goals.

Low team morale is usually not the only team problem to be resolved (several examples will be presented shortly). All major team problems need to be identified and prioritized by the project evaluator. The results of the team evaluation (step 4) are the main source of information for this task. This is then followed by a decision as to which team problems must be resolved before the project can resume.

The following list (which is also summarized in Table 9.1) includes several guidelines on where to look for team problems (it is derived from the team evaluation checklist in the previous section). Focus on the types of problems that could cause a project to slip back into catastrophe mode after it is resumed.

These guidelines can be considered as a virtual "template" to be placed over the results of the earlier team review. Wherever there is a match, a resolution is needed before the project can resume.

1. **Project team structure**

   Review the project team checklist in Section 9.1. Then identify problems related to the structure of the team, such as the following:

   - An unclear reporting structure.

   - An unreasonable or unworkable team organization (the developers are inadequately paired, matched, or teamed together).

   - For large, multi-team projects, look for problems in the internal team structure and between teams. For instance, does each team represent a logical part of the project (a major function, a support task, and so on), and are responsibilities allocated reasonably? Are the teams well coordinated (for example, during integration and testing).

   - Ensure that support teams (or individuals) included in the project structure are working well together (look at software quality assurance, configuration control, testing, and field support). For example, is the test team considered the "good guys" or the "bad guys"? Is configuration control considered a nuisance?

2. **Project team functions**

Consider the project's main tasks and functions:

- Look for project functions and tasks that have not been well assigned. Are they well defined? Do the team members know what they are expected to deliver?
- Identify unstaffed key team functions.
- Identify project functions and tasks that are not compatible with the new project goals.
- Ensure that there are no tasks, functions, or responsibilities that have been assigned but are not related to the project's goals. This would mean that some of the work that a team member is doing is not for the project. For example, is someone working on a great idea that has not been approved? Or is someone helping out another project unbeknownst to his or her own project manager?

3. **Team members**

Review the individual team members checklist in Section 9.1. Then

- Identify internal team compatibility problems: Do the team members work well with their colleagues?
- Consider the team members' skills and level of experience and look for deficiencies that may prevent the successful completion of their assignments.
- Are there any team members who should be replaced? Look for substantial problems of competency, dedication, and compatibility.

4. **Team leaders**

This refers to large multi-team projects.

- Look for problems related to the way the teams are led.
- Consider whether the team leaders' skills and level of experience are adequate for the success of their team's assignments.
- Are there any team leaders who should be replaced? Look for substantial problems of competency, dedication, and leadership.

5. **Project manager**

Review the project management checklist in Section 9.1. Then consider problems that are preventing the project manager from successfully leading the project. These may be general project problems that are preventing the manager from functioning properly and that have had an effect on the team (for example, lack of senior management support, insufficient development budget, or a lack of development tools).

Review the project manager's suitability:

- Consider whether the project manager's skills and level of experience are adequate for the success of the project.
- Consider the relationship with the team.
- Consider the relationship with the project stakeholders (management, customers, marketing, and so on).
- External problems: Determine whether there are partner-, subcontractor-, or vendor-related problems.
- Consider whether the project manager is the right person to lead this project.

This is a fairly broad list of potential team problem areas. If every problem area is considered by the evaluator, this list will exceed the scope of the disentanglement process. This can usually be overcome because early indicators on where to look (for team problems) will have already come from the previous steps in the process (for example, project status evaluation, team evaluation). In short, by the time the evaluator reaches step 7, a great deal will be known about the project's problems.

Table 9.1 Where to Look for Team Problems

Teamwork	• Cooperation versus discord, conflict, or disputes • Level of enthusiasm • Level of morale
Project team structure	• Reporting structure • Team organization • For large projects: inter- and intra-team relationships • Support teams
Project team functions	• Functions not adequately defined • Unstaffed team functions • Functions incompatible with project goals • Non-required work
Team members	• Internal team compatible problems • Skills and experience
Team leaders	For large projects: • Leadership problems • Skills and experience

Project manager	• Suitability problems:
	  – Relationship with team
	  – Relationship with stakeholders
	• External problems (subcontractors and vendors)

When using this list, do not go into low-level details unless it is completely necessary. Furthermore, as a rule of thumb, problems that do not absolutely need to be resolved at this stage should be left to the project manager for resolution after the project resumes.

9.3   Rebuild the Team

At this stage of the disentanglement process, we have evaluated the project status, defined a new set of achievable goals, and identified the main team problems. We now need to rebuild a team that can achieve the goals.

Rebuilding the project team means implementing changes in the staffing, structure, and operation (that is, how the team works) of the team to resolve the critical problem that have been identified. The following discussion discusses how to implement these changes and how to overcome the resistance that almost always follows.

> **Advisory:** When dealing with team members, you are dealing with the development organization's most valuable asset. In times of stress, this can be a delicate and sensitive task. When team issues become particularly complicated, it is wise to enlist assistance from a professional in the field (for example, the organization's human research manager). There are also several excellent reference texts on the subject (see, for example, Allcorn and Diamond [10], and Moorhead [11]).

9.3.1   Dealing with Change

As we have seen, rebuilding the team will require changes to the team or to the way it functions. This will require some or all of the following measures:

- Restructuring the internal organization of the team
- Restaffing some, or in rare cases, all of the team positions
- Redefining development procedures and work policies
- Changing the relationships between the team and the project stakeholders (such as their degree of intrusion into the team, or their authority to intervene)
- Changing the relationships between the team and other external groups, including vendors, subcontractors, administration service providers, and various business partners (this may affect their responsibilities, their involvement in the project, their level of commitment, and so on)

These measures may be triggered by the need to resolve team problems or as a consequence of the new project goals. In the first case, they will have existed before the disentanglement process started, and in the latter, they will have been created as a result of the process.

But whatever the reason for the changes, they will almost always be accompanied by resistance. This will likely come from within the team (especially if the changes involve replacing team members) and from the project stakeholders.

As discussed previously, dealing with resistance is a delicate task that requires a combination of tact and resolve. This means striking a balance between being sensitive to the concerns of the team members and the stakeholders while maintaining a firm resolve about the changes that must be made. These are, after all, changes without which the project cannot resume.

What can the evaluator do to mitigate this intricate step? The key is in the fact that the step does not come as a surprise; it is a formal part of the disentanglement process. Thus, the situation is best dealt with thorough preparation and by enlisting the assistance of allies. In this case, the most obvious ally is the initiating manager, but additional support should also be sought from among the other project stakeholders.

Resistance to change can also be mitigated by keeping the decision process completely candid and open (no behind-closed-doors decisions). This will reduce tension by ensuring that the reasoning behind all changes is clear and understandable to the team members and to all other involved parties.

> **Advisory:** It is important to keep in mind that changes to the team are a medium for achieving the new project goals; change is not a goal in itself. This is not a time to introduce into the project new cross-organizational or company policy changes. Introduce only those changes that are required to enable the team to achieve the project goals.

9.3.2   Implementing Changes

The team rebuilding step will always involve some changes to the team (we have seen that at a minimum, morale will always need to be restored). At this point in the step, the previous activities will have established whether changes to the structure, staffing, or processes of the team will also be necessary. These changes need to be determined, fully laid out, and launched (though not necessarily completed) before the final steps of the disentanglement process can begin.

The following set of guidelines covers the most common types of project team changes and discusses how to implement them. The required changes are determined by the project evaluator, but the implementation is the responsibility of the initiating manager (this is addressed more specifically in the guidelines).

As a general guideline, limit the changes to those that are absolutely necessary to successfully complete the project. For example, if the team structure is
adequate or if the development process works well enough, do not change them,
even if they can be improved.

1. **Restructuring the team**

   If you have determined that the team structure will prevent the team from
   achieving the project goals, redefine the structure. Use a functional structure for the team based on a natural functional decomposition of the project (see [5]) for both product functions (such as user interface, and data
   storage and retrieval) and development support functions (such as quality
   assurance and testing). Work with the project manager and with the development team to determine the appropriate team structure changes.

   At this stage, establish only a high-level version of the team structure and
   work with the project manager to formally introduce it. The project manager should then complete the lower-level details after the project is
   resumed.

2. **Replacing team members**

   Replace team members whom you have identified as being incompatible
   with the team and the needs of the project. To avoid spreading discontent,
   do not keep the team member in place until a replacement is found. Ensure
   that an adequate hiring budget is available and that the human resource
   department and senior management provide the necessary support to
   quickly locate a suitable replacement.

   This change should be implemented by the project manager, but if the
   project manager is being replaced, it should be implemented by the initiating manager.

3. **Replacing the project manager**

   Replace the project manager if you have determined that he or she cannot
   lead the team to achieve the project goals. To avoid spreading discontent,
   do not keep the project manager in place until a replacement is found. In
   the interim, the initiating manager should temporarily fill the position.

   The re-staffing of this position should be considered the most urgent matter on the project disentanglement agenda. Ensure that an adequate hiring
   budget is available and that the human resource department and senior
   management provide the necessary support to quickly locate a suitable
   replacement. Promote from within the team if there is a suitable project
   manager candidate in the team.

   This change should be implemented by the initiating manager.

4. **Changing process or policy**

   If you have determined that the development process is inadequate to achieve the project's goals, replace the existing development process or, if none exists, initiate a process.

   If the organization has an adequate process that has not been implemented correctly within the project, ensure that that process is used. Enlist the help of the initiating manager to have a senior software quality assurance professional assigned to oversee the project's development process (if none exists, hire a consultant).

   If the organization does not have an adequate process, adopt any suitable formal process, such as the IEEE Software Engineering Standards[6].[2, 3]

   Process changes should be implemented by the project manager together with the organization's software quality assurance manager.

5. **Changing relationship with stakeholders**

   If you have identified severe problems between the project stakeholders and the project team, you will need to redefine the relationship and ensure that senior management formally adopts the new relationship. This refers to such situations as stakeholders' over-involvement (intrusion) in development that hinders the team's work or under-involvement (indifference) that results in late discovery of product implementation errors.

   This change should be implemented by the project manager and the initiating manager.

6. **Changing relationships with external groups and organizations**

   If you have identified problems with an external group that could prevent the team from successfully achieving the project goals, you will need to change the relationship between the project and the group. This includes such groups as vendors, subcontractors, administration service providers, and various business partners.

   The change can be either a redefinition of the relationship with the group, the replacement of the group with another that will fulfill a similar role, or the removal of the dependency on the group (that is, the removal of the group with no replacement needed).

   If the group is a major player in the project, senior management should be involved in redefining the relationship (this should underline the expectation for better cooperation from the group).

---

[2] Refer to Boehm and Turner [5] for a discussion on how to adapt conventional software development processes to agile development.

[3] The IEEE software engineering standards comprise five volumes. Select a small subset of the standards that covers at least the following activities: planning, testing, requirements, design, reviews, user documentation, and maintenance.

This change should be implemented by the project manager and the initiating manager.

7. **Rebuilding morale and team spirit**

We discussed earlier the importance of high team morale and enthusiasm for a team to be successful. But we have also seen that when a failing project is halted, team morale is always low. Before the project can be re-started, this must change.

When all other major problems are resolved and the redefined project appears achievable, team morale will rise. It is then the responsibility of the project manager to rebuild team spirit. This is also the time for verbal encouragement by members of senior management in order to demonstrate their support for the project and the team (this will also improve morale).

Rebuilding the team should take between one and two days. In order to keep within that limit, keep the changes on a relatively high level whenever possible, and leave the details to be completed by the project manager and the team after the project is re-started.

9.3.3 Dealing with Opposition

As discussed earlier, opposition to change should be expected. The main causes will be career and job security concerns, political biases and personal interests, and the natural emotional resistance to change. But there will also be objective constructive criticism where valid questions will be raised requiring proper consideration.

Generally, subjective, political, and emotional opposition is best handled with the help of allies, especially the initiating manager. Constructive criticism should, of course, be handled by addressing the issues that are raised.

Here are some of the points that are often raised and the recommended responses:

1. **The project is already in trouble. Additional change will increase the risk.**

It was the current approach that got the project into trouble. If we do not change the way the team works, the trouble will get worse and the project will likely be cancelled. It is true that there is risk associated with change, but taking risk is part of doing business. The only way to totally eliminate risk is to do nothing, which will keep us where we were: on track for failure.

2. **Changes to the team will further demoralize the team members and further endanger the project.**

The project has reached a point where we either save it or lose it. These changes are essential if we are not to lose the project entirely. The team will not be further demoralized if it sees that it has the necessary staff and facilities to deliver the project goals. Similarly, the project will not be further endangered if it is redefined with achievable goals and a capable team.

3. **The project manager was picked by one of the key stakeholders who will not agree to a replacement.**

The project is in serious trouble and a necessary condition for its rescue is that all decisions be purely professional. If all major stakeholders do not agree to this condition, it is unlikely that the project can be saved. The decision to replace the project manager is purely professional, and the reasons can be reviewed with any stakeholder who wishes to do so. The decision can then be challenged for professional reasons but it cannot be vetoed for extraneous reasons.

4. **New policies or processes will only add more overhead to the team's work.**

The current policies and processes have not worked well. Continuing with them will likely condemn the project to failure. It is true that too many processes and burdensome policies can overwhelm a project, but that is not our intention.

The objective of the new policies and processes is to help the project achieve its goals within an acceptable schedule, and it is unlikely that the objective will be achieved without them. Be assured that we have kept the new policies and processes within reasonable limits.

5. **We must continue working with this external organization for strategic business reasons.**

After reviewing the project's relationship with the organization, we have concluded that rather than helping the project, the organization is hindering it. We will be pleased to share with you the information that led us to that conclusion. While we recognize the importance of business alliances and strategies, we must weigh the value of this project against the importance of the business considerations.

If the professional reasons do not outweigh the business considerations, we can continue working with the external organization, but we must be fully aware of the cost reflected in the risk that we will be taking. Also, if we continue working with this external organization, senior management must discuss this problem directly with the management of the organization to ensure a better working relationship in the future.

6. **As a key stakeholder, I expect to know what is going on and I need to walk around and talk to the team members regularly. I cannot wait for the next project report or review to hear about problems.**

We recognize your need to monitor the project, and we will ensure that you are kept informed. But questioning the team members daily will disrupt the project and prevent us from getting it back on track. We would like to meet with you separately to agree on a special reporting procedure that will meet your needs without disturbing the project team.

7. **Though I am a key stakeholder, I am too busy to get more involved in the project. I can't participate in every project review.**

The project needs your input to ensure that it does not go off track again. This means that you, or your representative, must participate in regular project reviews to provide feedback on the project's progress. You must bear in mind that if you do not provide feedback whenever the project needs it, you may find out about problems at a time when their correction is prohibitively expensive (generally, the longer you wait to correct a problem, the more costly the correction).

As in previous cases of discord with stakeholders, it is always wise to prepare your response in advance. The previous examples of arguments against change have many variants. You will usually begin to hear them well before you need to announce your decisions about the rebuilding of the team. As part of your preparation, ensure that all information is readily available, the course of your decisions is documented, and your allies are briefed and ready to support you.

> **Advisory:** If you have kept the team rebuilding process open and the discussions visible to the extent possible (excluding personal issues), you will be able to deal with the objections as they arise. This is usually much better than having to deal with all objections and dissent together at the end of this disentanglement step.

9.4 Rebuilding Large Project Teams

Rebuilding large teams means having to deal with more attention (budgets are larger), more developers (the team is larger), and probably more stakeholders (see Figure 5.2). It also means that the potential problems areas described in Table 9.1

are broader and therefore more difficult to deal with. But large projects are more difficult to deal with at every step, as we have seen throughout the disentanglement process, so that many of the recommendations discussed in previous steps will be valid at this stage too.

There are, however, several additional points to consider when rebuilding large teams:

- **Multiple teams**

  Dealing with large projects usually means dealing with multiple teams and team leaders. When implementing changes that require implementation by the project manager, plan also to involve the relevant team leaders.

  When implementing changes that require the involvement of the project team, consider whether you need to involve the whole project team or just the affected members. For example, if the project has a test team and the testing process is being changed, you will want to ensure that the test team members fully understand the new process. However, members of other project teams may not need the same level of involvement.

- **The project evaluation team**

  When projects and teams are large, the disentanglement process is performed by a team of project evaluators rather than an individual evaluator (see Section 5.3.2). This requires considerable coordination between the evaluators, especially in light of the tense atmosphere that accompanies the changes described in Section 9.3.2. This is why the project evaluation team should be a highly cohesive group.

- **Resistance can be overwhelming**

  In large projects, resistance from senior project staff and key stakeholders can overwhelm the evaluation team.

  In such cases, ensure that the support of the initiating manager is strong and highly visible. It is then the responsibility of the initiating manager to bring in additional members of senior management if their support becomes necessary.

- **Large teams can be overwhelming**

  Don't be overwhelmed by the size of the team, and don't lose control of your schedule: Keep the effort within one to two days. Whenever possible, leave the low-level details to be completed by the project manager and the team after the project resumes (for example, when introducing new development processes).

- **Promote from within the team**

  When project positions need to be restaffed, favor the promotion of suitable candidates from within the team whenever possible. This includes senior team members, team leaders, and the project manager positions. This will usually have a favorable effect on morale and will save the time required for new team members to get up to speed.[4]

Another point to be aware of is that large teams can mean a large number of changes. How will it affect the rebuilding of the team?

Certainly, rebuilding a large team can be one of the more laborious steps in the disentanglement process, particularly if many changes are required. However, the amount of effort required by the evaluation team for this step should not come as a surprise. The size of the development team is known from the start of the process, and indications regarding the extent of the changes will usually become apparent as the process proceeds (and before this step is reached). An appropriately staffed evaluation team should be in place well before this step begins, to ensure that rebuilding the project team does not take longer than the allocated time (one to two days).

There is also a positive side to large project teams. The likelihood of enlisting support for the process from team members is greater when the team is larger.[5] And, as we have seen, support from within the team can be a significant asset.

> **Advisory:** There is substantial risk in introducing many changes to the project team. If the necessary changes are substantial, allocate up to one half day to review and re-evaluate the changes. Then if you are still convinced that they are all necessary, proceed with their implementation.

9.5   What Can Go Wrong (and What to Do About It)

Many of the problems associated with rebuilding a project team derive from people's natural resistance to change. But genuine problems should also be expected to arise, especially whenever there is a need to quickly locate new staff or when new processes need to be introduced midway through the project. A good approach is to treat all problems as genuine.

---

[4] While this point is applicable to small projects, too, it is especially important for large projects due to the time it takes for new senior team members to absorb large amounts of information about the project.

[5] There are several assumptions inherent in this assertion, the most fundamental being that at least some team members will generally support a process that is designed to save their project. Experience shows that this is largely true.

The following list covers some of the things that can go wrong when rebuilding a team and the responses to help deal with them. In addition, much of the discussion in the "What Can Go Wrong" section of Chapter 6, "Step 4—Evaluate the Team," is relevant here, too.

- **Unable to recruit replacement staff.**

  This problem is particularly severe for senior positions when suitable candidates cannot be found. It is most serious when the project manager position cannot be filled.

  Action: If non-senior positions cannot be immediately staffed, the task can be left to the project manager after the project resumes. Nonetheless, staffing should be completed as soon as possible.

  Filling senior positions is more urgent. The project will not get back on track until the project manager position is staffed. As an emergency measure, the initiating manager can fill in while a suitable candidate is being sought. Similarly, for large teams, the project manager can fill in while a suitable team leader candidate is being sought.

  Generally, finding suitable candidates is dependent on the vigor of the recruitment effort, the priority assigned to the task by the recruiting group (the human resources department or an external recruiter), and by the budget available for the position. If any of these factors is lacking, enlist the help of the initiating manager to reinforce the sense of urgency in the search.

- **New processes have no champion.**

  This problem occurs when development processes have been changed or new ones have been introduced, but there is no one to follow through and ensure that they are implemented correctly. Without a process champion, it is unlikely that new processes will be successfully assimilated by the team.

  Action: If the organization has a software quality assurance professional, that person should be the champion. Otherwise, identify within the development organization (not just within the project team) a senior developer who is experienced in formal software engineering processes. Then enlist the help of the initiating manager to have the process champion responsibility assigned to this person. If a suitable experienced person cannot be located within the organization, hire the services of an external consultant.

- **There is opposition to change.**

  Severe resistance to change can be a serious problem and can stall or completely defeat the disentanglement process. This problem occurs when key players or stakeholders prevent necessary changes to the project team from being implemented.

  Action: It is wise to expect opposition and to plan ahead for it. The way to do this is discussed in Section 9.3.3.

- **There is a lack of management support.**

  As discussed earlier, rebuilding the development team is a difficult task and, in most cases, it cannot be completed successfully without the support of the organization's senior management. Many stakeholder- and team-related problems are almost impossible to resolve unless the parties involved know that management is fully behind the disentanglement process.

  Action: This problem should be resolved in the early stages of the disentanglement process because it affects virtually all the process steps. The actions to resolve the problem are discussed in the "What Can Go Wrong" section of Chapter 3, "Step 1—Stop."

- **Team morale remains low.**

  This problem occurs when the new project goals and the rebuilt team are not sufficient to revive team morale. Occasionally, some of the project and team changes may themselves be part of the morale problem. This is a serious problem because, as noted at the beginning of this chapter, team enthusiasm and morale are a key factor in making a team successful.

  Action: Make the resolution of this problem a high-priority activity. Enlist the help of the development organization's human resources manager. If the organization does not have an HR function, work with the initiating manager to identify the problem. Meet individually with the key members of the team and then with all the team members together to identify and discuss the morale problem. Then work with the project manager and the initiating manager to resolve the problem (see [8] and [9] for two excellent readable texts about teams). If none of this works, hire a good external team consultant.

9.6   Summary

Rebuilding a competent team is a key step in the disentanglement process. The objective is to build (or rebuild) the team by resolving the main team problems on both the overall team level and the individual team member level. This chapter discusses how to rebuild a competent project team in preparation for restarting the project.

This step of the disentanglement process is closely linked to the evaluation of the project team (step 4). The key subjects of the team evaluation can be used as a checklist for identifying potential team problems. The following list includes guidelines for deciding which team problems must be resolved:

1.   Project team structure: Identify problems related to the structure of the team, such as an unclear reporting structure or unworkable pairing or matching of team members.

2.   Project team functions: Look for project functions and tasks that have not been well assigned or staffed.

3.   Team members: Identify internal team compatibility problems and consider skills and competencies.

4.   Team leaders: In large teams, consider team leaders' skills and competencies.

5.   Project manager: Consider problems that are preventing the project manager from successfully leading the project and review the manager's suitability for the job.

Rebuilding the project team means implementing changes in the staffing, structure, and operation of the team, including the following:

- Restructuring the internal organization of the team
- Restaffing none, some, or in rare cases, all of the team positions
- Redefining development procedures and work policies
- Changing the relationships between the team and the project stakeholders
- Changing the relationships between the team and other external groups

Rebuilding the team should take between one and two days. In order to keep within the limit, keep the changes on a relatively high level whenever possible, and leave the details to be completed by the project manager and the team after the project is restarted.

Opposition to change should be expected. The main causes will be career and job security concerns, political biases and personal interests, and the natural emotional resistance to change. Generally, subjective, political, and emotional opposition is best handled with the help of allies, especially the initiating manager. Constructive criticism should, of course, be handled by addressing the issues that are raised.

Rebuilding a large team means having to deal with more attention, more developers, and probably more stakeholders. Because the project team is large, consider whether you need to involve all members of the team. Don't be overwhelmed by the size of the team, and don't lose control of your schedule.

The following things can go wrong when rebuilding a team:

- Unable to recruit replacement staff: For non-senior positions, leave the staffing to the project manager. For senior positions, enlist the help of the initiating manager to reinforce the sense of urgency in the search.

- New processes have no champion: Have the organization's SQA professional champion the process, or assign a person with significant formal software engineering experience.

- Opposition to change: Plan ahead to handle opposition (it should be expected). Use allies, and recruit the help of the initiating manager.

- Lack of management support: Resolve this problem in the early stages of the disentanglement process.

- Team morale remains low: This is a high-priority problem. Enlist the organization's HR professional or hire a consultant to help solve the problem (it must be solved before the project can resume).

Exercises

1. Review the airborne subsystem case at the beginning of Chapter 6 and review the list of potential team problem areas in Section 9.2 of this chapter.

   Where would you expect problems in the airborne subsystem project? Consider especially the project team structure (item 1 in the potential team problem list), the team members (item 3), and the project manager (item 5).

   Review the list of potential team changes in Section 9.3.2. As the project evaluator, which changes would you expect to implement in the airborne subsystem project?

   Make any necessary assumptions about the project and document them. Explain your conclusions.

2. Review examples of a rescued software projects by searching your local library, the Internet, or other sources. Locate at least one example where significant changes were made to the project team. How do these changes compare to the areas listed in Sections 9.2 and 9.3.2? Where there any changes implemented in the rescued projects that were not covered in Section 9.3.2? After reviewing this chapter, is there anything that you, as the project evaluator, would have done differently? Explain.

3. Class project: Have the students search their library for any prominent book that deals with team morale in technical projects. Find the top three recommendations in the book for rebuilding morale when a project is in serious trouble.

    In the classroom, compare the recommendations in the different books that were referenced. Discuss how similar or dissimilar they are. What are the three most common recommendations?

4. Class project based on exercise 1. Choose a mediator. Then divide the class into three groups: (a) the project team, (b) the project stakeholders, and (c) a team of three evaluators.

    Have the project team elect a project manager. Have the stakeholders define their relationship and interest in the project (all should be different). Have the evaluators elect a chief evaluator.

    The mediator will then conduct a debate of the project team changes. The evaluation team's role is to defend the changes and enlist allies from the development team and the stakeholders. The mediator should take notes of the key points made.

    After the debate, review and discuss the mediator's notes and determine whether the airborne subsystem project disentanglement process can proceed.

10

Step 8—Risk Analysis

Step 10   Early Warning System
Step 9   Revise the Plan
Step 8   Risk Analysis
Step 7   Rebuild the Team
Step 6   Can Minimum Goals Be Achieved?
Step 5   Define Minimum Goals
Step 4   Evaluate the Team
Step 3   Evaluate Project Status
Step 2   Assign an Evaluator
Step 1   Stop

Having redefined the goals and rebuilt the team, we are now ready to begin preparing for the resumption of the project. First we need to ensure that we are prepared to deal with any major problem that may occur after the project resumes. This involves risk analysis, and it is an essential part of *any* orderly development process. It is particularly important in a project that is emerging from a catastrophe because this is a project that has already been demonstrated to involve significant risk. Risk analysis ensures that the project does not become entangled again. It also provides a degree of confidence in the revised project plan (the next step in the process) by demonstrating that preparation has been thorough.

Risk analysis is a form of insurance—the basic idea is that if problems do occur, solutions will be readily available. Like all insurance, risk analysis usually comes with a price. The cost of preparing for the occurrence of a problem is primarily the cost of having the alternative solution at hand, while the problem may or may not occur. In some cases, the cost may be minimal: the time needed to analyze and document the solution and the time to track the problem. In other cases, the cost may be substantial: for example, the price of an alternative piece of development equipment. In any case, a problem that has been analyzed and resolved ahead of time is far simpler to deal with than a problem that occurs unexpectedly.

In many cases when a project is in serious trouble, risk analysis is the medicine we didn't take. If we had, the problems likely could have been either overcome or considerably alleviated. Here is an example:

> In mid-September 1999, Hurricane Floyd struck North Carolina. According to state flood maps, a major hurricane was a 500-year event, a flood predicted to occur only once in five centuries. But with Hurricanes Fran in 1996 and Bonnie in 1998, the state had already experienced two 500-year floods in just three years. Floyd would make it three in four years.

> A year before Floyd struck the Eastern Seaboard, a North Carolina-based company, Carobyte Software Inc. (CSI), was awarded a major software development contract for the 2000 Olympic games in Sydney, Australia.[1] The company performed risk analysis because that is what the contract required it to do, but the analysis was no more than superficial. A team member later recalled that he had suggested that they prepare for a hurricane, but his suggestion had been brushed aside.

> CSI's development facilities were located in the eastern part of the state where Floyd hit the hardest. Two buildings were completely flooded, which caused the results of one year of development work to be almost entirely lost. CSI was never able to recover sufficiently to deliver the system in time for the Olympic games. The company lost three million dollars, the cost of one year's work, and another two million dollars trying to recover. As a result, CSI also had to defend itself in lengthy litigation that ended only when the company eventually went out of business.

---

[1] While the basic facts are essentially accurate, some of the details have been altered.

A post-mortem (an appropriate name in this case) of the events concluded that had CSI simply stored backups at a remote location, the project would have survived (and, assumedly, the company, too). The conclusions also noted that the two serious hurricanes in the previous three years should have alerted CSI management to the possibility that one might happen again during the project.

The management of CSI made a very common mistake; they thought that because another severe hurricane was unlikely, the risk could be ignored. But risk analysis must take into consideration not just the likelihood that a problem will occur, but also the damage that it will cause if it does occur. For example, few homeowners insure their garden against frost even though it is common in cold winter climates (the damage would be low), while many homeowners have fire insurance even though fires are rare (the damage would be high).

Whether CSI learned from its experience, we will never know. It is likely, however, that if the company had not collapsed, it would have better prepared for subsequent hurricanes. Furthermore, someone would have wondered what other risks beside hurricanes should have been anticipated and planned for. This is the essence of risk analysis. Hopefully, most companies will not require a hurricane to recognize its importance.

Of course, risk analysis alone does not guarantee project success. Even a failing project may have performed some degree of risk analysis when it began. But the disentanglement process will have sufficiently redefined the project to warrant a revision of any existing analysis. Furthermore, the project's catastrophic situation would usually indicate that any earlier risk analysis would have been poor or ineffective. The availability of the project evaluator, an experienced veteran, is an opportunity to correct this.

This chapter describes the basic technique[2] for the management of software project risks and explains how to apply it to a disentangled project. The technique should be implemented by the project evaluator together with the project manager before the disentangled project is restarted. Risk analysis is, however, an ongoing activity that will require the involvement of the project team throughout the development of the project.

10.1   Risk Analysis Overview

This section provides a brief overview of risk analysis. Readers seeking a practical technique can go directly to Section 10.2.

---

[2] For a more rigorous discussion of the formal theory of risk management, see [1] and [2].

All software project managers have to deal with the risk that problems will occur during the development of their project. The degree to which they do so effectively is a key factor in determining project success. And like all important success factors, dealing with risks should not be an ad hoc activity. Effective risk management requires an orderly process.

In many cases, potential problems can be anticipated. In such cases, the manager can plan for the possibility that a problem will occur by estimating its probability, evaluating its impact, and preparing solutions in advance. This is referred to as *risk analysis* and is an effective means of combating potential development problems.[3]

Is risk analysis required in every software project? In even the simplest project, there is some penalty for failure, so the answer must be yes. But as projects become larger and more complex, risks increase both in number and in complexity, and accordingly the need to manage them increases too (see Figure 10.1). A simple example is that the risk of new hardware being late is much more severe in a twenty million dollar project than in a two million dollar project.

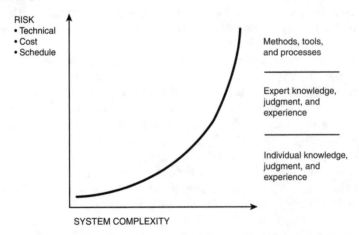

Figure 10.1   The need to manage risks increases with system complexity (from Higuera [5])

Another important question is when should risk analysis be performed? Is there a point when it becomes too late? Risk analysis should be performed as early as possible, and it is too late only if all anticipated problems have already occurred. Though this may sound obvious, it is significant because if a project has been launched without risk analysis, it is perfectly acceptable (even desirable) to perform risk analysis partway through development. This, of course, is the situation with the current step in the disentanglement process.

---

[3] *Risk analysis* is often more broadly referred to as *risk management*, especially when emphasizing the continuous nature of the practice.

Any problem that can disrupt the project is subject to risk analysis. Flooding or a power grid blackout is an external risk—an event that comes from outside the project. Excessive project team turnover is an internal risk. High project complexity and the introduction of a new programming language are technical risks.

Projects are also subject to behavioral risks, when emotions, customs, attitude, and other behavioral factors can have a negative effect on the development of the project. However, we will not deal with these types of risks in this overview (see Gemmer [3] for a discussion of the subject).

The SEI explains when a problem is not a risk:

> A company is developing a flight control system. During system integration testing, the control system becomes unstable because processing of the control function is not quick enough during a specific maneuver sequence. The instability of the system is not a risk since the event is a certainty—it is a problem [4].

The SEI also summarizes the meaning of successful risk management:

> A successful risk management practice is one in which risks are continuously identified and analyzed for relative importance. Risks are mitigated, tracked, and controlled to effectively use program resources. Problems are prevented before they occur and personnel consciously focus on what could affect product quality and schedules [4].

A technique for achieving this is described in the following sections.

10.2   The Risk Analysis Process

This section describes a systematic approach to risk analysis as it should be applied to a disentangled project. This discussion concentrates on dealing with the main risks that could prevent the project from being successfully completed. Less-critical risks should also be integrated into this high-level version of risk analysis, but only after the disentangled project resumes. The analysis should take about one day to complete.

Advisory: Risk analysis is a complex practice, which, when applied in full, can produce significant benefits for a software project. However, at this stage of the disentanglement process, a simplified version of the practice is all that is needed. After the project resumes, a more thorough version of the practice may be implemented (see [1] and [2]).

10.2.1 Anticipating Problems

The first stage in analyzing the risks of a disentangled software project is a high-level review of the main risk areas. The objective is to anticipate problems that could considerably disrupt the development of the project. This is achieved by convening a brainstorming session with the project evaluator, the project manager, and the key development team members. Other people may also be invited to participate in the session based on their experience and technical or administrative knowledge. This might include people from other project teams, support groups, the company's legal department, or the purchasing department. The session should be limited to a half-day.

Table 10.1 contains a sample list of potential project risk areas. The list should be expanded as needed based on the special characteristics of the development organization and of the disentangled project.

Table 10.1   Sample List of Potential Project Risk Areas

1.	Project scope and deliverables (consider the new minimized project goals)
2.	Process and organization (such as methodologies, standards, policies on)
3.	Technical issues (such as complexity, experience)
4.	Team issues (consider the rebuilt project team)
5.	Schedule constraints (consider stakeholder needs and expectations)
6.	Project development resources
7.	Management issues
8.	Customer and user issues
9.	Other stakeholder issues
10.	Support team issues (such as quality assurance, test teams, field support)
11.	External groups (such as subcontractors, vendors, partners)
12.	Resource issues (development tools, facilities)
13.	Budget issues
14.	Administrative issues
15.	Natural and social issues (such as weather, health, legal, industrial action)
16.	Other areas relevant to the specific project being disentangled

The outcome of the brainstorming session is a list of all anticipated problems and their potential effects on the project. Table 10.2 presents an example of an anticipated problem list.

Table 10.2   Example of an Anticipated Problem List

Problem	Description
1. Late delivery of hardware	If the hardware is not delivered by June 1, as planned, the integration phase will be delayed.
2. Internet communications too slow	If the information to be accessed from the Internet site is too slow, it will not support the amount of data to be transmitted.
3. No operating system expert	The system requires use of low-level operating system protocols. John Adams is the only OS expert in the company, and he may not be available for this project when needed.
4. System response time excessive	The required system response time to the input may exceed the five seconds specified in the requirements.
5. High staff turnover	The schedule is tight with only minimal slack time. If there is more than average staff replacement during development, the project will be late.
6. Communications too slow	The standard communications software is too slow. The design is based on the new binary communications package. This package has never been used with this system, and may not be suitable.
7. Later delivery of database subsystem	The database subsystem is contracted to Software Development Inc. (SDI), which has committed to delivery by April 15. SDI may not deliver on time, causing a delay in the final integration and test phase.

While the objective is not to list every conceivable problem that the disentangled project may experience after it resumes, it is necessary to identify those problems that should reasonably be considered in relation to the project. In any event, the following analysis stage is designed to isolate only those problems that could have significant impact on the project and that can reasonably be expected to appear.

10.2.2   The Analysis Stage

The analysis of the anticipated problems list requires the evaluation of each problem in order to

1. Estimate the probability that the problem will occur.
2. Estimate the impact of the problem on the project.
3. Attribute a measure of severity to the problem (this is explained next).

For each anticipated problem, the probability and the impact should be estimated by a team that includes at least the project manager, the project evaluator, and a third person with expertise in the field of the anticipated problem. All items on the list are best estimated during a single problem evaluation meeting to assure that the relative severity between problems is not distorted. The objective is to avoid situations where late delivery by supplier A is estimated at 0.8 by one estimator, and late delivery by supplier B is estimated at 0.6 by another, while both estimators would agree that the probability is equal. Having both persons in the same room at the same time reduces this relative distortion.

The next stage of the analysis measures the level of severity of each anticipated problem on the list. A simple and effective way of producing the measure of severity is to

1. Assign an expectation number between 1 and 10 based on the probability that the problem will occur, with 10 representing high probability, and 1 representing low probability (that is, multiply the probability by 10).

2. Assign a number between 1 and 10 based on the impact of the problem on the project, with 10 representing high impact and 1 representing low impact.

3. Multiply the value produced in step (1) by the value produced in step (2) to produce the measure of severity for the problem.

Table 10.3 presents an example of the calculation of the measure of severity, using the anticipated problems described in Table 10.2.

Table 10.3   Example of the Calculation of the Measure of Severity

Problem	Expectation	Impact	Severity
1. Late delivery of hardware	6	5	30
2. Internet communications too slow	4	2	8
3. No operating system expert	5	5	25
4. System response time excessive	5	3	15
5. High staff turnover	5	8	40
6. Communications too slow	2	8	16
7. Later delivery of database subsystem	3	9	27

After the measure of severity has been calculated for each anticipated problem, the list is sorted according to the severity of the problems, with the most severe problem at the top of the list. A decision can then be made that any problem with a severity level less than some value (say 10) will not be considered (this is called the *severity threshold*). The remaining problems are then evaluated and a detailed course of action is chosen for each problem. The action includes a *mitigation plan* to reduce the likelihood that the problem will occur and a *contingency plan* to reduce the damage if the problem does occur.

The information is then entered into a *risk action table*. For each entry in the table, a member of the development team is assigned as *tracker*, to track the problem, and to ensure the mitigation plan is implemented and to alert project management when the contingency plan needs to be put into effect. This stage is demonstrated in Table 10.4.

Table 10.4   Example of a Risk Action Table

Problem	Severity	Mitigation Plan	Contingency Plan	Tracker
1. High staff turnover	40	Hold regular employee reviews, resolve individual problems, and increase remuneration.	Have contract ready with consultancy company; hire consultants.	Y. Knot
2. Late delivery of hard-ware	30	Conduct regular reviews with hardware vendor management.	Identify alternate source for hardware; prepare tentative order.	Will Doo
3. Late delivery of the database subsystem	27	Define a smaller database system subset for system integration.	Use database simulator for integration.	U. Hope
4. No operating system expert	25	Select team candidate for intense OS training program.	Hire an OS expert consultant.	I. Hope
5. Commu-nications too slow	16	Get assistance from project Alpha's communications experts for part-time involvement.	Use communications system from project Alpha.	Mark Time
6. System response time excessive	15	Assign the software performance improve-ment task to an experienced team member.	Procure faster hardware from alternate vendor.	B. Patient
7. Internet communi-cations too slow	8	(Not considered)	(Not considered)	

The analysis stage of risk analysis is also performed on a high level (similar to the problem anticipation stage); this means that it should deal only with severe problems that can disrupt the disentangled project after it resumes. As mentioned earlier, other less-severe problems may be dealt with later after the project resumes.

The analysis stage should take no more than a half-day so that the entire risk analysis of the disentangled project, including the brainstorming session, should take about one day.

Advisory: Projects rarely deal with risks that are unique. Most problems have been dealt with before in previous projects. Prior to formulating mitigation and contingency actions, review previous projects to find solutions that have worked successfully in the past and use them in the risk action plan.

Advisory: There is never only one mitigation plan or only one contingency plan for each anticipated problem. Like insurance, plans vary in their degree of coverage, and their costs vary correspondingly, too.

You should balance the investment in mitigation and contingency plans with the problem's level of severity (higher severity requires broader coverage), the complexity of the solutions (sometimes they are surprisingly simple), and the project's available budget.

10.2.3 Implementing Risk Action Plans

There are steps in the disentanglement process that require the project evaluator to trigger special activities that are carried out *after* the process is completed and the project is resumed. These are activities that are solely designed to protect the project from slipping back into catastrophe mode. Risk analysis is such a step (the early warning system, step 10, is another). After the disentangled project resumes, the risk action plan must be implemented and kept current (it has little value otherwise).

The following guidelines explain how this should be done:

- **Mitigation plans**

    Mitigation plans are started by the project manager and the team as soon as reasonably possible after the project resumes. In most cases, the earlier these preventive measures are started, the greater the likelihood that they will succeed. It is the responsibility of the trackers to raise a red flag if the plans are not adequately implemented. In most cases, all mitigation plans should be put into action within one month or less of project resumption.

- **Contingency plans**

  Generally, contingency plans can be perceived as plans of action that are shelved for possible later use. However, in some cases, parts of the contingency plan may need to be implemented by the project manager and the team well before the risk problem can occur (for example, hurricane contingency plans should be in place well before the hurricane season).

  Occasionally the entire plan needs to be implemented *before* the anticipated problem occurs, such as the development of a simulator in case the delivery of a critical component is delayed. If the component is delivered on time, the simulator can then be discarded.

  The tracker is responsible for triggering the contingency plans in one or both of the following instances:

  1. The anticipated problem occurs or becomes imminent.
  2. The contingency plan requires advance preparation.

- **Updating**

  Risk action plans should be updated periodically to keep them relevant. (review, brainstorm, and analyze them at least every three months) Also, new risks that may surface should be included in the list and assigned to a team member for tracking. The project manager is responsible for updating the plans.

From the perspective of the disentanglement process, the risk analysis step is complete when the anticipated problem list has been prepared and analyzed, the risk action plans have been assigned for tracking, and the process has been comprehended and adopted by the project manager and the team. From a broader project perspective, risk analysis ends when the project ends.

Advisory: If the organization has a software quality assurance group or a software engineering process group, enlist the assistance of that group to ensure that the risk analysis activities continue after the disentangled project resumes.

10.3 Risk Analysis: An Example

The following example illustrates the risk analysis process. The example includes the main stages of the process but is greatly simplified. In reality, the risk analysis tables would be more extensive, and the anticipated problems more detailed.

Warranty Proxy Inc, (WPI) provides consumer warranty services for other companies. WPI has decided to replace its aging remote access database system with a faster, more reliable access system. The new system will connect the company's employees and customers at several remote locations to the service center database. It will also include software that will provide consumers limited access to their product warranty information via the Internet (for example, type of product, manufacturer, warrantee period, consumer ID, previous problems, open problem tickets). Consumers will access the company's databases using standard Web browsers.

The company's current system uses several high-capacity computers to maintain its databases. The company's current network of personal computers provides a level of access to the service center database depending on the user's access permissions.

WPI invited its largest customers to observe a test run of the new system, but the system was not ready on time. Two subsequent test dates were also missed. This tarnished the company's reputation with its customers. As a result, WPI's management initiated a major review of the project to decide whether to save or cancel it. After a thorough overhaul, project resumption was approved, and the new test run date was set for March 15.

Here is the current situation: The WPI development team has performed risk analysis on the overhauled (disentangled) project. The brainstorming session has identified three potential problems that could disrupt the much-publicized test run:

1. The remote personal computers will be using standard off-the-shelf software to access the service center database. The access software is not entirely compatible with the database, and a conversion program is being developed. The problem has not yet been fully studied and there is concern that the conversion program may take too long to develop.

2. The new firewall security system for the service center database computers may not be installed and ready for the March 15 test run.

3. The local health department has issued a warning that a severe flu epidemic may break out in February. This could result in the incapacitation of several key development team members.

Tables 10.5, 10.6, and 10.7 are the risk analysis tables for WPI's remote access project. Both the late firewall delivery and the software incompatibility problem have been identified as major risks. The possible flu epidemic is perceived as a minor risk (the severity threshold was set at 20).

Table 10.5   Anticipated Problem List

Problem	Description
1. Incompatible access software	The incompatibility problem is not fully understood, and the conversion program may take too long to develop.
2. Late delivery of firewall security system	The firewall security system may not be delivered in time for the test run and secure remote access may not be available at that time.
3. Flu epidemic breaks out	Key team members may become incapacitated.

Table 10.6   Severity of Risks

Problem	Expectation	Impact	Severity
1. Incompatible access software	5	8	40
2. Late delivery of firewall security system	8	6	48
3. Flu epidemic breaks out	5	3	15

Table 10.7   Risk Action Table

Problem	Severity	Mitigation Plan	Contingency Plan	Tracker
1. Late delivery of firewall security system	48	Meet with firewall vendor and impose penalties for late delivery.	Have firewall vendor deliver older system as a temporary solution for the test run.	Indira Hope
2. Incompatible access software	40	Assign top expert in the field to the team. Have two additional experts available and ready if needed.	Develop a special software module that limits access during the test run to functions that are known to be compatible. Load this module on all test access computers during the test run.	William Doo
3. Flu epidemic breaks out	15	(Not considered)	(Not considered)	

The project manager is responsible for getting the firewall vendor involved in the mitigation and contingency plans, and the legal department is involved in inserting the penalty clause into the vendor contract. The project manager will also enlist experts to help resolve the software incompatibility problem (if necessary, senior management's support will be requested). A team member will also be assigned to develop the special software module for the test run and to have it ready in case it is needed.

A team member, Indira Hope, has been assigned to track the firewall system delivery. She will raise an alarm if high-level meetings with the firewall vendor are not held within a month and if the purchase contract does not include a significant penalty clause. She will also ensure that the vendor is ready to deliver an older version of the firewall if the new version is not ready on time. She will initiate an immediate order for the older system to be installed when she is convinced that the new system will be late (she will monitor the status regularly).

Another team member, William Doo, is responsible for tracking the software incompatibility problem. He will raise an alarm if a competent expert is not assigned to the project to help resolve the problem. He will also monitor the development of the special software module, and he will trigger its inclusion in the system if he concludes that the compatibility problem will not be resolved in time for the test run.

10.4   What Can Go Wrong (and What to Do About It)

Risk analysis is usually not a particularly controversial step. When it is not implemented, it is usually because of a lack of familiarity with the process rather than a lack of support for it. Consequently, most problems related to the process are technical in nature; problems either relate to implementing the risk action plan or disagreeing about the severity of a problem.

As part of the disentanglement process, risk analysis also has to contend with issues of support that are derived from earlier steps of the process. Stakeholders, and especially senior management, may be reluctant to invest in the cost of insurance for potential problems. However, if the evaluator has so far successfully negotiated new project goals and a rebuilt team, there is a fairly reasonable likelihood that support for risk analysis can be established too.

The following list covers some of the things that can go wrong when performing risk analysis and suggests ways of dealing with them:

- **Significant problems were overlooked.**

  After the brainstorming session is complete, additional potential problems may be discovered. The problems may be discovered after the analysis stage is complete or even during one of the two remaining steps in the disentanglement process

  Action: At any stage before a serious potential problem materializes, the risk analysis process can be reactivated, and the risk action list can be updated. In fact, it is almost inevitable that this will happen.

  Apply the analysis stage to the problems that have been discovered, and if their severity passes the threshold that was established for the project, enter them into the risk action plan table.

- **Required brainstorming participants do not participate.**

  This problem occurs when brainstorming participants from outside the project are needed (product and development experts, finance staff, system administrators, and so on) and do not turn up.

  Action: Contact all invited participants several hours before the brainstorming session begins and request that they confirm their participation. This will provide time to resolve the problem.

  Decide how essential the missing participants are to the brainstorming session. If they are not essential, consider proceeding without them. Otherwise, attempt to recruit suitable replacement participants or request assistance from the initiating manager to ensure participation.

  If the problem cannot be resolved before the session begins, brainstorm the other problems on the list for which all invited participants are present. Hold a second session later when full participation has been ensured (the delay should be no more than one day).

- **The risk action plan lacks support.**

  This problem occurs when the cost of "insurance" is not made available. This means that the budget for mitigation and contingency plans is withheld or the staff required to implement the actions is not made available.

  Action: This is similar to problems of inadequate management support discussed in the "What Can Go Wrong" section of previous disentanglement steps.

  Meet with the initiating manager and, if necessary, with other members of senior management and explain the importance of ensuring that the project does not slip back into catastrophe mode. Clarify that the cost of implementing the actions is very small in comparison to the damage should the risk event occur.

If lower funding might be approved, consider a cheaper action plan. This plan will have a lower cost, but will include a less effective mitigation or contingency plan. However, this will usually be better than nothing.

If support is still withheld, formally record that the project is proceeding with the risk unresolved at the direction of the organization's management (this should be part of the final written report on the disentanglement process).

- **There is insufficient staff to track all risks.**

  Ideally, each team member should track no more than a single anticipated problem on the risk action list. However, if the team is small or the action list is long, there may be more problems to track than available team members.

  Action: Assign up to two problems for tracking to each team member. Do not assign problem tracking to the project manager.

  If this solution becomes a burden on the team members and interferes with their ability to perform their duties, or if the assignment of two problems to a team member still leaves problems unassigned, recruit a special person to the team as the project's risk action tracker.

- **Participants disagree about problem severity.**

  It is difficult to apply a totally objective technique for determining the problem expectation and impact numbers (and hence, the severity number). This can be a problem if brainstorming participants disagree on the numbers that should be assigned.

  Action: The project evaluator should apply an arithmetic average to determine the problem expectation and impact numbers. If significant disagreement remains, the project manager should make the final determination.

- **Participants disagree about severity threshold.**

  It is difficult to apply a totally objective technique for determining the threshold for problems to be included in the risk action list. This can be a problem if brainstorming participants disagree on the threshold to be used.

  Action: The project evaluator should apply an arithmetic or mode average to determine the threshold. If significant disagreement remains, the project manager should make the final determination.

Advisory: When analyzing additional problems that are discovered after the initial risk analysis activity is completed, review all previous severity levels before calculating the severity of additional problems. This will help maintain a degree of consistency in the way the severity level is calculated.

Advisory: If the number of problems in the risk action list is exceptionally large, this may be an indication that the project is extremely high risk. In such cases, it may be advisable to reconsider the advisability of resuming the project.

10.5 Summary

This chapter describes the basic technique for the management of software project risks and explains how to apply it to a disentangled project. The technique should be implemented by the project evaluator together with the project manager before the disentangled project is restarted.

In many cases, potential problems can be anticipated. In such cases, the manager can plan for the possibility that a problem will occur by estimating its probability, evaluating its impact, and preparing solutions in advance. This is referred to as *risk analysis*.

The first stage in analyzing the risks of a disentangled software project is a high-level review of the main risk areas. The objective is to anticipate problems that could considerably disrupt the development of the project. This is achieved by convening a brainstorming session with the project evaluator, the project manager, and the key development team members.

The anticipated problems list is then analyzed to

1. Estimate the probability that the problem will occur.
2. Estimate the impact of the problem on the project.
3. Attribute a measure of severity to the problem.

Next, the severity of each anticipated problem on the list is calculated.

1. Assign an expectation number between 1 and 10 based on the probability that the problem will occur.

2. Assign a number between 1 and 10 based on the impact of the problem on the project.

3. Multiply the value produced in step 1 by the value produced in step 2 to produce the measure of severity for the problem.

At this point, only problems with severity above a threshold value are considered. The information is then entered into a *risk action table*. For each entry in the table, a member of the development team is assigned as *tracker* to track the problem, ensure the mitigation plan is implemented, and to alert project management when the contingency plan needs to be put into effect. The following points explain how this is done:

- Mitigation plans are started by the project manager and the team and tracked by the assigned tracker.

- The tracker triggers the contingency plans if the anticipated problem occurs or if advance preparation is needed.

- Risk action plans should be reviewed periodically to ensure that they are still relevant.

The following things can go wrong when performing risk analysis:

- Significant problems were overlooked: Apply the analysis stage to the problems that have been discovered.

- Required brainstorming participants do not participate: Attempt to recruit suitable replacement participants or enlist help from management to ensure participation.

- Lack of support for the risk action plan: Explain the risks to senior management. If support is still withheld, record that the project is proceeding with the risk unresolved.

- Not sufficient staff to track all risks: Assign up to two problems for tracking to each team member.

- Disagreement about problem severity: Use an average of proposed severity numbers or the project manager should make the final determination.

- Disagreement over severity threshold: Use an average of proposed threshold numbers or the project manager should make the final determination.

Exercises

1. Review the CSI case described at the beginning of this chapter. As part of CSI's attempt to recover after hurricane Floyd, perform risk analysis for the project. Identify at least six potential problems, and prepare the risk analysis tables. Document any assumptions about the project that you make.

   Discuss the role of risk analysis in helping the project overcome the loss of one year of work. In your opinion, could risk analysis have helped the project survive? Explain.

2. A new cable television service company is preparing to establish service in eight months' time. The company provides service to subscribers for a fixed monthly fee that depends on the extent of the service that they have ordered. The company also screens new movies, each of which can be viewed by a subscriber by telephone request to the company.

   The company is now in the process of ordering equipment, purchasing facilities, and signing up customers. A software company has been contracted to develop a billing system for the subscribers. The system will interface with the equipment to receive information on new movie screenings, and it will interface with the customer database for regular monthly billing information.

   Prepare a list of the ten most critical problems that you anticipate in the development of the billing project. Discuss the reasoning behind your selection of problems.

3. Calculate a measure of severity for each of the potential problems you identified in Exercise 2. Explain your assignment of project impact and probability values.

   Suggest an alternative method for assigning a measure of severity to anticipated problems that also takes into consideration the cost of the contingency plans.

4. Suggest contingency plans for the anticipated problems you identified in Exercise 2. Consider two different alternative plans for each problem. Consider the cost of each alternative plan, and then select the best one based on the alternative method for assigning measures of severity that you suggested in Exercise 3.

   Prepare a contingency table containing the contingency plans that you have selected.

5.   Class exercise: Divide the class into groups of three or four students. Assign Exercises 2, 3, and 4 to each group. Request that each group present their risk analysis to the rest of the class. Discuss (a) the different anticipated problem lists, (b) the different contingency plans, and (c) the different methods for assigning a measure of severity (did any two groups suggest similar methods?).

11

Step 9—Revise the Plan

Step 10   Early Warning System
Step 9   Revise the Plan
Step 8   Risk Analysis
Step 7   Rebuild the Team
Step 6   Can Minimum Goals Be Achieved?
Step 5   Define Minimum Goals
Step 4   Evaluate the Team
Step 3   Evaluate Project Status
Step 2   Assign an Evaluator
Step 1   Stop

At this stage of the disentanglement process, most of the pieces are in place. But before the project can be restarted, the pieces must be combined into a formal plan and the missing parts filled in. Then, after approval of the revised plan, the project will duly emerge from catastrophe status and the team can prepare to resume development (though there will still remain one more disentanglement step before the process is complete).

Can an effective plan be completed within the remaining time left for the disentanglement process? While project planning is never a simple task, it will be relatively straightforward at this stage because much of the work will have been completed and the main points agreed upon, so that much of the planning will be fairly automatic. As we shall see, this provides an excellent opportunity to ease the task even further by using automated planning tools.

Furthermore, for the purposes of the disentanglement process, the full details of the plan are not required. At this stage, the plan's objectives are to provide a medium for receiving formal approval to restart the project, to help establish the cost-effectiveness of the disentangled project, and to provide the basis for a more detailed development plan (to be completed after development resumes). Thus, many low-level details may be excluded at this time.

Of course, this step is not always smooth sailing. There will still remain agreements to be finalized and approvals to be given, and there is no assurance that they will be easy to conclude. There is also a risk that the key players will interpret previous agreements in different ways or that they will reopen them for last-minute changes.[1] This can be a major headache for the project evaluator. However, a disentanglement process that has proceeded successfully this far will usually not break down at the last minute.

This chapter discusses the revised project plan and explains how to produce it from the results of the previous disentanglement steps. The discussion includes an overview of project planning and a set of guidelines for adapting a conventional development plan to the needs of the disentanglement process.

The planning activity should a collaborative effort by the project evaluator and the development team, especially the project manager. As this is the final approval step before the project resumes, it also requires the active support and involvement of key project stakeholders, particularly members of senior management.[2]

---

[1] See the Navy helicopter project anecdote in footnote 4 of Chapter 8, "Step 6—Can Minimum Goals Be Achieved?"

[2] While key stakeholder involvement is needed throughout the disentanglement process, it is especially required during this critical step.

11.1   Software Planning Overview

We will start by reviewing several basic concepts of software project planning. As mentioned earlier, parts of the detailed planning will be left until after the project resumes. However, before we discuss what can be left for later, it is important to review what the complete plan must eventually include. In particular, we will see how a project with significant pre-prepared planning information (as in disentanglement) can complete an initial version of the plan fairly quickly. In the next section, we will discuss the application of these concepts and methods to the special circumstances of the disentanglement process.

Planning is one of the basic elements of project management, and it is unlikely that a project will be completed successfully without it. There is nothing profound in this assertion; people generally plan complicated activities. It is common, for example, to consult a map before leaving on a long automobile trip; this might include checking the weather and emergency road service, and choosing the routes, the rest stops, the refueling points, and possibly even a schedule to rotate the driving among the passengers.

Most software projects are developed according to some type of plan. It may be a professional plan created according to a formal process, or it may be informal and rudimentary. Many of the leading software process organizations, such as IEEE, ISO, PMI, and SEI, have produced various processes, standards, and guidelines for project planning.

In the following discussion, we will review some of the basic concepts from the SEI's Capability Maturity Model, and we will look at an outline of the software project plan from the IEEE. We will then consider the use of tools that can significantly lessen the burden of complying with these processes.

11.1.1   Software Project Planning Concepts

What is the objective of a software project plan, and what are the main activities associated with preparing it? SEI has proposed a set of concepts as part of its *Capability Maturity Model* (CMM) (see [3], [4]). The set of concepts covers all the components that must be contained in an effective project plan.

As noted before, several of these components will be available from previous steps of the disentanglement process (for example, estimates, risk analysis, and requirements/goals). They must nonetheless be included in the project plan and are listed here for the sake of completeness.

In its description of the CMM, the SEI states that the purpose of software project planning is to establish reasonable plans for performing software engineering and for managing the software project. It describes the planning principles (which it calls "the goals of the plan") as follows:

1. Software estimates are documented for use in planning and tracking the software project.

2. Software project activities and commitments are planned and documented.

3. Affected groups and individuals agree to their commitments related to the software project.

Here are some general guidelines from the SEI on how this should be accomplished:

- For each software project, a plan is developed, according to a documented procedure, that covers the software activities and commitments.

- The requirements allocated to software form the basis for the software development plan.

- A software life cycle with defined stages is used as a framework for the plan.

- The plan includes documented size, cost, schedule, and resource estimates developed according to a written procedure and based on historical data.

- Estimates for critical computer resources are documented, reviewed, and agreed upon.

- All affected groups and individuals understand the estimates and plans and commit to support them.

- Senior management reviews the estimates and plans before external commitments are made.

- Software risks associated with the cost, resources, schedule, and technical aspects of the project are identified and evaluated, and contingencies are documented.

- Planning and estimation data are collected for use in planning subsequent projects and for input in management oversight review meetings.

These basic points are useful as a reference list to assist the project manager in mapping out the project planning activities. They also help ensure that often-accepted notions such as "the *agreed upon* commitments" (were *all* the commitments really agreed upon?) and "the inclusion of *all* affected groups" (were *all* groups really consulted?) are reflected in the project plan.

11.1.2 The Software Project Development Plan

Among the many organizations that have produced standards for software project plans, the IEEE standards are among the most widely used. We will choose the

IEEE standard as an example of a project plan format (another equally prominent and widely used standard is the ISO 9001:2000/7.3).[3]

Table 11.1 shows the IEEE Std. 1058 outline for a project management plan [2]. The plan is flexible and easily adapted to different types of project (large or small; simple or complex; with or without vendors, subcontractors, and development partners; and so on). Thus, not all elements in the outline are required for every project.

The standard includes guidelines for the application of each element, as well as references to other development process standards that are mentioned in the plan.

In Table 11.1, we see that the standard for the text of the plan essentially comprises four main parts:

1. Front matter and introductory sections: This includes the Title page, Signature page, Change history, Preface, Table of contents, List of figures, List of tables, and sections 1, 2, and 3.

2. Organization and implementation: This includes sections 4 and 5.

3. Process, methods, and tools: This includes section 6.

4. Other related processes and plans: This includes sections 7 and 8.

Although all parts are important for the success of the project, it is part 2 that contains the essence of the plan. Many of the sections in the other parts of the standard often contain substantial boilerplate text.

The production of a project development plan does not end at the beginning of the project; it ends at the end of the project. In effect, a project plan is a living entity, and it will quickly lose its value unless it is kept updated. This is particularly true of such items as estimation, risk analysis, and work and resource allocation, as well as the schedule and milestones. This means that it is perfectly reasonable to expect items of the plan to change as the project develops.

Table 11.1   Outline of a Software Project Management Plan (from IEEE Std. 1058 [2])

Title page
Signature page
Change history
Preface
Table of contents
List of figures
List of tables
1.   Overview
1.1   Project summary
1.1.1   Purpose, scope, and objectives
1.1.2   Assumptions and constraints

continues

---

[3] Note that the IEEE uses the term "software project *management* plan" rather than "software project *development* plan" (many organizations use the two terms interchangeably, as we will in this discussion).

Table 11.1   continued

		1.1.3	Project deliverables
		1.1.4	Schedule and budget summary
	1.2	Evolution of the plan	
2.	References		
3.	Definitions		
4.	Project organization		
	4.1	External interfaces	
	4.2	Internal structure	
	4.3	Roles and responsibilities	
5.	Managerial process plans		
	5.1	Start-up plan	
		5.1.1	Estimation plan
		5.1.2	Staffing plan
		5.1.3	Resource acquisition plan
		5.1.4	Project staff training plan
	5.2	Work plan	
		5.2.1	Work activities
		5.2.2	Schedule allocation
		5.2.3	Resource allocation
		5.2.4	Budget allocation
	5.3	Control plan	
		5.3.1	Requirements control plan
		5.3.2	Schedule control plan
		5.3.3	Budget control plan
		5.3.4	Quality control plan
		5.3.5	Reporting plan
		5.3.6	Metrics collection plan
	5.4	Risk management plan	
	5.5	Closeout plan	
6.	Technical process plans		
	6.1	Process model	
	6.2	Methods, tools, and techniques	
	6.3	Infrastructure plan	
	6.4	Product acceptance plan	
7.	Supporting process plans		
	7.1	Configuration management plan	
	7.2	Verification and validation plan	
	7.3	Documentation plan	
	7.4	Quality assurance plan	
	7.5	Reviews and audits	
	7.6	Problem resolution plan	
	7.7	Subcontractor management plan	
	7.8	Process improvement plan	
8.	Additional plans		
Annexes			
Index			

11.1.3   Tools for Project Planning

A key objective is to complete the planning within the tight schedule of the disentanglement process. For this purpose, planning tools can be extremely valuable.

There are many tools of varying levels of sophistication. These tools perform some or all of the following five main functions:

1. Automatically generate the project plan based on interactive entry of project information.

2. Prompt the user to provide missing information or to correct inconsistent or otherwise erroneous information.

3. Help estimate, allocate, budget, and schedule activities.

4. Evaluate different scenarios for the project plan.

5. Help track and monitor the project.

Planning tools are sometimes integrated with other software engineering tools. The following three examples show three different levels of integration: standalone planning, partial integration, and full integration:[4]

- Microsoft's Project is a tool intended to be used by project managers, business managers, and planners to help manage schedules and resources by rapidly setting up projects, communicating project data, and tracking and analyzing projects. This is a standalone planning tool.

- Borland's CaliberRM is an interactive tool that uses a requirements-oriented approach, usable by all project stakeholders, with an embedded planning application. It covers both the requirements management process and the project planning process (the two tools were developed separately and were later integrated).

- IBM Rational has an integrated suite of software engineering practices (part of the Rational Unified Process, or RUP) that includes project planning and estimating tools and techniques guidance, which is delivered through a Web interface. The suite covers all major areas of the software development process (including planning).

There is an obvious advantage in integrated software engineering tools: They generate compatible information, have similar interfaces, save learning time, and avoid multiple entries of the same data. But for someone seeking a single service, integrated tools can be an unnecessary burden. For example, an integrated planning tool might take longer to learn, and it might be more complex to operate than a standalone tool.

---

[4] None of these tools are endorsed here. They are mentioned just as examples of the many tools that are available.

Planning tools can be especially helpful if a substantial part of the input has been already prepared. In fact, the combination of an automatic planning tool and prepared planning information can drastically reduce the time required to prepare a professional project plan. One such example claims to "deliver a CMMI compliant project plan in 30 minutes"[5] (see [1]).

Planning tools also have the ability to examine "what ifs." For example, schedules can be extended or shortened to see the impact on staffing and budgets. Similarly, features can be added or removed to see the impact on the schedule, staffing, or the budget. Furthermore, some tools have the ability to examine the effect of a tight schedule (i.e., planning with very little flexibility to account for unexpected events) and to evaluate the likelihood of project delays.

The advantages of automatic tools are greatest for large projects. In fact, it is almost impossible to manage an exceptionally large project without using some process and software engineering tools. Conversely, very small projects may be better off without using tools; manual planning may be quite sufficient.

> **Advisory:** Planning tools have the ability to include a buffer in the schedule to compensate for unknown and unexpected tasks and events (this is often referred to as *spare*). The buffer may be introduced in any of several ways (in the estimates, as part of the schedule, and so on). Make sure you use this option. Review Section 8.1.2 for the suggested buffer level (spare) for a disentangled project.

11.2   Planning a Disentangled Project

We have stated that not all items in the project development plan are required in full detail at this stage of the disentanglement process. In this section, we will identify the items that are required and we will discuss how to adapt them in order to produce a plan that meets the needs of the process.

At this point, the limited objectives of the plan are the following:

1. To provide a formal representation of the disentangled project

2. To provide the medium for receiving formal approval to restart the project

---

[5] CMMI (Capability Maturity Model Integration) is the SEI's broad organizational adaptation of CMM that integrates similar approaches for improving management, engineering, and business activities.

3. To help establish the cost effectiveness of the disentangled project

4. To provide the basis for a more detailed development plan (to be completed after the project resumes)

These are the objectives required to enable the project to resume. It is not necessary at this time (though it is desirable) to complete the detailed allocation of tasks to the team members, to finalize support plans (for example, quality assurance or testing), or to complete other low-level details of the plan. This is further discussed in the following guidelines.

> **Advisory:** Numerous advanced methodologies and techniques have been developed for cost estimating and scoping a software project. Examples include Boehm's COCOMO II, function point analysis, and stepwise estimation. There are many excellent reference texts on the subject (see, for example, Jones [6], Boehm et al. [7], Garmus and Herron [8], and Bennatan [5]).

11.2.1 Guidelines for Producing a Disentangled Project Plan

The following list provides the project evaluator and the project manager with guidelines for adapting the planning process (as discussed in Section 11.1) to the disentanglement process and quickly producing an appropriate formal plan.

1. **Build on the previous plan.**

   Review any previous planning work that was done on the project. Make a quick decision about the quality and value of any relevant material that exists. In general, it is advisable to take advantage of relevant planning work that already exists, assuming that the quality is acceptable and that it does not require more of an effort to reuse it than to redo it.

2. **Use the output from previous steps.**

   Base the plan on the new agreed-upon project goals, the restructured team, the agreed framework for the schedule, and the high-level risk analysis, all of which resulted from steps 5, 6, 7, and 8 of the disentanglement process.

3. **Use the organization's standard or an industry standard.**

   If the development organization has adopted a formal project planning standard, use it. Otherwise, choose any widely used industry standard (for example, IEEE 1058 is a reasonable choice).

4. **Use tools to expedite plan creation.**

    As mentioned previously, tools can be very effective in reducing the time required for planning. If the organization has adopted a computer-based planning tool, use it. Otherwise, acquire a planning tool quickly (see Section 11.1.3). Do not choose an integrated suite of tools, and do not choose one that is overly sophisticated and takes too long to learn. Recruit a consultant who can help use the planning tool immediately.

5. **Required plan items for the disentanglement process.**

    The items required for the disentanglement process are primarily those in the organization and implementation part of the plan (see Section 11.1.2). They are listed here based on the IEEE outline (see Table 11.1). Refer to IEEE Std 1058 [2] for a detailed description of the items.[6]

    Mandatory:

    Title page and Signature page

    1.1.3 Project deliverables

    4.3 Roles and responsibilities

    5.1.1 Estimation plan (high level only)

    5.1.2 Staffing plan

    5.2.1 Work activities (high level only)

    5.2.2 Schedule allocation (high level only)

    5.2.3 Resource allocation (high level only)

    5.2.4 Budget allocation (high level only)

    5.4 Risk management plan (critical risks only)

    Desirable:

    1.1 Project summary

    4.2 Internal structure

    5.1.1 Estimation plan

    5.1.3 Resource acquisition plan

    5.2.1 Work activities

    5.2.2 Schedule allocation

    5.2.3 Resource allocation

    5.2.4 Budget allocation

    5.3.5 Reporting plan

---

[6] A description of the standard is also available online at http://standards.ieee.org/reading/ieee/std_public/description/se/1058-1998_desc.html.

6.4 Product acceptance plan

7.7 Subcontractor management plan

Nice-to-have:

All others

6. **Work closely with the team.**

The creation of the plan should be a collaborative effort of the project evaluator, the project manager, and the development team. This is essential because the project manager and the team will be responsible for adding missing details when the project resumes and maintaining the plan throughout the development cycle.

7. **Work with key stakeholders.**

Shorten the approval cycle by getting early feedback on the plan from key stakeholders. The final plan should not be the first plan they see. Many agreements will have already been reached so that it is reasonable to expect most of the stakeholders to be supportive of the main points of the plan.

8. **Use the planning tool to deal with disagreements.**

The planning tool, with its ability to evaluate different scenarios, can be a powerful asset in dealing with disagreements and requests for last-minute changes. These can often be resolved by trying out different scenarios and testing the impact of changes on the schedule, the budget, staffing, and the other resources.

9. **Establish the cost effectiveness of the project.**

There is now sufficient budget and resource information available to determine the cost effectiveness of the project. This activity requires the assistance of a financial analyst. Request that the project initiator have an analyst assigned to the project. Work with the analyst to evaluate the cost effectiveness of different scenarios by using the project planning tool.

10. **Allocate time for the plan.**

Allocate up to two days to complete the project development plan. The effort can start early by overlapping with previous steps of the disentanglement process. If approval of the plan becomes mired, start the next step in the process, but step 10 cannot be completed until the plan is formally approved.

Advisory: A note on cost effectiveness: In analyzing the cost of completing a software project, only future costs (not costs already expended) should be considered. The cost of project completion should then be compared to the value, or return on investment, of the completed project (see Section 2.2).

Thus, when deciding whether to continue a project, ROI is calculated based on future, not past, costs.

11.2.2 Additional Considerations

Following are some of the questions that usually arise during the planning process:

1. How early should planning begin?

2. Of the many possible planning scenarios, how do we choose the one that is right for our project? How should different scenarios be examined and compared? Is it a trial-and-error process?

3. If time allows, how many of the desirable items should be added to the plan? What is the benefit in adding desirable items?

4. If the organization has no orderly development processes, is this not a good opportunity to introduce them?

5. In an organization that has no orderly process, what should we expect? Will the team embrace a new planning process? If not, can we skip planning?

- **Start planning early.**

  The first eight steps of the disentanglement process lead up to this step. Thus, planning really begins with the first step of the process. Activities such as locating a planning tool, recruiting an expert, selecting a standard, evaluating the original project plan, and so on, should start as early in the process as possible.

- **Select a scenario.**

  To a limited degree, features, budget, staffing, and schedule can be traded off one for another (see [5]). At this stage of the disentanglement process, there is very little flexibility in the schedule and feature set (the project goals), so they should be resolved first with whatever degree of flexibility remains.

Start by initially selecting a scenario with a feasible feature set and schedule (the other parameters, such as budget and staffing levels, can initially be sidelined). In step 6, we will have established the existence of at least one such feasible scenario. This will produce various possible settings for the budget, staffing level, and other key parameters.

Next, vary the feature set and schedule within their limited degree of flexibility (if they are both inflexible, skip this stage). This means setting the feature set and calculating various project delivery dates and vice versa. The intention is to examine the possibility of increasing the features (adding important features that were removed in step 5) or reducing the delivery schedule.

When the schedule and feature set have been established, try out different budget and staffing levels. Many planning tools can optimize these project scenarios automatically based on the priorities and other criteria entered by the user. However, remember that even a generous budget and an unrestricted staffing level may not be enough to produce an acceptable plan if the fixed feature set conflicts with the schedule.

- **Add desirable items to the plan.**

The amount of detail in the disentangled project plan is determined by (a) the mandatory list of items in guideline 5 and of Section 11.2.1 and (b) the amount of time available. If the creation of the plan moves relatively smoothly and there is swift agreement from the key stakeholders, this step of the disentanglement process may be concluded in less than the allocated two days. While it is acceptable in this case to move on to the completion of step 10, there may be an advantage in devoting the remaining time to include more detail from the desirable list in guideline 5. This can place the development team members in a better starting position when the project resumes by providing a clearer picture of the project and their assignments.

The decision to include more detail should be made by the project evaluator based on the time consumed by the overall disentanglement process, the degree of urgency in getting the team back to work, and the expected benefit of additional detail at this time (recall that the project is expected to resume within a few days, at which time the additional detail will be added in any case).

- **Avoid introducing new processes.**

Sections 6 and 7 of the IEEE standard assume the existence in the development organization of a set of software development life cycle processes. If these processes do not exist, this is not the time to formally introduce them. For the remainder of the project, the project manager should produce a rudimentary set of common development practices (for testing, documentation, and so on). These practices should be summarized in a freestyle common practices document. It then becomes the project manager's responsibility to ensure that the practices are applied by the team.

This activity is a formal project task to be included in the project development plan (as part of Section 5.2.1 in the IEEE plan outline). The common practices document must be produced immediately after the project resumes and should be updated and improved during the development of the project. (This rudimentary solution should not be considered a permanent solution for future projects.)

- **Deal with opposition to new rudimentary practices.**

In ad-hoc organizations, there will almost always be some opposition to the introduction of orderly processes, no matter how simple or rudimentary they are. The intent, therefore, is both to minimize opposition and maximize acceptance (one does not necessarily produce the other). Thus the goal of the introduction of rudimentary practices is to provide an acceptable, but basic, level of orderly development without creating too much opposition. (Opposition can be dealt with after the project concludes and new processes are formally introduced into the development organization.)

So, the use of orderly development and planning practices cannot be skipped, even if the development team does not readily embrace them. The practices provide a very minimal level of orderly development, and without them, the project cannot be permitted to resume.

Advisory: All components of a project plan cannot be pre-set; there must be some flexibility. Thus, if the schedule is firm, ensure that budget, staffing level, and feature set are not also all fixed (or another catastrophe will ensue).

Advisory: Within the new schedule, allow ample spare time and resources for the implementation of the plan by the project team. "Ample spare" is dependent on the degree of high-level detail, the complexity of the project, the estimated level of risk, and evaluator's confidence in the accuracy of the high-level estimates. When in doubt, use 20% to 33% as ample spare (but do not duplicate spare that has already been included in the new estimates). See also the discussion on this subject in Section 8.1.2.

11.3   What Can Go Wrong (and What to Do About It)

As mentioned earlier, this step in the disentanglement process is not always smooth sailing. There is always the possibility that key stakeholders will interpret previous agreements in different ways. Also, because this step is close to the end of the process, there is a risk that stakeholders will want to reopen the agreements for last-minute changes (in some cases, this may be justified). As noted earlier, however, a disentanglement process that has proceeded successfully this far will usually not break down at the last minute.

The following list covers some of the things that can go wrong during the creation of the project plan and provides solutions for dealing with them:

- **Approval of the plan takes too long.**

  Approval can be delayed due to severe disagreements. Disagreements are usually about the final versions of the schedule and budget and other key elements of the plan. This can disrupt the disentanglement process in its final stage.

  Action: The following methods will help expedite approval:

  As suggested previously, use the planning tool to demonstrate that probable effect of opposing positions.

  Recruit the initiating manager to help secure agreements and signoff.

  As a last resort, explain to the stakeholders that without agreement and approval of a feasible plan, the disentanglement process cannot proceed.

- **Planning takes too long (even though planning information is available).**

  If the planning information is truly available, planning might be taking too long for the following reasons: (a) the plan contains too much detail, or (b) the team members working on the plan do not have the required planning experience.

  Action: (a) To avoid too much detail, keep the plan on a high level, as described in Section 11.2. Prioritize the information being introduced into the plan. Start with the highest-priority items and work through the list. After the allocated time has elapsed, the highest-priority items will have been included in the plan and the remaining items can usually be left to be completed by the project team when the project resumes.

  (b) The project evaluator cannot produce the plan in the allocated time without effective assistance. If the team is unable to provide assistance, recruit mentors for the team from other projects in the development organization, or hire a consultant for this purpose.

- **Previous agreements are reopened.**

  Many of the main elements of the plan will have already been agreed upon with the key stakeholders during previous steps (for example, project goals, staffing, overall schedule). If the agreements are reopened, it may set the disentanglement process back significantly.

  Action: Consider if there is substantial justification for reopening the agreements. If so, renegotiate the agreements and, in parallel, inform the initiating manager that the disentanglement process may be completed late (beyond the prescribed two weeks). If not, recruit the initiating manager to assist in suppressing the attempts to reopen agreements.

- **The original project plan is poor.**

  In this situation, the development plan prepared at the beginning of the project has little or no value. This may be because the plan was crudely or defectively created, it was never maintained and updated, or the project has changed significantly since it was originally launched.

  Action: There is no requirement to reuse parts of a bad plan. Disregard it and prepare a completely new plan for the disentangled project.

- **The existing planning tool is unsuitable.**

  If the development organization has a planning tool, it is usually advisable to use it in the disentanglement process (see Sections 11.1.3 and 11.2.1). However, if the tool is overly complex, outdated, or otherwise unsuitable, the disadvantage in using it may outweigh the advantage.

  Action: If you are convinced that the existing planning tool is unsuitable, do not use it. Encourage the organization to acquire a different planning tool (the expense is usually minor). If that does not work, consider producing the plan manually.

- **The planning tool seems to generate an inflated schedule or budget.**

  This problem appears when, after entering the project information into the planning tool, it produces a plan with an unacceptable schedule or budget.

  Action: Most professional planning tools work reasonably well. If the schedule or budget is unacceptable, it is usually due to one of the following two reasons:

  1. The input to the planning tool was entered erroneously.
  2. The schedule and budget are perfectly reasonable based on the information entered into the tool.

Check the input to ensure that it was entered correctly. If it was, examine the goals, deliverables, tasks, and staffing and consider different scenarios. If none are acceptable, it may be necessary to repeat steps 5, 6, and 7 of the disentanglement process.

- **The planning tool is too complicated.**

Some planning tools require significant training before they can be used effectively. If no expert user is available to help, it will be impossible to take advantage of the tool during the short time allocated for planning the disentangled project.

Action: Hire an expert to operate the planning tool (contact the manufacturer of the tool for names of experts). If no expert can be located in time, encourage the organization to acquire a simpler planning tool (the expense is usually minor). If that does not work, consider producing the plan manually.

- **There is a lack of cooperation in producing the plan.**

The potential for this problem to occur is common to most of the disentanglement steps. It is, however, rare for it to appear at this stage of the process. The problem may appear as an unwillingness by team members to assist in the preparation of the plan, as a lack of support from key stakeholders in reviewing and approving the plan, or as a lack of support from other teams, groups, and individuals from whom input is required.

Action: If the problem exists with the stakeholders or with external groups, enlist the support of the initiating manager to resolve the problem.

If the problem exists with just one or two team members, enlist the project manager's help in dealing with them—assuming that the project manager is not part of the problem. Otherwise, the solution will need the help of senior management by making their support clearly visible.

If the problem is with the project manager, a three-way meeting between the initiating manager, the evaluator, and the project manager may be the best solution.

- **The project is not cost effective.**

This problem occurs when the financial analyst determines that the plan is not financially viable.

Action: Evaluate different scenarios using the planning tool. If no feasible plan is financially sound, present the scenarios and analyses to the initiating manager, who must then decide how to proceed. The possible decisions are (a) to proceed with the project because it has strategic business importance, (b) to renegotiate the scope of the project with the key stakeholders in order to reduce it to a financially viable project, or (c) to cancel the project.

> **Advisory:** In resolving problems, resist any attempt to remove the *spare* from the plan to reduce the schedule and the required resources (see an earlier Advisory and Section 8.1.2). In project development, the purpose of spare is to cover the unexpected, and in software development it is always wise to expect the unexpected. In fact, the removal of spare from a project plan is an almost sure way to produce a new project catastrophe.

11.4 Summary

At this stage of the disentanglement process, most of the pieces are in place. But before the project can be restarted, the pieces must be combined into a formal plan and any missing pieces filled in. The disentanglement process sets a tight schedule for preparing the plan: just two days. Is this achievable?

It can be done, because by this last step of the process, much of the planning work will have been completed and the main points agreed upon. Furthermore, it is not yet necessary to prepare a detailed comprehensive plan. At this stage, the plan has limited objectives: to provide a medium for receiving formal approval to restart the project, to help establish the cost effectiveness of the disentangled project, and to provide the basis for a more detailed development plan (to be completed by the project manager after development resumes). Thus, at this point, many of the low-level details can be excluded.

Effective use of development tools can dramatically reduce the time required to produce a plan. In fact, the combination of an automatic planning tool and existing data led the proponents of one such tool to claim that they could "deliver a CMMI-compliant plan in less than 30 minutes."

The extensive existing literature on planning is immediately applicable to planning in the context of a project emerging from a catastrophe. The SEI CMM model lists the important concepts of good planning (some of which will already have been completed in earlier steps of the disentanglement process). Among the most of important of these are the documentation of estimates, activities, and commitments, and agreement on commitments from all affected groups and individuals.

An important planning standard that can be used is the IEEE Std 1058 (see Table 11.1). As already mentioned, planning for a disentangled project does not require the preparation of *all* the items prescribed in these standards. The required items include project deliverables and high-level estimation, staffing, and scheduling. If time permits, several additional planning items can be included.

Development tools come in many varieties. Some (for example, Microsoft Project) are designed for planning only, while others (such as IBM RUP Tool Set) provide an integrated suite for the entire development cycle. Important considerations when deciding which tool to use include its learning curve and its simplicity of operation. For these reasons, if the organization has already adopted an existing tool, it is often best to stay with it.

Although by this step of the disentanglement process most of the work is done and disagreements resolved, it is not always smooth sailing. For example, affected groups and stakeholders might withhold their final approval of the plan and demand changes, and stakeholders may require that agreements be reopened at the last moment. These problems should be handled tactfully. Often, the assistance of the initiating manager must be enlisted. Using the planning tool to examine various "what-if" scenarios could also be effective in resolving differences.

Exercises

1. Locate two formal project plan standards (other than IEEE Std. 1058) and compare them with the IEEE standard. How would you adapt them to the needs of a disentangled project? Explain.

2. Review the CCSI project in Section 7.2.2.

   Choose any formal project development plan standard. Prepare a simplified project development plan for the CCSI project. Propose three different scenarios for the project plan by changing the schedule, staffing, budget, and list of features. Make any required assumptions about missing details, and list them.

3. Class project: Review the CCSI project in Section 7.2.2.

   Designate a class discussion moderator and a project evaluator. Divide the class into two groups: the project stakeholders and the project development team (elect a project manager).

   The evaluator and the development team are requesting the stakeholders to sign off on the new project plan. However, the stakeholders are reconsidering the list of deliverables for the first release of the system. Convene a meeting, moderated by the class moderator, with all parties to discuss the reopening of the list of deliverables. The moderator should list all main arguments that are raised, together with their responses.

Review the moderator's list and draw conclusions about the discussion. Discuss when agreements should be reopened and when they should not. What could have caused the disentanglement process to fail? What should be done to ensure the process is successful?

4. Team project (covering disentanglement steps 1 to 9): Search the Internet and locate a description of the Denver Airport baggage handling system software project failure that was discussed in Chapter 1, "An Introduction to Catastrophe Disentanglement." Prepare a plan to disentangle the project. You are the evaluator.

   Create a list of people to be interviewed. Based on the description of the project's problems, consider the responses that you would most likely get from the reviews of the overall team performance, the project manager, and the individual team members.

   Perform steps 3 to 9 of the disentanglement process, and generate the necessary summaries, the midway report, and the project development plan. Make any required assumptions about missing details, and list them.

   Prepare a file with all relevant documents and findings.

12

Step 10—Create an Early Warning System

Step 10   Early Warning System
Step 9   Revise the Plan
Step 8   Risk Analysis
Step 7   Rebuild the Team
Step 6   Can Minimum Goals Be Achieved?
Step 5   Define Minimum Goals
Step 4   Evaluate the Team
Step 3   Evaluate Project Status
Step 2   Assign an Evaluator
Step 1   Stop

A critical part of fixing something is making sure it remains fixed. This almost universal concept is certainly true of a disentangled software project—there is little value in rescuing a project only to have it slip back into failure again. In this last step of the disentanglement process, the resilience of the rescue plan cannot be taken for granted; it must be built into the solution.

This concept applies in many fields, not just software development. It is aptly illustrated in one of the escapades of Hannibal, the famous Carthaginian general, who in the third century B.C. led an army (and a herd of elephants) across the Alps into Northern Italy. While Hannibal lost many of his men crossing the freezing Alps, he made up for his loss by recruiting willing volunteers along the way. The problem was, however, that he didn't have enough food to feed them all, and as quickly as he recruited them, they died, not so much from the cold as from exhaustion (aggravated by a lack of food). Worse, many of his loyal veteran soldiers were dying too.[1]

Hannibal decided to disentangle the catastrophe by imposing a strict limit on the number of men who would be recruited into his army, and he assigned several of his lieutenants to decide when someone would be accepted into the ranks. His new process worked well, and from that point on Hannibal made good time toward Italy.

Until his men started dying again. Apparently, his lieutenants, at some point, could no longer turn away the many Gallic recruits who were eager to fight Rome, and so the ranks again began to swell and the rations began to dwindle. History tells us that Hannibal lost more than 15,000 men on the march into Northern Italy.

Hannibal created a good process, but it wasn't resilient—he didn't have a monitoring system to sustain his new recruiting process. Without it, his project (the march to Italy) gradually reverted back to its previous state of catastrophe. What Hannibal needed was a system for reviewing the status of recruiting operations and the distribution of food and a correction procedure to be triggered if matters began to deteriorate again. Hannibal needed an early warning system.

A disentangled software project is no different. It is essential that any rescue plan include a procedure to ensure that the project does not slip back into catastrophe mode. This procedure acts as an early warning system that triggers corrective action before a problem becomes a severe catastrophe again.

Of course, not every problem need sound the alarm. An effective early warning system must be able to differentiate between problems that can reasonably be expected to be resolved by the project team and severe problems that can disrupt the project entirely. This requires the application of some type of alarm triggering technique, which can be simple or quite elaborate, depending on the sophistication of the system that is used.

---

[1] To be historically accurate, Hannibal's problems started in Iberia, where the trek began, and the tradeoff between food and men was a problem throughout the long march to Italy. But undoubtedly, the problem was worst during the march over the Alps.

For example, Liu, Kane, and Bambroo [1] have developed an elaborate alarm-triggering technique using fuzzy logic.[2] Their method utilizes the quantifiable aspects of software development from three different dimensions: product, process, and organization. It then applies intelligent risk-detection rules utilizing not only individual metrics from each dimension, but also various combinations from the three.

Other methods are based on the measurement of actual versus planned progress; this is the approach used in Chapter 2 to determine whether a troubled project is a catastrophe. A more advanced version of this approach is called *earned value project management* [2] and requires intricate planning and monitoring of the project.

In contrast to the catastrophe determination method discussed in Chapter 2, the goal of an early warning system is to find potentially severe problems while they are still relatively simple to correct, and well before they become a catastrophe. Virtually all methods used to achieve this goal include five basic elements: data collection, status reviews, alarm triggers, corrective action, and follow up.

The sophistication (or complexity) of the method is mainly indicated by the amount of project data that is collected and by the technique used to trigger an alarm. The other three elements (status reviews, corrective action, and follow up) are not differentiated by the degree of sophistication or complexity; these elements should always be thorough, irrespective of how simple (or sophisticated) the method that is used.

How sophisticated should an early warning system be to ensure the resilience of a disentangled project? As noted in previous chapters, this is not the time to introduce complex methodologies, and the previous five basic elements suffice for most projects. However, if the organization has already adopted a software engineering process that incorporates an advanced alarm-triggering technique (such as earned value), that technique should be used.

This chapter describes a simple early warning system for a disentangled project. The description covers the five basic elements, provides guidelines on how to implement them, and proposes a simple technique for sounding the alarm when the project is in danger of slipping back into catastrophe mode.

The chapter covers topics that are important for all the main project players: the development team, members of senior management (who play a key role in the procedure), and the other key stakeholders. The implementation of the early warning system will provide the additional structure needed for all parties to feel confident about restarting the project.

---

[2] Fuzzy logic is a branch of mathematical logic that has been extended to handle the concept of partial truth-values between *completely true* and *completely false*. It is a powerful problem-solving methodology with innumerable applications in information processing. Fuzzy logic provides a simple method for drawing definite conclusions from vague, ambiguous, or imprecise information, similar to the way humans make decisions.

12.1   The Elements of an Early Warning System

As we have seen, there are five basic elements to an *early warning system* (or EWS) procedure, as illustrated in Figure 12.1:

1. The collection of development data (or metrics)
2. Periodic project status reviews
3. Identification of potential alarm-triggering problems (or risks)
4. Initiating corrective action
5. Follow-up activities

When the disentanglement process is implemented within an organization that has successfully installed an advanced software development process, we can presume that all or most of these basic elements will already be in place. So in many of these organizations, an effective EWS will already exist and should be used for the disentangled project when it is restarted (this is further discussed in Section 12.7).

But catastrophe projects often occur in organizations where the development process has broken down or where no effective development process exists at all. This means that this last step in the disentanglement of the project requires the swift establishment of an effective procedure that institutes the five basic EWS elements. Is this a reasonable expectation?

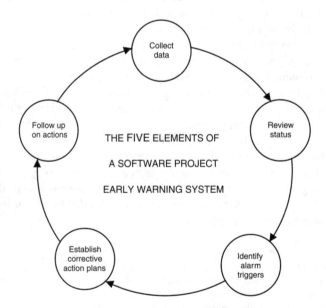

Figure 12.1 The five elements of a software project's early warning system

The following case study illustrates how a large development organization successfully installed such a procedure simultaneously for multiple projects. One would assume that for a single project, it would be easier.

In the early 1990s, a major U.S. communications company recruited a new general manager for its Communications Infrastructure Division[3] after several painful failures had occurred in the division's product development group. Customer complaints about the quality of the division's products were mounting, and customers were turning to the company's competitors. Even more painful, this was happening in a company that had made quality synonymous with its name. Mac Bryant, the new general manager, had strong business and development backgrounds and was entrusted with turning the division around.

Immediately upon his arrival, Bryant launched several activities, which, it turns out, were quite similar to the first few catastrophe disentanglement steps. He brought several outsiders into the company and immediately had them work with the division's senior managers to determine the true status of the division's projects. Here's some of what he learned:

- Problems were everywhere, but more than anywhere else they were in software development.

- Although all the developers claimed that software development was following an organized process, it wasn't. Some of the projects had makeshift processes, but each project had its own version, and the processes were not complete, they were not being followed consistently, and few of the developers knew what they were.

  Projects did have schedules, estimates, and progress reports, but they were inaccurate and of little or no value.

- Project development data (metrics) was not being collected in any reliable way.

- Project reviews were being held sporadically, they followed no reasonable or consistent review process, the results were rarely documented, and there was rarely any follow up.

- There was little or no contact between the development organization and the division's customers.

Bryant designated a quality manager (QM) to work with him on these problems. The QM set up biweekly project reviews (the frequency was later changed to monthly). The reviews were held in a large presentation hall during a full day starting at 6:30 a.m. (coffee, fruit, and donuts were served), and all the division's projects were reviewed. The reviews were attended by Bryant, the QM, all senior division managers, and the senior

---

[3] The basic details (excluding names) of this case study are factual.

staff from each project, as well as representatives of the division's major customers.

The first review was a disaster. Bryant and the QM asked each project manager some very tough questions. Adequate answers were rare because no one knew how to prepare the review. Most of the day was spent with Bryant and the QM explaining how the presentations for the next review were to be prepared. A few action items were set for each project and the project managers were instructed to report on the items at the next review.

The QM followed through on the action items during (not at the end of) the two weeks between the first two reviews and provided assistance and guidance to the project team in completing their action items. She also provided guidance on how to collect the raw data for the presentation slides, the methods of analysis (such as Pareto charts[4]), defect and error reports, progress reports, and so on.

The second review was more successful, and almost everyone, including the project team members, began to feel better about their own work. There were, of course, some project staff members who were slow to jump aboard the new review process, and they were given extra help.

By the third review, every project team had a plan that the project manager could explain and defend. The project teams also had six weeks of data, which enabled them to begin some very basic "planned versus actual" or "earned value" analysis. This became the basis for the division's early warning system. Whenever a project drifted negatively more than 10% beyond its planned value, it automatically raised a red flag. At the end of every review, the red flags were assigned either corrective action or a date when a corrective action plan was to be submitted to the QM. Needless to say, all red flags were reviewed at the beginning of every project presentation (and sometimes more frequently).

It took Bryant two months to get all of the division's projects reorganized (two large projects were cancelled), another two months (four in all) to get them back on track, and another two months (six in all) to feel confident that projects were under control.

When Bryant came to the Communications Infrastructure Division, he mainly knew that the organization was in deep trouble. But he was not sure why (though he did have some ideas). The division could not provide him with reliable information about status, progress, and the resolution of problems. He suspected that

---

[4] A Pareto chart is used to graphically summarize and display the relative importance of the differences between groups of data. See http://www.asq.org/learn-about-quality/cause-analysis-tools/overview/pareto.html.

he had several catastrophes on his hands that needed urgent attention. So his first action was to find out the true status of his projects, and he did this with the help of an experienced professional whom he recruited from outside of the organization. In effect, Bryant started by implementing steps 2 and 3 of the disentanglement process (later, most of the other steps were also implemented, particularly for the most severely troubled projects).

There are a number of lessons to be learned from this case study:

- First, orderly project reviews can be introduced gradually, though not over too long a period (it took Bryant's division six months to come up to speed, but only two months to produce effective reviews, and just one month—a period covering two reviews—to start gaining some value from the reviews).

- All the elements of an EWS are best introduced with the help of a professional (in Bryant's division, it was the QM).

- Initially, the elements of an EWS can be quite simple. They can gradually be expanded and become more sophisticated. We will see later that for disentangled projects, the process can remain fairly simple throughout the life of the project (as noted previously, the disentanglement of a project is not a good opportunity to introduce unessential new processes).

- The collection of reliable data, the accurate reporting of status, and the other elements of the basic warning system will be taken seriously by project staff when they see that senior management is taking them seriously, too.

A key conclusion from the Bryant case is that the elements of an EWS *can* and *must* be introduced into a development organization, even if it is an ad hoc organization. Introducing an EWS process into a disentangled project should take up to one half day. In the following sections, we will discuss how the EWS works.

12.2 Development Data Collection

According to a common saying, you cannot show progress if you cannot measure. How many managers and other stakeholders would be satisfied to hear simply that a project is "making good progress"? The obvious rejoinder from any recipient of such a report would be "How do you know?" which is simply an inquiry into what the rosy report is based upon. As we shall see, an effective status report must be based on measurable data, such as "the number of levels 1 and 2 defects has dropped by 50% in the past week."

In the development of a software project, the number of defects is a metric; it is a quantitative measure of an attribute of the development project. In Chapter 2, we used metrics to help determine whether a project was a catastrophe (for example, the size of a schedule overrun presented as a percentage of the schedule).

In this section, we will briefly discuss the role of metrics in reporting project status, and we will then review how the data is collected and analyzed for an EWS.

> **Advisory:** In an ad-hoc development organization (that is, with no orderly development processes), the first management process that should be introduced is an EWS procedure (with its five elements). It will provide management with the status of the organization's projects, which is the minimum information needed to make decisions. An EWS procedure is also an excellent stimulant for initiating other processes.

12.2.1   The Role of Project Development Data

We will start by looking at the importance of project data for the effective management of a project.

Using data as the basis for management decisions (in contrast to subjective methods, such as intuition) is referred to as *management by data*. It is widely recognized as a preferred method of management (especially in the technology and business arenas), but it is not as broadly implemented as one might expect, and especially not in software development (see [5]). Is it because software development organizations do not collect data?

A recent survey found that most software development organizations (82%) actually do collect development data (some do so consistently and some do so occasionally). But the survey also discovered that many of them do not use the data very effectively. It appears that some organizations simply do not know what to do with the data they collect [4].

But even if software organizations do not always take full advantage of the data they collect, we might still assume that the data is available, and all that is needed is to feed it into an EWS mechanism. The survey findings in Figure 12.2 show that this is not the case. While 82% of software organization collect development data, a much smaller percentage (22%) does not do so extensively and consistently.

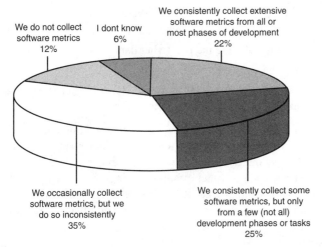

Figure 12.2   The percentage of surveyed software development organizations that collect metrics (from [4])

What can these findings tell us about the creation of an EWS? We will shortly see (in Section 12.2.2) that extensive metric collection is not needed for an EWS, but *consistent* collection most certainly is. Management by data cannot work effectively if the data is not consistently available. For example, it might be impossible to follow up on corrective action if there is no data to show the progress that has been made (the fact that data was available when the problem was identified does not help). So the data in Figure 12.2 tells us that the introduction of an EWS into a software development organization will usually have to start with the introduction of a data collection process.

According to Figure 12.2, a quarter of surveyed organizations collect data consistently but not completely (they collect from only a few development phases). Need the collection of data be *complete* as well as consistent? Though completeness may be desirable, it is not as important as consistency. It is perfectly legitimate for an organization to decide which data it wishes to collect. According to the IEEE software metrics standard, an organization can employ whichever metrics it deems most appropriate for its applications [9].

In addition to the IEEE, several other international organizations have also produced widely used standards for software metrics methodologies (for example, the ISO—International Standards Organization [10]). However, we will focus on the essential parts of the IEEE metrics standard (IEEE Std. 1061), due to its considerable flexibility and its detailed guidelines.

The IEEE standard addresses software metrics collection and analysis within the context of project quality. The standard covers the following activities:

1. Establishing software quality requirements
2. Identifying software metrics (what do we want to measure?)
3. Implementing software metrics (what data do we need to collect?)
4. Analyzing the software metrics results
5. Validating the software quality metrics (ensuring the metric truly represents the attribute that we wish to measure)

The standard includes guidelines on how to identify and implement software metrics. This is achieved in a hierarchical (top down) manner, starting with high-level metrics (called *direct* metrics or *factors*) and successively breaking them down to lower-level metrics (each of which produces a single numerical value).

In the following example (adapted from the IEEE 1061 standard) a development organization wishes to measure the functionality that is being delivered by the project team.

a. The project's *functionality* would be defined as a factor (i.e., a high-level metric).

b. *Functionality* would decompose into *completeness, consistency, correctness, security, compatibility,* and *interoperability*. This means that functionality would be measured against these attributes (Is the functionality complete? Is it consistent? Is it correct? and so on).

c. For example, *completeness* would be measured as *ratio of number of completed documents or software components to total number of documents or software components*.

d. Similarly, *consistency* would then be measured as *ratio of number of documents or software components that are free of contradictions to total number of documents or software components*.

e. And so forth.

An important point highlighted in the standard is the need to clearly establish the benefit to be derived from each metric for which data is collected. This ensures that time is not wasted collecting data that has limited or no real value.

The standard also covers the use of automatic tools for data collection. This is an important subject because data collection is a tedious task, easily abandoned if performed manually. Automatic tools make data collection more practical and more sustainable (this is further discussed later in this chapter).

As the IEEE standard shows, metrics is a very broad activity, potentially covering all aspects of a software project—administration and management, as well as software development. However, comprehensive project metrics collection is more than is needed for an early warning system.

Advisory: At this point, it is important to re-clarify that the objective of this step is to avoid the introduction of broad processes that could prevent the disentangled project from restarting (the intent is to keep new processes to the minimum necessary for the successful completion of the disentangled project). However, if effective advanced processes already exist within the development organization, of course, they should be left in place.

12.2.2   Data Collection in a Disentangled Project

How is the broad subject of metrics applied to a disentangled project? Can a data collection process be introduced swiftly into an organization that has limited experience collecting metrics data? As we shall see, it can, because a partial and simplified version of data collection is all that is needed for an EWS.

At this point, we will consider only the project data required to ensure that a disentangled project does not slip back into disentanglement mode. This means focusing on data related to two main areas:

1. Problems

2. Progress

It also means temporarily disregarding data related to such areas as process improvement, efficiency, reuse, training, and the broader organization (unless these areas are already part of the project's existing metrics collection process).

How is project problem and progress data collected? This discussion will not go into the details of the various techniques for data collection. Many excellent texts on the subject already exist (in addition to the IEEE and ISO standards). The following list includes examples of reference texts that can be adapted to the needs of a disentangled project:

1. Kan's *Metrics and Models in Software Engineering* [6] is a comprehensive treatise on software metrics. It covers much more than the limited data needed for a disentangled project, but it is a good comprehensive reference source on the subject. The book discusses the fundamentals of measurement theory, specific quality metrics and tools, and methods for applying metrics to the software development process.

2. Garble et al.'s *Metrics for Small Projects: Experiences at the SED* [7] gives useful insight (and several examples) into the experience of applying metrics analysis to small software projects. The article shows that an

organized, comprehensive metrics program can bring order to the chaos of small-project management and form the foundation for a concerted process improvement effort. The authors describe their experience in applying metrics to one such U.S. Army organization.

3. Carleton's *Software Measurement for DoD Systems: Recommendations for Initial Core Measures* [8] provides guidelines and several good lists, as well as examples of analysis. The report presents recommendations for a basic set of software measures that *Department of Defense* (DoD) organizations can use to help plan and manage the acquisition, development, and support of software systems.

For a disentangled project that is under pressure to restart quickly, the information in these texts may be overwhelming (Where should you start? What should you include?). The list in Table 12.1 provides a starting point. It contains the basic data items that are required to produce an EWS for a disentangled project. The list should be used to extract the relevant parts from a professional software metrics guide (such as the previous three texts).

Table 12.1 should be expanded based on the specific characteristics of the disentangled project. But even before the table is expanded, the list can be used to immediately begin data collection.

Table 12.1   Basic Set of Data Items to Be Collected for a Disentangled Software Project

1.	Tasks completed in units of effort (for example, work days) and breakdown by types of task
2.	Tasks remaining in units of effort (for example, work days) and breakdown by types of task
3.	New defects found by level of defect
4.	Defects resolved (closed) by level of defect
5.	Testing completed by functions/modules by complexity/size
6.	Testing remaining by functions/modules by complexity/size
7.	Budget consumed (in units of currency)
8.	Budget remaining (in units of currency)
9.	Schedule consumed (in days)
10.	Schedule remaining (in days)
11.	Staffing level (number of people) and breakdown by type of staff
12.	Integration: number of functions/modules successfully integrated
13.	Integration: number of functions/modules remaining
14.	Product performance: measures of ease of use, response time, stability, and so on

Before data collection begins, there is another point to consider. As mentioned earlier, data collection is a tedious task and, if performed manually, there is a risk that it will not endure. This is particularly true if the project is medium or large (beyond 15 person-years); in such cases, it will be difficult or even impossible to manually collect data effectively.

Thus, in all cases (even for small projects), automated metrics tools are highly desirable aids for data collection (see [11] for information about available automated metrics tools[5]).

> **Advisory:** Avoid the introduction of complicated tools when restarting a disentangled project. New tools introduced into a disentangled project should be necessary, relatively simple, easy to use, and easy to learn.

12.3 Periodic Project Status Reviews

Generally, the purpose of a software project status review (sometimes called a management review) is to provide information to project staff, stakeholders, and other involved parties so decisions can be made regarding the project, approvals can be given (or withheld), and actions assigned at previous reviews can be tracked. A disentangled project review, which is part of the EWS, has the same purpose. The review provides information on the status of the project, identifies and monitors the resolution of problems, and ensures that critical problems are resolved.

Project reviews are mainly based on data. This is why the collection of development metrics is so important; without it, the review has little value. We saw this in the case study reported in Section 12.1 where the first review had no metrics and was virtually a disaster (the only benefit from it was an assurance that the next review would be better).

Project reviews should be periodic events, usually held every month, but in some cases more frequently (every one or two weeks) and occasionally less frequently (every two or three months). More frequent project reviews carry the burden of excessive overhead (a review and its preparation require the investment of substantial time and effort), while less frequent reviews carry the risk of unresolved problems left to deteriorate.

How should reviews be conducted? There are many standards for software project reviews; one such example is the IEEE Std 1028 [3], which covers a broad

---

[5] QSM's *Software Life Cycle Management* (SLIM) (http://www.qsm.com) is one example of a tool that includes metrics collection and analysis as well as an EWS (not endorsed).

range of project reviews (management reviews, technical reviews, inspections, and walkthroughs). Though these different types of reviews are all flexible and adaptable, when introduced together they can be quite a hefty undertaking for a software organization with limited development processes. Fortunately, a disentangled project's EWS does not require all the reviews described in the IEEE standard.

In the previous section, we discussed how to introduce metrics to a disentangled project. The approach for introducing reviews is similar: Introduce only those elements of a review process that are necessary for the successful completion of the disentangled project (unless more comprehensive reviews are already an effective part of the organization's process).

We will discuss the adaptation of a common project status review standard (such as the IEEE standard) to the needs of a disentangled project (others, such as the ISO project review standard [12] can, of course, also be adapted).

1. **The project status (or management) review**

   The IEEE standard covers a broad range of software project reviews: management reviews, technical reviews, inspections, walk-throughs, and audits. The minimum required for a disentangled project's EWS is the management review. According to the standard, the purpose of a management review is

   "To monitor progress, determine the status of plans and schedules, confirm requirements and their system allocation, or evaluate effectiveness of management approaches used to achieve fitness of purpose. Management reviews support decisions about corrective actions, changes to the allocation of resources, or changes to the scope of the project."

   This exactly fulfills the needs of a disentangled project's EWS.

2. **Review participants**

   Who needs to participate in a project status review? The review should be attended by

   - The key management decision makers
   - The review leader (who has the administrative task of running the review)
   - A recorder (who documents the main events and decisions of the review)
   - The project manager
   - Technical staff
   - Other team members
   - Optionally, a representative of the customer or user

Other individuals may be invited to participate in the review if their presence is required during the discussion of specific issues.

3. **Length of the review**

The review should take between two hours and a complete day (depending on the size and status of the project).

The review of large projects, or of projects with a long list of problems, may take a day to complete. The review of short projects (less than 15 person-years) or of projects that are running well with no major problems can be completed within two hours or so.

4. **The agenda**

The IEEE standard includes a broad range of subjects to be covered by the review. For a disentangled project, the subjects can be reduced to the following:

- A presentation of overview, scope, and objectives
- A report on the status of action items from the previous review
- A discussion of urgent issues and problems
- A presentation of the status and progress of the project

  Schedule

  Budget

  Staffing

  Development progress

  Defects

  Other development issues

- Project management problems and proposed solutions, including the status of risks
- Decisions and approvals
- Action items (including actions, owners, and completion dates)

5. **Preparation**

The IEEE Software Reviews Standard 1028 functions both as a guide and as a standard. It includes guidelines for preparing the review (such as providing appropriate facilities in which to hold the review), planning the review (such as scheduling and announcing the meeting, distributing material before the review, establishing an agenda and schedule), and conducting the review (such as establishing a review leader, and recording the proceedings).

12.4   The Project Alarm Trigger

Chapter 2 discusses how to determine whether a project is in serious trouble (a catastrophe). But how do you determine whether a project is headed in that direction (but is not, as yet, a catastrophe)? How can you know that a project needs to be urgently steered back on track before the cost of corrective action becomes very high? Answers to these questions are the core of the EWS triggering concept.

For the purpose of this discussion, we will differentiate between software project-related problems (that is, problems that are administrative, managerial, process-related, environmental), and software product-related problems (such as defects in the product being developed). Project and product problems should be classified according to their level of severity, as follows:

1. **Critical**

   Critical product problem: A product defect that renders the product unusable or near-unusable.

   Critical project problem: A project-related problem that, if not corrected, can prevent the project from being completed successfully.

2. **Serious**

   Serious product problem: A product defect that renders a major product feature unusable, but the overall product is still effectively usable and can achieve its main purpose.

   Serious project problem: A project-related problem, which, if not corrected, can

   - Significantly affect customer satisfaction. There is evidence indicating that 20% or more of users/customers who were expected to use/purchase the product will not use/purchase it.[6]
   - Cause the project to overrun its budget by more than 20%.
   - Cause the project to overrun its schedule by more than 20%.

3. **Minor**

   Minor product problems: A product defect that makes the product difficult to use, but all major product features continue to function effectively. This category also includes all other product defects that are not critical or serious.

   Minor project problems: A project problem that is neither critical nor serious.

---

[6] Harsher definitions can be used to describe serious customer satisfaction problems, depending on the characteristics of the product being developed (for example, a medical life support software system would require a more stringent definition).

Critical and serious problems can trigger an alarm based on such attributes as the number of problems, the length of time spent on the problem list, and lack of adequate progress toward resolution. For example, in a strategic or life support software system, a single critical problem that has existed for more than one review period may trigger an alarm. In projects that deal with non-critical situations (for example, a time and attendance system), a triggering mechanism may be more elaborate.

Triggering mechanisms are often based on aging, which means that critical and serious problems move up the ladder of severity as time passes without them being resolved. Following is an example of a triggering mechanism (sample parameter values appear in parentheses):

1. Assign X points (for example, 5) to a new critical problem.

2. Increase the point value of a critical problem by Y points (for example, 2) every reporting period (for example, every week).

3. Assign Z points (for example, 1) to a serious problem.

4. Increase the point value of a serious problem by U points (for example, 1) every reporting period (for example, every week).

5. Calculate the total number of points for all critical and serious problems.

6. If the total number of points exceeds a triggering value V (for example, 20), trigger a warning alarm.

The values of X, Y, Z, U, and V depend on the characteristics of the project, the product being developed, the development organization, the product's customers and users, and the history of the development organization (how well problems have been resolved in previous projects). There are two rules governing the XYZUV values:

1. The values must be preset before the project resumes.

2. Changes to the values during the development of the project should be restricted and infrequent.

These two rules ensure that the trigger mechanism is not changed frivolously or recklessly in order to avoid the need to seriously contend with problems.

Overall, a good project alarm-triggering method is based on a broad view of the project (not just a single problem). However, an alarm may be triggered when the implications of a single problem are overpowering (the likelihood of project failure is unmistakable).

We mentioned previously that development organizations that already have an effective EWS in place should apply that process when a disentangled project resumes. For other organizations, a simple yet effective approach is to start with the sample XYZUV values in the previous example, and refine them as the project proceeds. Though, as the XYZUV rules state, the values should not be refined too often.

12.5   Initiating Corrective Action

Corrective action generally describes the course of action to be followed in order to resolve a problem. In this discussion, we will be dealing mainly with the resolution of *critical* problems—those that could potentially cause a project to fail. These are the actions resulting from critical problems that were identified during project management reviews. In a disentangled project, these actions are usually very closely monitored by management because they relate to a project that has previously almost failed.

There are many excellent texts that discuss how to resolve software development problems (see, for example, [13] and [14]). Our discussion here is confined to stressing the importance of doing so formally and systematically. This means that solutions must be

- **Documented**

  The proposed course of action must be formally, clearly, and systematically documented.

- **Evaluated**

  The ability of the proposed course of action to solve the problem must be clearly established.

- **Practicable**

  The feasibility of the solution within the constraints of the project must be clearly established.

- **Preferred**

  The superiority of the solution must be established from among other possible courses of action.

The formal resolution of a serious problem may take significant time and is usually not concluded during the project review in which the problem is identified. In such cases, the resolution of the problem becomes an action item to be presented at the next review. In order to ensure that this critical action is carried out, a follow-up procedure is required.

12.6   Follow-Up Procedure

Follow up of critical action items, as part of an EWS, is a straightforward procedure. Basically, it functions the same as any other type of problem follow up. Its purpose is to ensure that critical actions (solutions to problems) are successfully implemented. However, because we are dealing with a disentangled project (that has previously almost failed), follow up is given added importance.

Follow up should be carried out in a formal manner. This requires the following:

1. **Assign a coordinator.**

    A senior person who is not part of the project team should be assigned the role of follow-up coordinator. (This responsibility is often assigned to the development organization's QA manager.)

2. **Provide authority.**

    The follow-up coordinator must be given the authority to ensure that the designated course of action is followed and successfully implemented by the project team (as well as any other parties involved in the solution).

3. **Confirm the status.**

    The status of the course of action, as reported at the next review meeting (or in intermediate status reports), must be formally confirmed by both the project manager and the follow-up coordinator.

The responsibilities of the follow-up coordinator are limited to ensuring that the designated course of action is implemented within the schedule that was agreed at the review. All other implementation decisions remain the responsibility of the project manager.

Advisory: As important as it is for the follow-up coordinator to monitor the resolution of problems, it is no less important to ensure that this role does not turn into a close, ongoing supervisor. Care must be taken to ensure that follow-up activities do not excessively interfere with the project team's work. The extent of the follow-up coordinator's involvement in the project should be the minimum needed to ensure the implementation of the course of action and should be limited to the time it takes to complete that action.

12.7   What Can Go Wrong (and What to Do About It)

The creation of an EWS is one of the less controversial steps in the disentanglement process; all parties involved in the project usually support it. All the same, there are several problems that can occur during this step. But usually, none of the problems should prevent the disentanglement process from being completed, nor should they prevent the disentangled project from restarting.

The following list covers some of the things that can go wrong during the creation of an EWS and provides solutions for dealing with them:

- **There is a fear of excessive interference in project development.**

  This problem occurs when the project team objects to the EWS because of concerns that it will impede the development of the project. This can be due to requirements for additional administrative- or process-oriented activities or because of perceived limitations on the project team's freedom to choose solutions. If the concerns are not resolved, the problem can reduce the team's commitment to the success of the project.

  Action: The first step is to determine whether this concern is justified. The project evaluator and the project manager should enlist the assistance of an experienced software quality assurance (SQA) professional to review the EWS procedure. If the organization does not have a suitable SQA professional available, an external consultant should be hired to review the procedures and recommend changes (if needed).

  Though the resolution of this problem is not urgent (it need not delay the resumption of the disentangled project), it must be resolved within two to three weeks after the project resumes (to ensure that the team's commitment is not affected).

- **Management support is lacking.**

  This is the same type of problem that was discussed in several previous steps of the disentanglement process. In this case, the problem occurs if management shows little or no interest in the EWS procedure.

  Action: The resolution of this problem requires the involvement of the initiating manager. A clear message must be formally transmitted to senior management regarding the importance of management support for the EWS. In particular, the risk of slipping back into catastrophe mode must be made clear.

While this problem should not prevent the resumption of the disentangled project, it should be prominently addressed in the project evaluator's final report (see Chapter 13, "Epilogue: Putting the Final Pieces in Place").

- **The existing early warning system is deficient.**

Earlier in this chapter, the possible pre-existence of an EWS procedure within the development organization was mentioned, and, if it is an effective procedure, its use was recommended. However, the fact that the disentangled project reached catastrophe mode calls into question the effectiveness of any existing EWS procedure.

Action: The existing EWS should be closely examined to determine whether it is adequate and whether it was a factor in the creation of the original near-failure of the disentangled project. If it was a factor, the deficiencies in the procedure should be identified and corrected. This corrective task should be implemented by the organization's quality assurance manager or, if that role does not exist, by a suitable external consultant.

The use of an existing EWS procedure should be preferred if it is effective, or can be made effective with minimum changes. But if the existing procedure is particularly poor or overly complex, a simple replacement should be considered (similar to the procedure in the example discussed earlier).

- **There is no suitable follow-up coordinator.**

There is usually no real justification for the existence of this problem. When a follow-up coordinator cannot be located, it is often due to insufficient management support for the EWS procedure.

Action: The resolution of this problem requires the involvement of the initiating manager in order to adequately prioritize the role for the organization and to assign this responsibility to a suitable person. Then, if no suitable person can be found within the organization, an external consultant should be hired to fulfill the role.

Of all problems that can occur within this last step of the disentanglement process, the most severe is the lack of management support. If this occurs, it may well be that the problem was the original cause of the project catastrophe. However, on a more optimistic note, a catastrophe project that has successfully completed the first nine steps of the disentanglement process has most likely ensured management support (without which the first nine steps could not have been completed) and will likely complete this last step successfully, too.

12.8 Summary

This chapter describes a simple early warning system (EWS) for a disentangled project. The purpose of an EWS is to ensure that the disentangled project does not slip back into catastrophe mode.

The EWS includes five basic elements:

1. The collection of development data (or metrics): It is only necessary to consider project data that is required for the EWS. This means focusing on data related to problems and progress. It also means temporarily setting aside data related to such areas as process improvement, efficiency, reuse, training, and the broader organization (unless these areas are already part of the project's existing metrics collection process).

2. Periodic project status reviews: The purpose of a software project status review (or management review) is to provide information to project staff, stakeholders, and other involved parties so decisions can be made regarding the project, approvals can be given (or withheld), and actions assigned at previous reviews can be tracked. Project reviews should be periodic events.

   The review, which should take between two hours and a complete day (depending on the characteristics of the project), should be attended by key management decision makers, the review leader (who has the administrative task of running the review), a recorder (who documents the main events and decisions of the review), management staff, technical staff, and other team members as needed, as well as optionally a representative of the customer or user.

3. Identification of potential alarm-triggering problems (or risks): Project and product problems should be classified according to their level of severity: critical, serious, or minor. Critical and serious problems can trigger an alarm based on such attributes as the number of problems, the length of time on the list, and progress toward resolution. Triggering mechanisms are often based on aging, which means that critical and serious problems move up the ladder of severity as time passes without them being resolved.

4. Initiating corrective action: Corrective action as part of an EWS is a straightforward procedure (it functions much the same as any other corrective action procedure). The procedure identifies and launches solutions to one or more problems that are identified during the project review. Solutions must be documented, evaluated for effectiveness, practicable (feasible), and preferred (superior to other possible solutions).

5. Follow-up activities: Follow up of critical action items, as part of an EWS, is also a straightforward and formal procedure. This requires the assignment of a follow-up coordinator, who has the necessary authority to ensure the solution's course of action is carried out. The follow-up coordinator must then confirm (with the project manager) the status of the action item.

The following list covers some of the things that can go wrong during the creation of an EWS:

- There is fear of excessive interference by the EWS in project development: The EWS procedure should be reviewed by a software quality professional who should then recommend changes (if needed).

- Management support is lacking: The risk of slipping back into catastrophe mode must be made clear to senior management.

- The existing EWS is deficient: If a project becomes a catastrophe, the effectiveness of any existing EWS becomes suspect. Review the EWS and correct or replace.

- There is no suitable follow-up coordinator: If no suitable person can be found within the organization, an external consultant should be hired.

Exercises

1. Review the literature in your local library or scan the Internet and find an example of a software project early warning system. (It does not have to be called an "early warning system." Search for the functionality, not the name.) Compare the EWS that you have found to the example described in this chapter.

2. Consider the data items listed in Table 12.1.

   (a) For each data item, suggest different alternative methods of collecting its data.

   (b) Compare the alternative methods, and determine which ones would be more intrusive on the development process, and which would be less.

   (c) Consider when you would prefer to use the more intrusive methods and when you would prefer to use the less intrusive methods.

   Explain your answers and any assumptions that you have made.

3. Review the Communications Infrastructure Division case in Section 12.1. Assume that the division has 10 projects: three are large, three are medium, and four are small. One of the three medium projects and one of the large projects are critical (that is, life supporting). Consider the following options: (a) several different alarm triggering mechanisms for each type of project, and (b) a single common alarm triggering mechanism for all projects.

    Suggest a mechanism for options (a) and (b) and explain your reasoning for each option.

    Compare options (a) and (b). What are the advantages and disadvantages of each?

4. Scan the Internet for a description of the Denver airport baggage delivery software project catastrophe, discussed in Chapter 1. What EWS did the project use? How were project reviews conducted? How were serious problems identified? How were solutions implemented? Could an effective EWS have saved the project? Explain.

5. Class project: Select a review coordinator. Select an EWS procedure. Divide the class into two groups: (1) the Denver airport baggage control software project development team, and (2) the project review participants.

    Have the project team present the status of the project to the review participants. The review participants, led by the review coordinator, should identify serious problems using the EWS that was selected. The coordinator should take notes of key points in the review.

    After the review, discuss the coordinator's notes. What lessons can be learned from the Denver project?

13

Epilogue: Putting the Final Pieces in Place

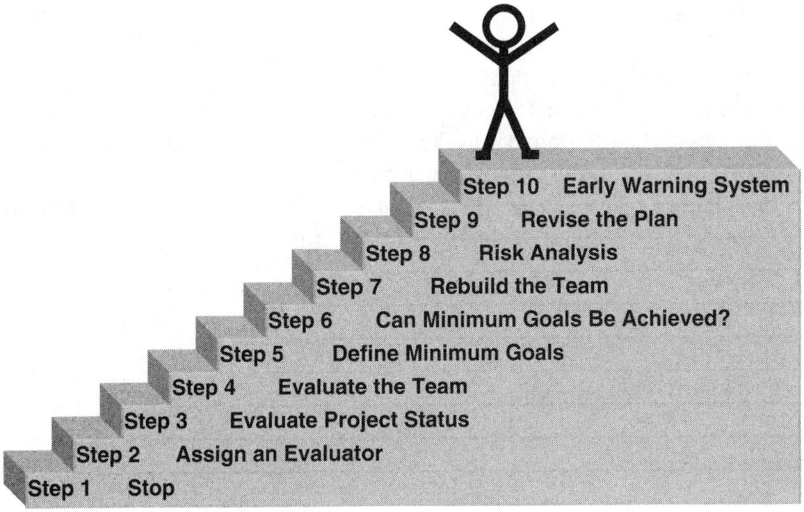

What happens after the catastrophe disentanglement process is concluded and the project resumes? We can, of course, justifiably expect the development of the disentangled project to proceed according to the new plan and, in due course, to have the software product delivered successfully. But there is more. If you have had a fire extinguished in your home, you will want to know how it started and how you can ensure that it does not happen again. No correction process can be complete without ensuring that the problem it corrected does not recur.

This is especially true of the disentanglement of a catastrophe project; catastrophes are not something that development organizations will want to repeat. One way to ensure that severe mistakes are not repeated is to conduct a post-project review of the course of events that led to the catastrophe. This is a valuable learning process in which an organization studies the events surrounding the project so they can better manage them in the future. After all, the best way to save a project is to ensure that it does not become a catastrophe in the first place.

In this final chapter, the post-project review is one of several topics that complement the discussion of the disentanglement process. The chapter also covers the human factor, which is so important in this process, and will focus on some important aspects of the development team members. This is followed by a bird's eye view of project disentanglement, as illustrated in a high-level timeline for the overall process. Then the project evaluator will be assigned one final task (the final report) before returning to his or her original duties.

This chapter will conclude with a discussion of a real-life example showing the successful application of the disentanglement process.

13.1   Post-Project Reviews

Getting a failing software project back on track is an admirable accomplishment, but an even greater one is not having it go off track in the first place. Therefore, part of the catastrophe disentanglement procedure is preventing future recurrences of similar catastrophes. This is achieved through a special review process held after the project has ended (successfully or otherwise).

The *post-project review* (sometimes rather morbidly called a *post-mortem*) is a process intended to promote an understanding of why a project evolved the way it did; what was done right, what was done wrong, and what can be done better next time.[1] The review is a structured process that is not intended to find the guilty or to lay any blame and is best done with a trained facilitator.

---

[1] A useful overview of a generic after-action review process, which can be easily adapted for software projects, is given by former U.S. Army Chief of Staff Gordon Sullivan and Michael Harper in their text *Hope Is Not a Method* [4].

The output of the review includes a list of operational, procedural, and organizational changes and actions to ensure that mistakes are not repeated and successes are. In fact, the U.S. Army's recommendation, summarized in Table 13.1, is that 50% of the review be devoted to discussions on how to do better in the future; the remaining time should be devoted to what happened (25%) and why (25%) (see [1]).

Table 13.1 The Post-Project Review

• What happened? (25%)
• Why did it happen? (25%)
• How can we do better in the future? (50%)
• Who is to blame? (0%)

In an excellent overview of the critical success factors in software projects, John Reel offers some examples of the advantages of software post-project reviews:

> A post-mortem will also help you develop a profile for how your team and company develop software systems. Most companies and teams have personalities that strongly impact the development cycle. As you go through post-mortem analyses, these personalities emerge as patterns rather than as isolated incidents. Knowing the patterns allows you to circumvent or at least schedule for them on your next project [2].

A key point is that post-project reviews become more useful the more they are used. Project profiles in a development organization can be both positive and negative, and as more analysis is conducted of both successes and failures, these profiles can be understood and reinforced (if they are positive) or corrected (if they are negative).

Consider the following case from the early days of software offshore outsourcing:

> A large U.S. communications company opened a subsidiary in Bangalore, India. The subsidiary was intended to be a flagship example of excellence in software development, and when it became operational, it was accredited SEI PMM level 5.[2]

> The subsidiary was given several small projects that were developed successfully. However, the first large strategic project was wrought with problems, and there was significant dissatisfaction with the delivered product. The U.S. parent company became frustrated with their subsidiary and was on the verge of canceling the offshoring program when it decided to conduct a post-project review of the troubled project.

---

[2] Carnegie Mellon's *Software Engineering Institute* (SEI) established its five levels of software development competency and originally called them the *Process Maturity Model* (PMM). The *Capability Maturity Model* (CMM) came later.

The key staff from the Indian subsidiary came over to the U.S. to participate in the review, which was conducted during two days. The review findings were as follows:

1. The Indian subsidiary had excellent development staff that should have been able to develop the strategic project successfully.

2. The problem was cultural. The U.S. and Indian staff were not communicating well because they were unfamiliar with each other's customs and culture. For example, in India, criticism of a developer by a U.S. manager was considered grounds for dismissal. Subsequently, several key Indian developers were lost without the U.S. managers understanding the cause of their departure. Additionally, the members of the staff in India were reluctant to correct their U.S. counterparts, even when such correction was vital.

One of the outcomes of the post-project review was a course of cross-cultural training for the U.S. and the Indian staff and managers. After the training was completed, the working relationship between the parent company and the Indian subsidiary improved significantly.

Cross-cultural problems are an excellent example of the type of issues that may not emerge without a formal review. In the case of the Indian subsidiary, the U.S. staff members were unaware of the consequences of their actions (criticism would lead to the loss of good staff, and a tough business atmosphere seemed hostile to the Indians), and the Indian staff members did not understand that by avoiding valid confrontation with their U.S. counterparts they were hindering their position rather than advancing it.

With the growth of offshoring and of global development, cultural issues are becoming more common (and so is cross-cultural training). Examples of other common issues that often surface during software post-project reviews include the following:

- **Process:** The impact on projects of excellent or poor development processes.
- **Management:** Insufficient or too much management involvement in the project.
- **Customers:** Too much or too little customer or user involvement in the project.
- **Product Definition:** A poorly defined product (for example, lack of requirements or too many requirements changes).
- **Budget:** Insufficient development budget.
- **Schedule:** Impossible schedules, making project failure a forgone conclusion.
- **Training:** Insufficient training for the project staff.

- **Staffing:** Unsuitable staff, recruiting problems, high attrition rate, low compensation, and so on.
- **Testing:** Lack of an independent test organization.
- **Support:** Poor support from other groups (for example, quality assurance, hardware support, system administration, the human resource group, field support).
- **Tools:** Insufficient, unsuitable, or outdated development tools.
- **Environment:** Poor development environment.
- **Morale:** Low staff morale.

The responsibility to conduct post-project reviews is organizational; this means that it will only happen if it is part of the development organization's culture. Generally, senior management needs to ensure the review process is introduced into the development organization. But the best champion for the process is the quality assurance manager (if the organization has such a position).

For a disentangled project in an organization with no existing post-project review process, the initiating manager should initiate the review.

13.2 The Human Factor

The process of disentangling catastrophes is traumatic—not just for the project team, but for the organization itself. Clearly, halting a project does not add to the motivation of a project team. Similarly, declaring a project to be a catastrophe does not add to the prestige of a development organization—though the courage to make such a decision often deserves praise.

While a highly motivated team is certainly one of the primary factors for project success, the fear of demotivating a team or tarnishing an organization's image should never be a reason to allow a team to continue in the wrong direction. Catastrophe disentanglement should be viewed like corrective surgery; just as the body undergoes trauma in order to heal, so does the development organization.

One of the problems with the rather drastic measures of catastrophe disentanglement is that the knowledge that an organization will take such measures can inhibit the flow of accurate information (particularly bad news) to senior management. But successful corrective action, just like successful surgery, depends on the flow of truthful and accurate information, even (in fact especially) when the news is bad.

The ability to bring bad tidings and make unpopular decisions is a desirable, if not entirely common, part of an organization's culture. Former Intel CEO, Andy Grove says: "…if you are a middle manager you [may] face…the fear that when you bring bad tidings you will be punished, [and] the fear that management will not want to hear the bad news from the periphery." Grove continues "Fear that might keep you from voicing your real thoughts is poison. Almost nothing could be more detrimental to the well-being of the company." [5]

Grove's point is that effective corrective action requires accurate information— a reality not unfamiliar to us as automobile drivers: We cannot effectively steer a vehicle on the road if we cannot get accurate data from our body's senses. Thus, an organization that wants to be able to effectively evaluate its activities with processes such as the one described here needs to promote the flow of accurate information by ensuring that

- The process is open and fair (not secretive).
- The staff is briefed about the process and the reason it is being adopted.
- The organization promotes a mistake-tolerant culture.[3] Blame and punishment need to be eliminated from the evaluation process (mistakes should be addressed in normal performance reviews alongside successes and achievements).

Grove's views are important for the disentanglement process because the success of the process is heavily dependent on the cooperation of the organization's development team. The team members need to feel comfortable cooperating within a process that will appear to be associated with failure. In this situation, cooperation will not always come naturally if the organization promotes a culture where everyone is expected to succeed all the time. Thus, the message from senior management must be that every organization that creates something fails sometimes, and doing so is legitimate.[4] Secondly, the message should clarify that being associated with the disentanglement process means cooperating with turning failure into success (certainly an admirable act).

For a more detailed discussion of the human factor, see Allcorn and Diamond [6] and Moorhead [7].

13.3   The Catastrophe Disentanglement Timeline

In the preceding discussion of the disentanglement process, the description of each step includes a recommended duration. The durations of the steps, after the

---

[3] For an interesting discussion of a mistake-tolerant business culture, see Harvard Business School Professor Richard Farson and co-author Ralph Keyes' interesting article, "The Failure-Tolerant Leader" [9].

[4] Of course, while occasional failure is legitimate, it is not something any organization would want to glorify.

project is stopped, are summarized in an overall timeline for the process, which is illustrated in Figure 13.1.

In reviewing the timeline, recall that the steps can partially overlap, though no step can conclude before all the preceding steps are concluded. Also, more than two tasks can overlap, though this is not illustrated in Figure 13.1.

As stated in Chapter 1, "An Introduction to Catastrophe Disentanglement," the total amount of time to be allocated for the disentanglement process, from the point it is stopped, is two weeks (ten days). While every effort should be made to keep within the two-week schedule, in rare cases an extension may be unavoidable. At a number of points in the previous chapters, obstacles were discussed that could prolong the process (for example, when minimized goals are still unachievable). If this occurs, an attempt should be made to keep the extension within two days, and then, if possible, the work week should be extended to six days so that the overall process is still contained within a two-week calendar period.

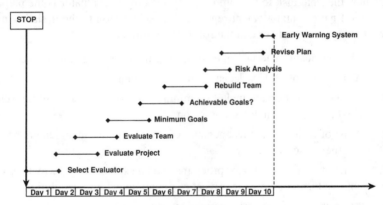

Figure 13.1   The catastrophe disentanglement timeline

It is important to keep within the committed disentanglement process schedule for the following reasons:

- Every extra day that the project is halted is costly.

- One of the goals of the disentanglement process is to inspire a new mindset within the project team and within the development organization regarding the importance of adhering to committed schedules.

- If the disentanglement process cannot keep to its schedule, confidence in the project's new schedule will be low and confidence in the disentanglement process will decline (according to common wisdom, confidence in success is half the battle).

- Experience shows that if the process is permitted to slip by one day, it will most likely slip by more.

All the same, as in all other cases, common sense must ultimately prevail. There is no sense in enforcing a two-week schedule only to produce a project that will become entangled yet again. As soon as it appears that an extension will be necessary, the project evaluator and the initiating manager should meet to establish a strategy to ensure that the extension is contained and minimized.

13.4   The Final Report

The disentanglement process is a valuable learning experience for the development organization. It is not just an opportunity to learn and improve the process; it is also a source of information for the post-project review that will follow.

Thus, the final task to be completed by the project evaluator is the preparation of the final disentanglement report and its submission to the initiating manager. This report should contain the following information:

1.   All significant material collected during the disentanglement process.

2.   A summary of all key decisions made and their justification.

3.   The new project plan, including minimized goals, project staffing, schedule, budget, risk analysis, and so on.

4.   A list of major problems encountered during the disentanglement process and their resolution.

5.   A list of unresolved major problems and an explanation of why they were not resolved and how the project can continue without resolutions.

6.   An overview of the early warning system.

7.   Recommendations and suggestions.

8.   A two-page executive summary.

Most of the information for the final report will have been generated during the disentanglement process. The finalization of the report should take between one and two days and should be prepared *after* the disentangled project resumes. Accordingly, the project evaluator should plan for 12-day assignment (ten days for the disentanglement process and two days for the final report).

This report is produced even if the disentanglement of the project is not successful or if the project is cancelled. In that case, the report is produced after the process is terminated. The report will include the relevant information from items 1, 2, 5, 7, and 8 in the previous list and any other information from the list that was collected or generated.

13.5 Case Study

The following case study demonstrates the application of the disentanglement process. The description of the case covers the evolution of the problems in a critical project, the launching of the disentanglement process, and the main events that followed. The case also demonstrates how the minimization of goals can provide an effective solution for a perilously late project.

A failing project is often like a hand in a cookie jar; to get some cookies out, you first have to let some go. Such was the case at Motorola with the software for a wireless telephony control and maintenance center (CMC) that we delivered several years ago as part of a two hundred thousand subscriber project to one of the emerging Eastern European countries (see [1]). The specially tailored CMC was a last-minute add-on to the wireless telephony contract and, consequently, was not well defined.

The CMC was developed with a subcontractor team based on an existing control system, and the first phase of the project was devoted to producing a voluminous set of requirements, none of which could be omitted (according to the customer). The schedule was dictated—16 months, which was set as close as possible to the date the subscriber telephony system was to become operational. Needless to say, every month was critical.

Five months into the project, key dates were already being missed. Seven months into the project, doubts began arising among senior management about whether the project would be ready on time. Nine months into the project, senior management was trying to calculate how much the late delivery penalties would cost, and a frantic marketing team was looking for alternatives. At all junctures, the development team was adamant that they would deliver the project on time.

At the end of nine months, amid significant resistance from the development and marketing teams, the project was brought almost to a complete halt (some tasks did continue). Two activities were then launched: (i) a total external review of the project, and in parallel, (ii) negotiations were reopened with the customer on the CMC requirements.

1. The project status was evaluated and it was confirmed that the then-current rate of progress would lead to a major project overrun. The team was moving forward at a steady pace, but there was no way that they could meet the delivery date, or any date close. The cost of such an overrun would be enormous. This indeed was an approaching catastrophe.

2. Because the CMC was critical for the operation of the whole system, the customer was cooperative in re-evaluating the project's software features. Thus, a new set of minimal requirements was prepared.

3. The project was rescheduled with two release dates: the first with the minimal feature set and the second with the remaining features.

4. On the development team side, instead of using a single team for development, installation, and support, a cooperative effort was launched together with a local support team.

5. Frequent progress reviews of the project were initiated by management with key members of the development team together with the customer.

As a result, a working CMC system was delivered on time, and the full telephony system became operational as planned. The additional CMC features were provided as part of a later second release.

Many of the disentanglement challenges of the CMC project were eased by a cooperative customer. The customer's representatives were highly technical and fully understood the project's problems and the need for compromise. By doing so, they helped achieved their two main goals: (a) the timely launch of the telephony system, and (b) a complete, functional CMC (which was delivered in the second release of the software).

The post-project review, which was held at the Motorola development center responsible for the telephony system, concluded that because the CMC was a small (though important) part of the overall telephony system, it had not received sufficient attention at the beginning of the telephony project. Consequently, the CMC project was launched too late, and this produced an impossible schedule. This conclusion led to improvements in the way future projects were managed at the Motorola development center.

13.6   A Concluding Note

Reading the list of problems in this book can be comparable to reading the label on a bottle of medicine. The fact that there are many warnings doesn't mean that everyone who uses the medicine will suffer from all the side effects. Similarly, not all troubled projects exhibit all the problems discussed here—it would be quite alarming if they did. The solutions and guidelines provided here should be regarded as a toolbox: Use only the ones you need.

As we saw in the survey data reported in Chapter 1, when software projects are in serious trouble, 45% of organizations almost always manage to get them back on track (see Figure 1.2). So we should certainly not be deterred by the challenge; the success ratio is impressive. The goal of the disentanglement process is to raise the percentage toward 100% of those projects that are worthy of being saved.

Of course, an even better goal would be not to have catastrophes at all (or at least to reduce their numbers). Most software catastrophes were troubled projects that went on for too long. Unfortunately, the recognition that a project is in serious trouble usually comes too late. In fact, part of the trauma of dealing with them stems from the realization that "This shouldn't have happened," or "We should have seen it coming," and, of course, the call to action: "Something has to change around here."

Returning to Johnson's *Who Moved My Cheese* at the opening of Chapter 1, the tale continues: "The little people were outraged, shocked, scared, and befuddled when the cheese disappeared. In their comfort, they didn't notice the cheese supply had been dwindling, nor that it had become old and smelly. They had become complacent."

How better to describe the failing of a software project?

References

Chapter 1

[1] Glass, Robert L. *Software Runaways: Lessons Learned from Massive Software Project Failures.* Prentice Hall, 1998.

[2] May, Lorin J., "Major Causes of Software Project Failures." *Crosstalk, The Journal of Defense Software Engineering*, July 1998.

[3] Applegate, Lynda M., Ramiro Montealegre, H. James Nelson, Carin-Isabel Knoop. *BAE Automated Systems (A): Denver International Airport Baggage-Handling System.* Harvard Business School Cases, 1996.

[4] Johnson, Kirk. "Denver Airport Saw the Future. It Didn't Work." *The New York Times*, August 27, 2005.

[5] Staw, B. M. "The Escalation of Commitment to a Course of Action." *Academy of Management Review*, Vol. 6, No. 4, pp. 577–587, 1981.

[6] Nuldén, Urban. "Escalating? Who? Me?" Information Systems Research Seminar in Scandinavia, Lökeberg, Sweden, 1996. www.viktoria.se/nulden/ Publ/Publicationwindow.html

[7] Keil, M. "Identifying and Preventing Runaway Systems Project." *American Programmer 8 (3)*: 16–22, 1995.

[8] Bennatan, E.M. "Software Project Failures," Parts I, II, and III. *Executive Update*, Vol 6, Nos. 13, 22, 24. The Cutter Consortium, 2005.

[9] Johnson, Spencer, and Kenneth H. Blanchard. *Who Moved My Cheese? An Amazing Way to Deal With Change in Your Work and in Your Life.* Putnam Publishing Group, 1998.

[10] The Royal Academy of Engineering and The British Computer Society working group. *The Challenges of Complex IT Projects.* The Royal Academy of Engineering, London, 2004.

[11] Bennatan, E.M. *On Time Within Budget, Software Project Management Practices and Techniques, Third Edition*. Wiley, 2000.

[12] Bennatan, E.M. "The State of Software Estimation: Has the Dragon Been Slain? (Part 1)." *Executive Update*, Vol. 3, No. 10. The Cutter Consortium, July 2002.

Chapter 2

[1] Bennatan, E.M. "The State of Software Estimation: Has the Dragon Been Slain? Part 1." *Executive Update*, Vol. 3, No. 10. The Cutter Consortium, July 2002.

[2] Bennatan, E.M. *On Time Within Budget, Software Project Management Practices and Techniques, Third Edition*. John Wiley & Sons, 2000.

[3] Goldratt, Eliyahu. *Critical Chain*. North River Press, 1997.

[4] Brooks, Fredrick P. *The Mythical Man-Month: Essays on Software Engineering, 20th Anniversary Edition*. Addison-Wesley, 1995.

[5] Schroeder, Larry D., David L. Sjoquist, and Paula E. Stephan. *Understanding Regression Analysis: An Introductory Guide (Quantitative Applications in the Social Sciences)*. SAGE Publications, 1986.

[6] IEEE. *Software Engineering Standards*. The Institute of Electrical and Electronic Engineers, Inc., New York, 1982, 1994, 1999.

[7] Bennatan, E.M. "A Fresh Look at Software Quality? Part 1—What Does Quality Really Mean?" *Executive Update*, Vol. 4, No. 3. The Cutter Consortium, July 2002.

[8] Wettemann, Rebecca. *ROI 101: Making the Business Case for Technology Investments*. CIO, May 14, 2003.

[9] Denne, Mark, and Jane Cleland-Huang. *Software by Numbers: Low-Risk, High-Return Development*. Prentice Hall, 2003.

Chapter 3

[1]   Piven, Joshua, and David Borgenicht. *The Worst-Case Scenario Survival Handbook: Travel.* Chronicle Books, San Francisco, 2001.

[2]   Keil, M. "Identifying and Preventing Runaway Systems Project." *American Programmer 8 (3)*: 16–22, 1995.

[3]   Nuldén, Urban. "Escalating? Who? Me?" Information Systems Research Seminar in Scandinavia, Lökeberg, Sweden, 1996. www.viktoria.se/nulden/Publ/Publicationwindow.html

Chapter 4

[1]   McConnell, Steve. *Rapid Development.* Microsoft Press, 1996.

[2]   G. R. Salancik. *Commitment and the Control of Organizational Behavior and Belief.* New Directions in Organizational Behavior, B. M. Staw and G. R. Salancik Editions. Chicago: St. Clair Press, 1977.

[3]   Nulden, Urban. "Escalation in IT Projects: Can We Afford to Quit or Do We Have to Continue?" Information Systems Conference of New Zealand (ISCNZ '96), 1996.

[4]   Kuo, T.W. *Sun Tzu: Manual for War.* Atli Press, 1989.

[5]   Bennatan, E.M. *On Time Within Budget, Software Project Management Practices and Techniques, Third Edition.* Wiley, 2000.

[6]   Brooks, Fredrick P. *The Mythical Man Month, 20th Anniversary Edition.* Addison-Wesley, 1995.

Chapter 5

[1]   Oz, Effy. "When Professional Standards Are Lax." *Communications of the ACM*, Vol. 37, No. 10, 1994.

[2]   Brooks, Fredrick P., *The Mythical Man-Month: Essays on Software Engineering, 20th Anniversary Edition.* Addison-Wesley, 1995.

[3]   Snow, Andrew P., and Mark Keil. "The Challenge of Accurate Software Project Status Reporting: A Two Stage Model Incorporating Status Errors and Reporting Bias." *IEEE Transactions on Engineering Management*, Vol. 49, No. 4, November 2002.

[4]   Rahanu, H., J. Davies, and S. Rogerson. "Development of a case-based reasoner as a tool to facilitate ethical understanding." Proceedings of the Fourth International Conference on Ethical Issues of Information Technology (Rotterdam, The Netherlands), 25-27 March 1998: 578-588

[5]   Humphrey, Watts S. "Why Big Software Projects Fail: The 12 Key Questions." *CrossTalk, The Journal of Defense Software Engineering*, May 2005.

[6]   IEEE Standard for Software Reviews. IEEE Std 1028-1997. *Software Engineering Standards*, Vol. 2. The Institute of Electrical and Electronics Engineer, New York, 1999.

[7]   Bennatan, E.M. *On Time Within Budget, Software Project Management Practices and Techniques, Third Edition.* Wiley, 2000.

Chapter 6

[1]   DeMarco, Tom, and Timothy Lister. *Peopleware: Productive Projects and Teams. Second Edition.* Dorset House, 1999.

[2]   Bennatan, E.M. "Software Teams—Your Most Important Asset: Part I: The "Make or Break" of a Project." *The Cutter Consortium*, Executive Update Vol. 5, No. 7, December 2004.

[3]   Bennatan, E.M. *On Time, Within Budget: Software Project Management Practices and Techniques, Third Edition.* Wiley, 2000.

[4]   Allcorn, Seth, and Michael A. Diamond. *Managing People During Stressful Times: The Psychologically Defensive Workplace.* Quorum Books, 1997.

[5]   Moorhead, Gregory. *Organizational Behavior: Managing People and Organizations, Seventh Edition.* Houghton Mifflin Company, 2003.

Chapter 7

[1] Bennatan, E.M. "The State of Software Estimation: Has the Dragon Been Slain?" *Benchmark Review*, The Cutter Consortium, Vol. 2, No. 8, August 2002.

[2] The Standish Group. "Extreme Chaos." The Standish Group International Inc., 2001.

[3] Sun Tzu. *Manual for War*. Translated by T.W. Kuo. Atli Press, Chicago, 1989.

[4] IEEE Standard Glossary of Software Engineering Terminology. IEEE Std 610, The Institute of Electrical and Electronics Engineers, New York, 1990.

[5] McGregor, Douglas. *The Human Side of Enterprise: 25th Anniversary Printing*. McGraw-Hill/Irwin, 1985.

[6] Humphrey, Watts S. "Large-Scale Work—Part II: The Project." *News @ SEI*, Issue: 2005 | 3.

Chapter 8

[1] Peters, Tom. *Thriving on Chaos, Handbook for a Management Revolution*. Pan Books, 1989.

[2] McConnell, Steve. "Feasibility Studies." *IEEE Software Journal*, Vol. 15, No. 3, May/June 1998.

[3] Boehm, Barry, and Richard Turner. *Balancing Agility and Discipline: A Guide for the Perplexed*. Addison-Wesley, 2003.

[4] Brooks, Fredrick P. *The Mythical Man Month* After 20 Years, Keynote Talk. The 17th International Conference on Software Engineering, April 23-30, 1995, Seatle, Washington.

[5] Boehm, Barry W., Ellis Horowitz, Ray Madachy, Donald Reifer, Bradford K. Clark, Bert Steece, A. Winsor Brown, Sunita Chulani, and Chris Abts. *Software Cost Estimation with Cocomo II*. Prentice Hall, 2000.

[6] Bennatan, E.M. *On Time Within Budget, Software Project Management Practices and Techniques, Third Edition*. Wiley, 2000.

[7] Greenwood, Darren. "IT firms 'best employers'—survey." *Computerworld*, December 1, 2000.

Chapter 9

[1]   Bennatan, E.M. "Software Project Failures, Parts I, II, and III." The Cutter Consortium, 2005.

[2]   Reel, John S. "Critical Success Factors in Software Projects." *IEEE Software Journal*, May/June 1999.

[3]   Rich, Ben R., and Leo Janos. *Skunk Works*. Little, Brown and Company, 1994.

[4]   Hackman, J. Richard. "The Five Keys to Successful Teams (interview with Mallory Stark)." *Harvard Business Review Working Knowledge*, July 15, 2002.

[5]   Bennatan, E.M. *On Time Within Budget, Software Project Management Practices and Techniques, Third Edition*. Wiley, 2000.

[6]   *IEEE Software Engineering Standards*. The Institute of Electrical and Electronics Engineers, New York, 1999.

[7]   Boehm, Barry, and Richard Turner. *Balancing Agility and Discipline: A Guide for the Perplexed*. Addison-Wesley, 2003.

[8]   Lencioni, Patrick M. *The Five Dysfunctions of a Team: A Leadership Fable*. Jossey-Bass, 2002.

[9]   Lencioni, Patrick M. *Overcoming the Five Dysfunctions of a Team: A Field Guide for Leaders, Managers, and Facilitators*. Jossey-Bass, 2005.

[10] Allcorn, Seth, and Michael A. Diamond. *Managing People During Stressful Times: The Psychologically Defensive Workplace*. Quorum Books, 1997.

[11] Moorhead, Gregory. *Organizational Behavior: Managing People and Organizations, Seventh Edition*. Houghton Mifflin Company, 2003.

Chapter 10

[1]   Boehm, B.W., and T. DeMarco. "Software risk management." *IEEE Software*, Vol. 14, No. 3, May-June 1997.

[2]   Murphy, Richard L., Christopher J. Alberts, Ray C. Williams, Ronald P. Higuera, Audrey J. Dorofee, and Julie A. Walker. *Continuous Risk Management Guidebook*. Carnegie Mellon University, Software Engineering Institute, 1996.

[3] Gemmer, Art. "Risk management: moving beyond process." *IEEE Computer,* May 1997.

[4] Carnegie Mellon University. *Risk Management.* Software Engineering Institute, 2005. http://www.sei.cmu.edu/risk/main.html and http://www.sei.cmu.edu/risk/risk.faq.html

[5] Higuera, R.P., and Y.Y. Haimes. "Software Risk Management." Software Engineering Institute, Technical Report CMU/SEI-96-TR-012, ESC-TR-96-012, June 1996.

Chapter 11

[1] Schaaff, Kevin, and Mike Busak. "Delivering a CMMI Compliant Project Plan in 30 Minutes." Software Engineering Process Group Conference (SEPG), 2005.

[2] IEEE. "Standard for Software Project Management Plans." Std. 1058, The Institute of Electrical and Electronics Engineers, 1998.

[3] Software Engineering Institute. "Key Practices of the Capability Maturity Model." SEI-93-TR-25 Version 1.1.

[4] Software Engineering Institute. "CMMI for Software Engineering, Continuous Representation." CMMI-SW Version 1.1.

[5] Bennatan, E.M. *On Time Within Budget, Software Project Management Practices and Techniques, Third Edition.* Wiley, 2000.

[6] Jones, Capers. "Software Cost Estimating Methods for Large Projects." *CrossTalk, The Journal of Defense Software Engineering,* April 2005.

[7] Boehm, Barry W., Ellis Horowitz, Ray Madachy, Donald Reifer, Bradford K. Clark, Bert Steece, A. Winsor Brown, Sunita Chulani, and Chris Abts. *Software Cost Estimation with Cocomo II.* Prentice Hall, 2000.

[8] Garmus, David, and David Herron. *Function Point Analysis: Measurement Practices for Successful Software Projects.* Addison-Wesley, 2000.

Chapter 12

[1]   Liu, Xiaoqing (Frank), Gautam Kane, and Monu Bambroo. "An Intelligent Early Warning System for Software Quality Improvement and Project Management." Proceedings of the 15th IEEE International Conference on Tools with Artificial Intelligence (ICTAI '03), 2003.

[2]   Fleming, Quentin W., and Joel M. Koppelman. "Earned Value Project Management… an Introduction." *CrossTalk, The Journal of Defense Software Engineering*, July 1999.

[3]   IEEE. "Std 1028, Standard for Software Reviews." The Institute of Electrical and Electronics Engineers, 1997.

[4]   Bennatan, E.M. "Measuring Up to Metrics: Part I—How I Became a Missourian." *Executive Update*, Vol. 6, No. 3, The Cutter Consortium, February 2005.

[5]   Bennatan, E.M. "Measuring Up to Metrics: Part II—Are Software Organizations Managing by Data?" *Executive Update*, Vol. 6, No. 4, The Cutter Consortium, March 2005.

[6]   Kan, Stephen H. *Metrics and Models in Software Quality Engineering, Second Edition*. Addison-Wesley, 2002.

[7]   Grable, Ross, Jacquelyn Jernigan, Casey Pogue, and Dale Divis. "Metrics for Small Projects: Experiences at the SED." *IEEE Software Journal*, March/April 1999.

[8]   Carleton, Anita D., Robert E. Park, Wolfhart B. Goethert, William A. Florac, Elizabeth K. Bailey, and Shari Lawrence Pfleeger. "Software Measurement for DoD Systems: Recommendations for Initial Core Measures." Software Engineering Institute, Carnegie Mellon University, Technical Report CMU/SEI-92-TR-019, ESC-TR-92-019, September 1992.

[9]   IEEE. "Standard for a Software Quality Metrics Methodology." IEEE Std 1061-1998, The Institute of Electrical and Electronics Engineers, 1998.

[10] ISO. "Software Engineering—Product Quality—Part 3: Internal Metrics." ISO/IEC TR 9126-3:2003, The International Organization for Standardization, 2003.

[11] The American Society for Quality (ASQ): http://www.asq.org/index.html

[12] ISO. "Software Reviews and Audits." ISO/IEC 12220-6, The International Organization for Standardization, 2000.

[13] Bennatan, E.M. *On Time Within Budget, Software Project Management Practices and Techniques, Third Edition.* Wiley, 2000.

[14] Pressman, Roger S. *Software Engineering: A Practitioner's Approach.* McGraw-Hill Science, 2004.

Chapter 13

[1] Meliza, Larry L. "A Guide to Standardizing After Action Review (AAR) Aids." Report number: A348953, U.S. Army Research Institute, Field Unit, Orlando, Florida, 1998. http://www.stormingmedia.us/34/3489/A348953.html

[2] Reel, John S. "Critical Success Factors in Software Projects." *IEEE Software Journal*, May/June 1999.

[3] Whitten, Neal. *Managing Software Development Projects.* John Wiley & Sons, 1995.

[4] Sullivan, Gordon R., and Michael V. Harper. *Hope Is Not a Method.* Times Business, Random House, 1996.

[5] Grove, Andrew S. *Only the Paranoid Survive.* HarperCollins Business, 1996.

[6] Allcorn, Seth, and Michael A. Diamond. *Managing People During Stressful Times: The Psychologically Defensive Workplace.* Quorum Books, 1997.

[7] Moorhead, Gregory. *Organizational Behavior: Managing People and Organizations, Seventh Edition.* Houghton Mifflin Company, 2003.

Glossary

Catastrophe project: A disastrous software development project that is completely out of control in one or more of the following aspects: schedule, budget, or quality.

Disentanglement: The act of producing an agreed-upon plan that will enable the successful completion of a catastrophe project.

Project evaluator: An experienced software professional, external to the development organization, who is assigned the task of leading the disentanglement process in order to get a catastrophe project back on track.

Initiating manager: The senior manager who initiates the disentanglement process for a catastrophe project.

Stakeholders: Individuals and organizations that have a significant interest in a project (for example, senior managers, customer, users, investors, and partners).

Minimized goals: A subset of a catastrophe project's goals that includes only the most essential goals.

Early warning system (EWS): A method that finds potentially severe project problems while they are still relatively simple to correct, and well before they become a catastrophe. (This usually includes metrics, reviews, an alarm-triggering mechanism, corrective action, and follow up.)

About the Author

E. M. Bennatan's extensive hands-on management experience stems from many years as senior director at Motorola, Inc., developing large software systems and leading multinational design centers. He has also been vice president of engineering at Midway Corporation, where he managed several hundred software and hardware engineers. A frequent lecturer and speaker on software project management, he is author of *On Time Within Budget: Software Project Management, Practices, and Techniques, Third Edition* (Wiley, 2000). Mr. Bennatan is currently president of Advanced Project Solutions, Inc. (www.AdvancedPS.com) and senior consultant for the Boston Cutter Consortium.

INDEX

V

W-Z